Windows on Learning:
Documenting Young Children's Work, 2nd Ed.
  JUDY HARRIS HELM, SALLEE BENEKE, & KATHY STEINHEIMER

Ready or Not:
Leadership Choices in Early Care and Education
  STACIE G. GOFFIN & VALORA WASHINGTON

Supervision in Early Childhood Education:
A Developmental Perspective, 3rd Ed.
  JOSEPH J. CARUSO WITH M. TEMPLE FAWCETT

Guiding Children's Behavior:
Developmental Discipline in the Classroom
  EILEEN S. FLICKER & JANET ANDRON HOFFMAN

What If All the Kids Are White? Anti-Bias Multicultural
Education with Young Children and Families
  LOUISE DERMAN-SPARKS & PATRICIA G. RAMSEY

The War Play Dilemma:
What Every Parent and Teacher Needs to Know, 2nd Ed.
  DIANE E. LEVIN & NANCY CARLSSON-PAIGE

Possible Schools: The Reggio Approach to Urban Education
  ANN LEWIN-BENHAM

Everyday Goodbyes: Starting School and Early Care—
A Guide to the Separation Process
  NANCY BALABAN

Playing to Get Smart
  ELIZABETH JONES & RENATTA M. COOPER

How to Work with Standards in the
Early Childhood Classroom
  CAROL SEEFELDT

In the Spirit of the Studio:
Learning from the Atelier of Reggio Emilia
  LELLA GANDINI, LYNN T. HILL, LOUISE BOYD CADWELL, &
  CHARLES SCHWALL, EDS.

Understanding Assessment and Evaluation in Early
Childhood Education, 2nd Ed.
  DOMINIC F. GULLO

Negotiating Standards in the Primary Classroom:
The Teacher's Dilemma
  CAROL ANNE WIEN

Teaching and Learning in a Diverse World: Multicultural
Education for Young Children, 3rd Ed.
  PATRICIA G. RAMSEY

The Emotional Development of Young Children:
Building an Emotion-Centered Curriculum, 2nd Ed.
  MARILOU HYSON

Effective Partnering for School Change: Improving Early
Childhood Education in Urban Classrooms
  JIE-QI CHEN & PATRICIA HORSCH
  WITH KAREN DEMOSS & SUZANNE L. WAGNER

Let's Be Friends: Peer Competence and Social Inclusion in
Early Childhood Programs
  KRISTEN MARY KEMPLE

Young Children Continue to Reinvent Arithmetic—
2nd Grade, 2nd Ed.
  CONSTANCE KAMII

Major Trends and Issues in Early Childhood Education:
Challenges, Controversies, and Insights, 2nd Ed.
  JOAN PACKER ISENBERG & MARY RENCK JALONGO, EDS.

The Power of Projects: Meeting Contemporary Challenges
in Early Childhood Classrooms—Strategies and Solutions
  JUDY HARRIS HELM & SALLEE BENEKE, EDS.

Bringing Learning to Life:
The Reggio Approach to Early Childhood Education
  LOUISE BOYD CADWELL

The Colors of Learning: Integrating the Visual Arts into
the Early Childhood Curriculum
  ROSEMARY ALTHOUSE, MARGARET H. JOHNSON,
  & SHARON T. MITCHELL

A Matter of Trust: Connecting Teachers and Learners in
the Early Childhood Classroom
  CAROLLEE HOWES & SHARON RITCHIE

Widening the Circle:
Including Children with Disabilities in Preschool Programs
  SAMUEL L. ODOM, ED.

Children with Special Needs:
Lessons for Early Childhood Professionals
  MARJORIE J. KOSTELNIK, ESTHER ETSUKO ONAGA,
  BARBARA ROHDE, & ALICE PHIPPS WHIREN

Developing Constructivist Early Childhood Curriculum:
Practical Principles and Activities
  RHETA DEVRIES, BETTY ZAN, CAROLYN HILDEBRANDT,
  REBECCA EDMIASTON, & CHRISTINA SALES

Outdoor Play: Teaching Strategies with Young Children
  JANE PERRY

Embracing Identities in Early Childhood Education:
Diversity and Possibilities
  SUSAN GRIESHABER & GAILE S. CANNELLA, EDS.

Bambini: The Italian Approach to Infant/Toddler Care
  LELLA GANDINI & CAROLYN POPE EDWARDS, EDS.

(continued)

Windows on Learning

Documenting Young Children's Work

Second Edition

Judy Harris Helm
Sallee Beneke
Kathy Steinheimer

Teachers College, Columbia University
New York and London

Published by Teachers College Press, 1234 Amsterdam Avenue, New York, NY 10027

Library of Congress Cataloging-in-Publication Data

Helm, Judy Harris.
    Windows on learning : documenting young children's work / Judy Harris Helm, Sallee Beneke, & Kathy Steinheimer. — 2nd ed.
        p. cm. — (Early childhood education series)
    Includes bibliographical references and index.
    ISBN 978-0-8077-4786-5 (pbk. : alk. paper)
    1. Project method in teaching. 2. Early childhood education—Documentation. 3. Portfolios in education. 4. School reports. I. Beneke, Sallee. II. Steinheimer, Kathy. III. Title.
LB1139.35.P8H45 2007
372.13'6—dc22   2007013221

ISBN 978-0-8077-4786-5 (paper)

Printed on acid-free paper

Manufactured in the United States of America

14   13   12   11   10   09   08   07   8   7   6   5   4   3   2   1

Contents

Foreword

In less than a decade since launching the first edition of *Windows on Learning*, Helm, Beneke, and Steinheimer have broadened and sharpened their mastery of how to document young children's experiences in preschool and primary settings.

In this expanded and extended exploration of the three important "windows" on children's experiences, every chapter is replete with rich, clear, and persuasive examples of how each of the three "windows" serves the important cause of early childhood education. Every page throughout the book includes rich and clear examples of the enormous power of good documentation to enhance all aspects of early education, including helping parents understand and participate in their children's experiences and advancing teachers' professional development.

The new introductory chapter puts the purposes of documentation in clear perspective. It explains how the authors' approach to early education and various documentation processes are based on the best available contemporary theories of development and learning. The ideas and practices that are recommended are richly illustrated with a wide variety of real examples of teachers' work with children. Each example is given in sufficient detail to ensure that readers who are just discovering the value of documentation in providing quality educational experiences to our children can readily adopt the strategies and techniques recommended. The inclusion of project planning sheets and checklists in Chapter 13 makes it much easier to use than the first edition. In addition, the authors offer helpful insights and suggestions about how state standards can be addressed when the project approach is incorporated into the curriculum and the work undertaken is carefully and fully documented.

If you have any doubts about the value of documentation to all those involved—children, their families, their teachers, and those who provide the resources—go straight to Chapter 9 and read the detailed account of the Movie Theater Project that Kathy Steinheimer undertook with the 3- and 4-year-olds in class Yellow 2 at the Valeska-Hinton Early Childhood Center in Peoria, Illinois. Even though I had heard bits and pieces about the Movie Theater Project, I found the documented report of its development in Chapter 9 to be breathtaking and certainly inspiring. Though the children in Steinheimer's group are identified as being "at risk," mainly on the basis of family income, the documentation that she shares with us clearly shows that her confidence in the children is not only justified, but clearly perceived by the children themselves.

Like so many of the projects described throughout this edition, one of the major points that becomes clear from the wide variety of examples throughout the book is that documentation can enhance the quality of the education and care we provide for our young children—but there has to be something to document! The authors include a useful brief introduction to using the project approach in the curriculum, which can provide a rich variety of children's experiences and learning to be captured in the variety of documentation methods the authors describe.

So, go to the windows available throughout this book and let the views they offer support and strengthen your own efforts to provide mind-engaging experiences for young children.

—Lilian G. Katz,
University of Illinois

Acknowledgments

The authors wish to express thanks for the contributions made by the following people to this work:

Lilian Katz, who mentored and encouraged us as we investigated this topic, and who provided invaluable criticism and advice in the first drafts of this book.

Sylvia Chard, for providing insight through her writing and teaching.

Ken Hinton, director of Valeska Hinton Early Childhood Education Center, for inspiration and support.

The teachers of Valeska Hinton Early Childhood Education Center—Stacy Berg, Jolyn Blank, Suzi Boos, Monica Borrowman, Anna Brown, Rachel Bystry, Judy Cagle, Beth Crider-Olcott, Michelle Didesch, Mary Ann Gottlieb, Gail Gordon, Renee Jackson, Valerie McCall, Pam Scranton, Tammy Shinkey, and Valerie Timmes—whose work is included in this book.

Illinois Valley Community College Early Childhood Education Center director Diane Christianson, teacher Rebecca Tonellie, and student teachers Ellen Bejster, Mindy Kramer, Theresa Leifheit, Linda Petelin, Arin Sorenson, and Robyn Tonelli.

Nancy Hertzog and the staff of the University Primary School at the University of Illinois.

Mary Jane Elliott, Don Shuler, Lee Makovichuk, Kim Fisher, Ruth Harkema, and Maggie Beneke, teachers who shared their work.

Dr. Maxine Wortham and Mary Ann Randle, for encouraging us to persevere in getting our thoughts on paper and smoothing the way for sharing the children's work.

Paula Ellberg, for her feedback.

Char Ward and the staff of STARNET at Western Illinois University, for their early recognition of our research and their encouragement.

Tom Layman, Octavia Durham, and Dexter Smith from the Chicago Metro Association for the Education of Young Children, not only for their support of the professional learning communities whose work is described, but also for their continued support of research in documentation, which led to the Power of Documentation Exhibit at the Chicago Children's Museum.

We are grateful for our colleagues Pam Scranton, Stacy Berg, and all the staff of Northminster Learning Center and their willingness to serve as a laboratory school for our ideas.

We could not have completed this book without the consistently calm and thoughtful editing and encouragement of Susan Liddicoat and her successor Marie Ellen Larcada, for their calm and thoughtful editing, and the patience and persistence of Shannon Waite of Teachers College Press.

Most of all, we wish to thank the children and their parents, who allowed us to share their stories.

Windows on Learning

Documenting Young Children's Work

Introduction

A visitor coming into the school for the first time is stopped by the children's work hanging on the walls. Drawings, paintings, and plans, carefully displayed in pleasing arrangements, attract his attention. A title tells the visitor that children are studying "The Pond." A large mural of a pond covers one wall. The visitor first admires the mural as children's art. Leaning closer, he is struck by the detail and care with which each element of the mural has been executed. Around the mural, he sees preliminary sketches of sections of the mural. Photographs show children sitting by a pond and in a meadow sketching the very plans that he now sees displayed.

The visitor is captivated by the look on the face of a child searching for information in a book. The child is intently involved in her work. Her small finger is on the picture in her book, and her small clipboard with her notes lies next to the book. The visitor can see that the child is comparing the picture in the book with her own drawing. The teacher's notes explain that the child is using books as a resource for the first time. As the visitor looks at the picture, he notices how very small the child is. Quickly searching the wall, he finds a summary written on a printed form and framed. "These children are 5 years old!" He wonders, "How did these children learn so much about the pond? How did they acquire the skills to do this kind of work?"

The visitor hears children coming down the hall. Peering down the corridor, he sees a small group of children settling onto the floor facing another display of children's work. They are carrying papers with them of work they have done. As he watches, he hears them discussing the work that they had previously completed, which is now displayed on the wall. The children are comparing the work on the wall with their latest work and talking about what they now know that they did not know before. The teacher is jotting notes on a Post-it pad and sticking the notes on a clipboard. Next to the notes she is making a list on a page entitled "Books and Materials Needed."

Turning the corner of the hall, the visitor almost stumbles over a large block structure of a water treatment plant. Labels made by the children designate the primary and secondary treatment pools. Having learned from his first experience with the mural, he immediately searches the walls to find the summary of this project. He sees that this study lasted 3 weeks and was completed by 3- and 4-year-olds. He also notices that this display includes teacher observations of how individual children's concepts changed.

As he enters the office to conduct his business, his first comment to the secretary is, "I can see that children are really learning at this school!"

◆　◆　◆

This book grew out of the experiences of teachers at schools like the one just described as they learned to document young children's work. The schools range from a comprehensive, state-of-the-art early intervention center in an urban setting, to a small school in a small town on the Mississippi River, to a community college laboratory school. Their path to documenting followed several routes. Some learned first to use an authentic assessment system, some learned how to use the project approach and document that process, and some learned how to document as they first learned how to teach in a teacher preparation program. What they had in common was wanting to know how to teach better, how to meet the needs of their children, and how to open the eyes of others to the wonderful world of young children's learning.

We shared that experience intimately with some of them. As a teacher, a lead teacher, and a teacher educator, we were involved in the experimentation, teaching children, asking questions, observing, applying, arguing, and reflecting. We developed frameworks to help us all understand, and we re-worked and reworded those frameworks until they began to take a form that could support our ideas and serve as a foundation for our thinking about documenting children's learning. We read widely and incorporated the work of many others, building on their pioneering efforts and using their points of view to enrich our own. We are grateful to those who came before us and took the time to write down what they had learned. You will see their remarks quoted throughout this book.

USING AN AUTHENTIC ASSESSMENT SYSTEM

Our first experience with documenting children's work was through the use of an authentic assessment system. Many teachers whose work is shared in this book use an authentic assessment system, with most using the Work Sampling System (Dichtelmiller, Jablon, Dorfman, Marsden, & Meisels, 2001). The Work Sampling System is a performance assessment that provides an alternative to group-administered, norm-referenced achievement tests in preschool through fifth grade. Its purpose "is to document and assess children's skills, knowledge, behavior, and accomplishments across a wide variety [of curriculum] on multiple occasions" (p. 4). The Work Sampling System consists of three complementary components: (1) developmental guidelines and checklists, (2) portfolios of children's work, and (3) summary reports completed by teachers.

Assessments based on the Work Sampling approach take place three times a year. They are designed to reflect classroom goals and objectives and to help teachers keep track of children's continuous progress by placing their work within a broad, developmental perspective. Through its focus on documenting individual performance of classroom-based tasks, Work Sampling enhances student motivation, assists teachers in instructional decision making, and serves as an effective means for reporting children's progress to families, educators, and the community (Dichtelmiller, Jablon, Dorfman, Marsden, & Meisels, 2001).

The Work Sampling System provides us not only a framework for systematically collecting and processing children's work but also for training in how to observe, how to collect, and how to analyze. It enables teachers to set up a plan so that all children's work is sampled in all areas of development. It also provides a systematic way to collect, store, and organize the portfolios. Through the training process, teachers learn about nonbiased and nonjudgmental observing and recording of behavior. The checklists provide a comprehensive and developmentally appropriate picture of what children can be expected to know and do across all domains of growth and learning. Especially valuable to the development of documentation skills is the collection and rating schedule that paces teachers through the process and provides an impetus for ongoing, systematic collection of children's work.

UNDERSTANDING THE PROJECT APPROACH

About half of the teachers in this book had participated in a class with Lilian Katz on the project approach. These teachers incorporated the knowledge about collecting, observing, and recording that they had gained through applying the assessment system to the task of adding the project approach to their curriculum.

The project approach is a good example of developmentally appropriate, active, engaging, and meaningful learning. A *project* is an in-depth study, over an extended period of time, of a topic that is of high interest to an individual, a small group, or a whole class (Helm & Katz, 2001; Katz & Chard, 2000). Skills and concepts are learned by children through their efforts to find answers to questions about a topic. Topics are posed by either the children, the teacher, or the teacher working with the children. Independent and group planning, construction, research, and representation are all ways that children learn in the project approach.

The project approach is similar to thematic teaching in its integrated approach to content but is different in the emphasis on child investigation and problem solving. Children become emotionally involved in the learning experience. The project approach is not new in education, but interest has been revived and extended by the changes in understanding of how children learn and the need to develop problem-solving skills in order to meet the challenges of a technological society.

Doing projects is an approach with great promise for all children. Helping parents and community members see the value of this approach depends upon the teacher's ability to provide comprehensive, good-quality documentation of what children are doing and learning. Careful and systematic recording of learning can enable the teacher to meet accountability needs while using this promising approach. Documentation can capture for the teacher, the parent, the school administration, and the public a vision of the intellectual development that occurs while children are involved in research. They can also see the strengthening of the variety of intellectual and social dispositions that occurs while the children work together, argue, hypothesize, and predict. Documentation enables the teacher to monitor the development of the project. It is a method of evaluating and improving the project as the project develops.

As the teachers with whom we worked began to collect and display documentation of the projects, we sought a conceptual structure upon which to focus our discussion and reflection about documentation. The first concept that we developed and shared was the framework of the windows described in Chapter 2. The second concept was the types of documentation web described in Chapter 3, which shows a variety of ways to document. The web and its pieces, which appear throughout the book, provide an impetus to document in many different ways.

We have discovered that it is in the careful documentation of children's learning in the project approach that teachers are most able to meet the needs for assessment and program evaluation without narrowing children's experiences. The project approach enriches and increases the complexity of the items that teachers are able to collect in an authentic assessment process. Work samples that result from project work are more informative than work samples collected when children are doing teacher-directed learning activities.

LEARNING FROM THE REGGIO EMILIA PRESCHOOLS

One of the reasons that interest has developed in the project approach is the demonstration of high-quality early childhood education in the preschools of Reggio Emilia in Italy. These schools also use projects extensively and have been extremely successful in demonstrating the wealth of knowledge and skills that are gained in these projects through their use of aesthetically displayed documentation.

Many educators in North America were first introduced to documentation when they visited "The Hundred Languages of Children," the touring exhibit from Reggio Emilia. The documentation that takes place in the schools of Reggio Emilia is extensive and rich. According to Lella Gandini (1993), documentation in these schools has several functions:

> To make parents aware of their children's experiences and maintain parental involvement; to allow teachers to understand children better and to evaluate the teachers' own work, thus promoting their professional growth; to facilitate communication and exchange of ideas among educators; to make children aware that their effort is valued; and to create an archive that traces the history of the school and of the pleasure and process of learning by many children and their teachers. (p. 8)

All of these functions are similar to the functions of documentation in our schools. However, according to founder Loris Malaguzzi (1998), the schools of Reggio Emilia

> have no planned curriculum with units and subunits. . . . Instead every year each school delineates a series of related projects, some short range and some long. These themes serve as the main structural supports, but then it is up to the children, the course of events, and the teachers to determine whether the building turns out to be a hut on stilts, or an apartment house or whatever. (pp. 87–88)

Although we may envy the curricular freedom in the Reggio Emilia preschools to follow the lead of the children, the reality is that it is more difficult to do in our schools. Following developmentally appropriate practices, "teachers make plans to enable children to attain key curriculum goals across various disciplines such as language arts, mathematics, social studies, science, art, music, physical education, and health" (Bredekamp & Copple, 1997, p. 18). In many schools in our educational system, there are state learning goals, standardized achievement tests, exit exams, or required public disclosure by program, school, or district of student performance. Since the first edition of this book in 1998, the emphasis on accountability and the introduction of standards and required research-based curriculum in many early childhood programs has even intensified. The gap between the culture of the preschools of Reggio Emilia and the culture of the schools in which we work has widened. Even teachers in private preschool programs without governmental requirements are often challenged to demonstrate their effectiveness. In addition, parents may have content expectations and share these when participating in goal setting for early childhood programs, especially where curriculum and learning experiences are negotiated with parents, families, and children. These factors have resulted in more emphasis on accountability in our documentation.

For a program to succeed, or a teacher to succeed, it is important that the teacher be able to provide evidence of how the learning occurring in the classroom relates to goals and objectives of the district or program. Even teachers with few restrictions on how they teach are often frustrated when they are unable to articulate to others the value of active, engaged, and meaningful learning experiences such as the project approach. We found that documentation enabled us to see children's learning more clearly, allowing us to more easily integrate content into emergent curriculum approaches. Documentation has also enabled us to help others understand how emergent curriculum approaches can be an effective way to meet content goals. Documentation has become a strategy for us to use to show the value of the learning experiences we provide our children.

Many of our teachers face the challenges of high mobility of both children and staff and an increase in the number of children in poverty (Helm & Beneke, 2003). Being involved with programs for children at risk, we know it is important to closely monitor each child's development. This does not mean focusing on children's deficits but rather identifying strengths, maximizing teaching effectiveness, and accessing resources as needed. This positive focus results in documentation that includes systematic collections of each child's work in each area of learning in addition to project documentation. As we continue to see children who struggle in school and increasing numbers of children with special needs and children learning a second language, we have become convinced of the importance of systematic documentation.

A lesson that we have learned from Reggio Emilia is the immense power of documentation. The preschools themselves, which are paid for by the city of Reggio Emilia, are a tribute to the ability of the staff to involve the families and the community. Their consistent, informative, high-quality documentation has, no doubt, contributed greatly to that involvement. We are inspired to persist in our exploration of documentation and to adapt many of the documentation processes of Reggio Emilia to our own schools.

INTRODUCING OUR SCHOOLS

We have drawn our examples in this book from many different schools. Numerous stories of documentation come from the Valeska Hinton Early Childhood Education Center, a public school early childhood program in Peoria, Illinois. It provides a comprehensive full-day, year-round program for children ages 3 through 6. Seventy-five percent of these children come from low-income families. The center is divided into four villages, or minischools, of five classrooms each. The villages are named for the colors—red, yellow, blue, and green. Teachers in each village meet weekly to plan and reflect.

Illinois Valley Community College is another site where extensive experimentation and development of the documentation concepts presented in this book have occurred. This small, rural community college in the north-central part of the state offers a 2-year child development degree. An on-campus child-care center functions as a laboratory for practicum students who are learning how to teach and as an exemplary center for area child-care programs.

A third major source for our work is new to this second edition. Discovery Preschool, a faith-based, Reggio-inspired program in Peoria, Illinois, provides a toddler program, a preschool program, a full-day kindergarten program, and after-school care. The teachers and administrators of this program have served as leaders in project work and documentation. Each year they host Open Door, a day of visitation and professional development that brings teachers from all over the country to observe the project approach, documentation, and authentic assessment in action.

Other schools are represented in this book by teachers who have shared their knowledge and experiences with documentation with us through workshops, conferences, and the Internet since the first edition of this book. With this second edition, we hope to expand this network by encouraging more teachers to adopt the practice of documenting young children's learning.

OVERVIEW OF THE SECOND EDITION

Part I of this book enables readers to learn about documentation. Chapter 1 provides the rationale for the study of documentation. In Chapter 2, readers will find the windows conceptual structure for thinking about documentation that guided the teachers. In Chapter 3, the web of types of documentation is introduced. Chapters 4 through 8 provide an indepth exploration of the variety of types of documentation, with samples collected by the teachers. Through children's work and teacher notes, readers will see what children learned and how they developed through use of the project approach.

In Part II, Chapters 9 through 11, readers will learn about documentation in action. New in this second edition, Chapter 9 provides a rich example of the power of documentation as the reader follows Kathy Steinheimer and her class through the Movie Theater Project. Through the teacher's and the children's documentation, readers will experience the progress of the Movie Theater as it grew, expanded, and concluded. Each type of documentation carries labels from the web to help readers relate this example to the concepts explained in the earlier chapters of the book. Throughout the book and especially in Chapter 10, teacher reflections will show readers how teachers use documentation to inform teaching and for their own professional development. In an expanded Chapter 11, readers will learn how documentation as described in this book relates to recommendations and requirements and for accountability and assessment.

In Part III, we offer some practical tips and advice that we have picked up through the years. Chapter 12 explains how to collect, organize, and share documentation with children, other teachers, parents, and the community. The last chapter provides useful forms for the documentation process that were previously published separately.

CONTINUING THE JOURNEY

We have found our study of documentation and how teachers and children use it to be a fascinating, adventurous journey. We share the work of these teachers and what we have learned with and from them in the spirit of supporting and encouraging others. We invite you to join us in this journey.

PART I
Learning About Documentation

CHAPTER 1

The Value of Documentation

document: —2. To support (an assertion or a claim, for example) with evidence or decisive information.
—*American Heritage Dictionary* (2000)

Documenting children's learning is one of the most valuable skills a teacher can develop today. The teacher who perceives how children learn and who can help others see that learning can contribute significantly to the child's development. The school visitor described at the beginning of the Introduction said, "I can see that children are really learning at this school." He was able to see what the children were learning because teachers had carefully collected, analyzed, interpreted, and displayed the evidence. This use of documentation is directly related to what research in the early childhood field has shown about how children learn.

APPLYING WHAT IS KNOWN
ABOUT CHILDREN'S LEARNING

Many early childhood teachers are aware of the literature on the importance of active, engaged, meaningful learning experiences and the importance of children's constructing their own knowledge through interaction with their environments and with others (Berk & Winsler, 1995; Gardner, 1991; Kamii & Ewing, 1996; Katz & Chard, 2000; Vygotsky, 1978). The work of Piaget demonstrates the importance of sensory experiences and concrete learning activities (DeVries & Kohlberg, 1990; Kamii, 1982; Kamii & Ewing, 1996). The National Association for the Education of Young Children (NAEYC) confirmed the importance of direct, firsthand, interactive experience in the position statement *Developmentally Appropriate Practices* (Bredekamp, 1987; Bredekamp & Copple, 1997).

Early childhood teachers are also aware of the importance of providing opportunities to develop positive dispositions toward learning, a concept described by Bruner (1996), Katz (1985, 1987), and Smith (1990). Dispositions are "relatively enduring habits of mind or action, or tendencies to respond to categories of experience across classes of situations" (Katz, 1985, p. 1). Dispositions are preferences of what we choose to think about (Smith, 1990).

> We are all disposed to think about some things but not about others—depending on our interest in them, and whether we feel they are within our competence . . . the disposition to think about particular matters rises and falls on the tides of positive and negative experience. (p. 124)

Teaching the young child is a matter not just of providing opportunities to learn knowledge and skills but also of developing attitudes toward learning and using those skills. An example of how dispositions have an impact on school skills is the disposition to read. How a child feels about reading and whether or not the child wants to learn to read can have long-range effects on the child's reading achievement. We know that skills involved in reading improve by actually reading. Thus, the disposition to be a "reader" must be strengthened and monitored (Katz, 1995). In the guidelines for constructing appropriate curriculum, NAEYC specified that "curriculum promotes the development of knowledge and understanding, processes, and skills, as well as the dispositions to use and apply skills and to go on learning" (Bredekamp & Copple, 1997, p. 20).

The literature applying recent research on brain development and thinking to education has also had an impact on early childhood teachers' commitment to active, engaging methods that foster positive dispositions (Hart, 1983; Howard, 2006; Sylwester, 1995, 2004; Zull, 2002). One insight from brain research is that learning is related to children's feelings and emotions, thus potentially influencing the important dispositions to learning (Howard, 2006; Wolfe, 2001). Not only are children less likely to practice and perfect skills if they are not positively involved, but children's feelings about an experience also affect how successful the child is in learning the skill in the first place (Sylwester, 1995).

A second insight from brain research is that learning is easier when experiences are interconnected rather than isolated or compartmentalized into subject areas (Howard, 2006). From brain research also comes the understanding that the brain adapts and develops through continuously changing and challenging environments (Kotulak, 1993). Children, especially in the early years of schooling, learn from hands-on, thought-provoking experiences because these experiences challenge children to think.

In addition, experience in the early years builds a foundation for symbolic and abstract thinking. "In the first years of life, young children . . . develop at least a first-draft level of competence with basic human symbol systems—language, number, music, two-dimensional depiction, and the like" (Gardner, 1993, p. 56).

Despite the prominence of recommendations for active, engaging, and meaningful learning experiences and the literature on brain development, teaching young children in ways that they learn best is not always supported by decision makers and parents. Educators have felt increasing challenges created by social and economic changes and the pressure to transfer methods that are not appropriate from the elementary years into the early years. This is based on a belief that beginning academic instruction earlier would result in higher achievement. Many early childhood programs place undue emphasis on rote learning and whole-group instruction of narrowly defined academic skills (Bredekamp & Copple, 1997).

In response, NAEYC issued its first position statement on developmentally appropriate practices (Bredekamp, 1987). This statement was very influential in challenging teachers to think about what was appropriate in early childhood classrooms. In a revised version (Bredekamp & Copple, 1997), 12 principles of child development and learning were articulated (see Figure 1.1). These accurately summarize our beliefs about appropriate early childhood programming.

WHY DOCUMENT?

Through documentation the teacher can make it possible for others to "see" the learning that takes place when developmentally appropriate teaching occurs. Documentation also provides the evidence needed for reliably assessing children's progress, for meeting accountability requirements, for monitoring individual students' growth and development, and for program evaluation.

Often as teachers become more and more committed to teaching children appropriately and fostering positive dispositions, they become concerned about the use of standardized group achievement tests to assess children's development.

Figure 1.1. Principles of child development and learning.

1. Domains of children's development—physical, social, emotional, and cognitive—are closely related. Development in one domain influences and is influenced by development in other domains.
2. Development occurs in a relatively orderly sequence, with later abilities, skills, and knowledge building on those already acquired.
3. Development proceeds at varying rates from child to child as well as unevenly within different areas of each child's functioning.
4. Early experiences have both cumulative and delayed effects on individual children's development; optimal periods exist for certain types of development and learning.
5. Development proceeds in predictable directions toward greater complexity, organization, and internalization.
6. Development and learning occur in and are influenced by multiple social and cultural contexts.
7. Children are active learners, drawing on direct physical and social experiences as well as culturally transmitted knowledge to construct their own understandings of the world around them.
8. Development and learning result from interaction of biological maturation and the environment, which includes both the physical and social worlds that children live in.
9. Play is an important vehicle for children's social, emotional, and cognitive development as well as a reflection of their development.
10. Development advances when children have opportunities to practice newly acquired skills as well as when they experience a challenge just beyond the level of their present mastery.
11. Children demonstrate different modes of knowing and learning and different ways of representing what they know.
12. Children develop and learn best in the context of a community where they are safe and valued, their physical needs are met, and they feel psychologically secure.

Source: Bredekamp, S., & Copple, C. (Eds.), 1997, pp. 10–15.

Meeting Accountability Demands

An important impetus for documentation is accountability. Funding of early childhood programs is under scrutiny, along with all other social service government expenditures. In light of severe competition for scarce public funds, providing evidence of program effectiveness has become essential. Results are more closely monitored than in the past with requirements to inform the constituencies of schools and other early childhood programs of their effectiveness. Many programs were required to show evidence of achievement on standardized achievement measures while others turned to standardized tests as a way to to meet demands for accountability.

However, group-administered tests are inappropriate for assessing young children. According to Samuel Meisels (1993, 2000), group-administered tests focus on the acquisition of simple facts, low-level skills, superficial memorization, and isolated evidence of achievement, and can actually create barriers to learning. Their content is generally abstract, verbally mediated, and potentially biased against children unfamiliar or uncomfortable with testlike activities and with middle-class manners and mores. Many educators have expressed special concern about the use of standardized achievement tests with young children. Gullo (2005) explains why young children are especially affected:

> During most of the early childhood years, it is difficult to measure and assess bits of knowledge and skills that are isolated from other types of knowledge and skills. Young children are not reliable test takers due to the many different confining personal, developmental, and environmental factors that affect their behaviors. In addition, just as children do not develop in an isolated manner, they do not acquire knowledge nor learn specific bits of information or skills without learning other things within the contextual framework. (p. 17)

Gullo also raises the issue of the importance of the context of learning and using knowledge and skills. Standardized achievement tests, with their narrow focus, do not provide information about how children integrate their learning and apply content knowledge to real-life challenges. An example of this is the child who can score well on spelling lists of memorized words but misspells those same words when they are used in writing a story or a letter. Problem solving, which involves knowing what skills to apply when, is also not easily assessed by conventional methods. There is a need to assess the child's ability to integrate and apply what is learned in the more formal parts of the curriculum, such as school skills like spelling, to less formal parts of the curriculum, such as project work. The importance of assessment is underscored by the National Research Council's Board on Testing and Assessment:

> Students will learn more if instruction and assessment are integrally related. *In the classroom, providing students with information about particular qualities of their work and about what they can do to improve is crucial for maximizing learning.* It is in the context of classroom assessment that theories of cognition and learning can be particularly helpful by providing a picture of

intermediary states of student understanding on the pathway from novice to competent performer in a subject domain. (Pellegrino, Chudowsky, & Glaser, 2001, p. 8; italics in original)

All of the concerns about standardized testing for the preprimary- and primary-age child provide additional impetus for learning to document. Teachers are being challenged to apply developmentally appropriate curriculum and teaching methods and, at the same time, to provide evidence of growth, development, and intellectual and social learning. The two circles in Figure 1.2 represent these two simultaneous challenges. Teachers want to meet demands of accountability placed upon them. They also want to know how to use informal methods for assessment and program evaluation that would show what children are learning and give credibility to the teaching and learning processes occurring in their classrooms. Figure 1.2 also shows how comprehensive, careful, systematic documentation of the learning that occurs when children are involved in meaningful learning experiences can meet the demands for both effective teaching and accountability.

Becoming Better Teachers

One of the most important reasons to learn about documentation is its power to inform teaching. "Documentation provides a basis for the modification and adjustment of teaching strategies, and a source of ideas for new strategies, while deepening teachers' awareness of each child's progress" (Katz & Chard, 1996, p. 2). Teachers who have good documentation skills are more likely to make productive decisions when planning educational experiences, interacting with the child and family, and accessing support systems for children. These decisions

Figure 1.2. Simultaneous challenges.

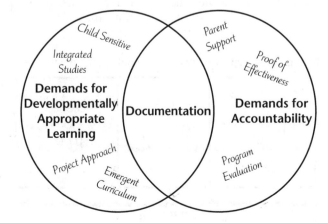

include how to organize the classroom, what to do next, what questions to ask children, what resources to provide, and how to stimulate the development of each child. The more information the teacher can gather on which to base these decisions, the more effective the teacher is likely to be.

Typical assessment of children's learning using standardized tests provides limited assistance in teacher decision making. Vygotsky's sociocultural theory of maximizing learning demonstrates the most serious insufficiency of traditional methods of assessment and of monitoring children's development (Berk & Winsler, 1995; Bodrova & Leong, 1996; Vygotsky, 1978). "Vygotsky suggested that what we should be measuring is not what children can do by themselves or already know but rather what they can do with help of another person and have the potential to learn" (Berk & Winsler, 1995, p. 26). According to Vygotsky, the teacher is most effective when teaching is directed toward a *zone of proximal development* for each child. Vygotsky presents learning as a continuum (see Figure 1.3). The *actual developmental level* is what the student has already mastered. The *zone of proximal development* is what the student is beginning to understand, what the student can do sometimes and not other times, and what the student can do with help. This is where progress in learning is maximized. The *potential developmental level* is new knowledge or skills that the child has not yet achieved. The student moves through this continuum as new knowledge is integrated with old knowledge and new skills are mastered. The zone of proximal development is dynamic and changing constantly as children acquire new skills and knowledge. As Bodrova and Leong (1996) explain:

> Vygotsky chose the word *zone* because he conceived development not as a point on a scale, but as a continuum of behaviors or degrees of maturation. By describing the zone as proximal (next to, close to), he meant that the zone is limited by those behaviors that will develop in the near future. (p. 35)

Figure 1.3. Vygotsky's zone of proximal development.

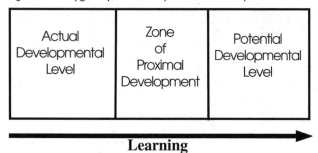

According to Berk and Winsler (1995), a major goal of education is to keep children working in the zone of proximal development. The teacher can do that by structuring the task and the environment and adjusting the amount of adult intervention to the child's current needs and abilities. To do this requires that teachers have in-depth and current understanding about the knowledge and skills of their students. This has great implications for assessment practices. To determine the zone, a teacher needs to assess a child's development, probe the child's thinking on the topic, and provide learning experiences that will build a bridge or scaffold to higher-level thought processes or *potential learning*. To do this successfully, it is important that the teacher know not only what a child can already do independently but also what the child can do with different levels of assistance. Teachers also need to know how children use their help and what hints are most useful (Bodrova & Leong, 1996).

Standardized tests do not assist the teacher in teaching to the zone of development. They focus on a limited sample of what the student has mastered. By using only information on what children already know, the teacher cannot as effectively assist the child in reaching the next stages of learning. In addition, the time delay between administration of standardized group tests and availability of results to teachers precludes using this data to inform teachers of the zone of proximal development.

Meeting Diversity Challenges

Teachers are also interested in documentation because of the demographic changes in classrooms. In many communities, children are coming to preschool with unmet needs, and the role of the teacher has become more complex. Changing demographics have increased the skills required for an early childhood teacher to be effective. Teachers are finding more and more children in their classrooms who are growing up in poverty, and the challenge of successfully supporting their growth and development is greater (Children's Defense Fund, 2004). Because mothers are returning to the workforce early in their child's life, even children from families with adequate income are spending a significant amount of their growth and learning time under the direction of early childhood teachers in group settings (Children's Defense Fund, 2004). With the increase in single-parent families and the increasing economic challenge to support young families, many parents have little time and energy to interact daily with their children or participate in their children's schools. Today's teacher, in addition to being responsible for effective teaching in the classroom, often takes more responsibility for assisting parents in understanding and supporting their children's learning.

Inclusion of children with special needs in regular education classrooms has also increased the complexity of teaching. Special needs include children who are gifted, have physical disabilities, have learning problems requiring individualized education plans, speak English as a second language, or have problems resulting from growing up in poverty. Teachers need to know what children do and do not know, as well as how they learn most easily so that methods can be adjusted to help them learn in the most effective way—teachers do not want to waste children's time and effort. It is also important to be sure that information teachers are using for decision making is unbiased and culturally sensitive. Documentation can help the teacher identify and provide the appropriate learning experiences for all children as well as more typically developing children.

Changes in typical approaches to meeting diverse needs are also common. Some of these changes have resulted in a greater need for documentation. For example, there are new approaches to meeting the needs of children in classrooms with a high percentage of children in poverty. In the past, teachers in such classrooms often focused on what children lacked with intensive drill and practice on discrete skills. Teachers moved children as a group through a fixed sequence of subskills, and assessment was through standardized tests. Several decades of studies of successful teaching in such classrooms now point to the value of deemphasizing the teaching of discrete skills in isolation from the context in which these skills are applied, fostering connections between academic learning and the world from which children come, and using the child and the child's experiences as a resource for learning (Knapp, 1995). The emphasis is now on strategies that provide extensive opportunities for engaging children in activities that require reading, writing, and problem-solving skills (Helm & Beneke, 2003).

In contrast to standardized achievement or subskill testing, which does not provide much of the information teachers need, comprehensive, quality documentation can assist teachers in teaching children from high-poverty backgrounds. Similarly, documentation can assist teachers in meeting special needs of other children through productive, efficient, and developmentally matched teaching methods.

Involving Children and Families

Watching children learn is exciting and rewarding to teachers. They understand the importance of developing a culture of a learning school where children see themselves as learners, parents see their children as successful learners, and members of the community value the learning that occurs. Early childhood teachers need to know how to develop documentation systems that involve children and families as participants as well as viewers. Teachers need to use a variety of ways to document so they can show all of the children's strengths and unique talents. They need to know how to collect and present evidence of children's learning so that people with a wide range of backgrounds and interests can understand the meaning of the documentation.

Teachers also want documentation to assist in developing partnerships with parents. A carefully planned and implemented documentation process can assist teachers in informing and reassuring parents. For example, a parent might express concern that his child is not writing real words at the beginning of kindergarten. A teacher who has collected samples of children's writing may be able to ease these fears by showing the child's progress through the writing samples that she has collected. By examining the samples and hearing what the teacher has to say about typical progress, the parent can see that children progress from letterlike shapes, to clear letters, to words. The parent can then appreciate how his child is progressing through the normal sequence and can share with the teacher what he has observed at home. The parent, whose anxieties are eased, will not endanger the child's disposition to write by placing undue pressure on the child, such as extensive drill and practice of making "correct" letters at home. Together the teacher and parent can develop ideas to use at home that will show the child how important writing and reading are. The parent can put his efforts into providing a literacy-enriched environment, and the teacher can share her documentation of the child's ongoing progress toward literacy.

Documentation can also assist parents in making decisions about their child's education. In the following note, a parent, Nancy Higgins, explains how she came to understand the project approach through a documentation display and how it assisted her in choosing a preschool program for her child.

My first actual encounter with projects occurred in late spring at an open house for prospective parents. Because my husband was out of town, I had to attend alone. I tried to analyze the project approach in the manner he might have. I was skeptical—the so-called traditional approaches had worked for me, so why wouldn't it also provide success for our child. . . . Walking around the school that night, I began to be impressed. I studied [the documentation on] a project on reflections. I marveled at the insights shared by the children. The critical thinking skills which their work exhibited was phenomenal. Direct quotations included sentences of greater length and complexity than I would have expected. Their vocabulary was very specific. I went home and attempted to describe what I had seen to my husband. . . . After our discussion, we became convinced that this was the place for our daughter to learn.

Having gained a clear understanding of the curriculum and teaching methods of the school, this parent felt confident about the decision to enroll her child.

Documentation can also assist the teacher in making decisions about when additional support systems are needed for a child. As a teacher becomes a skilled documenter, he can improve his knowledge and understanding of the typical development of children's knowledge and skills. When collecting a child's work over a period of time, he can see if a child is progressing as expected and if mastery of a skill is just around the corner. When the teacher does not see mastery or emerging skills, he can seek additional help, and special assistance can be provided for the child.

Providing a Vehicle for Reflection

Documentation reveals to us not only what children are learning but also what teachers are learning about teaching. Documentation can be a vehicle for self-reflection and a way to analyze, share, discuss, and guide the process of teaching by communicating with other professionals what is occurring in the classroom. Teachers teach by making dozens of decisions each day. Bredekamp and Copple (1997) recognize the importance of these decisions when they define "developmentally appropriate practice as the outcome of decision making" (p. vii). Teachers are challenged from a variety of sources to be-

come more reflective and to regularly analyze, evaluate, and strengthen the quality and effectiveness of their work. To do this, they need to accurately capture what is occurring in the classroom through documentation.

THE PROMISE OF DOCUMENTATION

Learning to document yields positive results when a teacher makes a commitment of time and effort. Teaching in developmentally appropriate ways is facilitated when teachers know how to obtain and provide evidence of children's learning (Bredekamp, 1987). In contrast to standardized achievement tests, comprehensive, good-quality documentation can do the following:

- Provide evidence of children's learning in all areas of a child's development—physical, emotional, social, and cognitive
- Offer insight into the complex learning experiences provided to children when teachers use an integrated approach
- Provide a framework for organizing teachers' observations and recording each child's special interests and developmental progress
- Emphasize learning as an interactive process by documenting what children learn when they are engaged in active exploration and interaction with adults, other children, and materials
- Show the advantages of providing activities and materials that are concrete, real, and relevant to the lives of young children
- Enable a teacher to assess what children know or can and cannot do so the teacher can modify the difficulty, complexity, and challenge of an activity

When teachers document children's learning in a variety of ways, they can be more confident about the value of their teaching.

CHAPTER 2

Windows on Learning: A Framework for Decision Making

window: —1. An opening constructed in a wall or roof to admit light or air.
—American Heritage Dictionary (2000)

For documentation to yield the benefits outlined in Chapter 1, the methods used must be simple, organized, and efficient so that they enhance rather than detract from a teacher's productivity. Using documentation to inform instruction can help a teacher know what activities to plan in her lessons, anticipate materials that will be useful in the classroom, and differentiate instruction for individual children.

Good-quality documentation enables the three major players in the child's educational experience—teachers, parents, and community—to respond more accurately to the true needs of the child in the education system. In this way, the education system can work more consistently with, rather than against, teachers in their efforts, thereby enhancing effectiveness. But how do teachers decide what and when to document? How extensive should the documentation be? How should the documentation be presented?

Answers to these questions depend on the use of sound theoretical frameworks for making decisions about focus, presentation, and extensiveness of documentation. We have found it helpful to use a concept of three windows. First, a window on a child's development provides a framework for the teacher to document and share with others an individual child's growth and development. Second, a window on a learning experience provides a framework for the teacher to document and share with others a specific learning experience of the class. Third, a window for teacher self-reflection provides the teacher with a framework for documenting his or her role in the learning. To visualize the use of these frameworks, begin with an image of a classroom where children are deeply engaged in project work. Constructions are coming together; scenes are unfolding in the dramatic play area; some children are totally absorbed in an individual activity; some children are working together, talking and planning; and teachers are in-

teracting with children. These activities are typical of the bustle of a classroom in which children's minds are fully engaged in a variety of meaningful activities. Now imagine that three windows have been inserted into the walls of this busy classroom, to enable others to look in. The windows represent three different ways of looking at the learning that is occurring in this classroom. Selecting a window to open guides the teacher in choosing the particular aspect of the project to be documented, the form of documentation, and the degree of elaboration in the description.

A WINDOW ON A CHILD'S DEVELOPMENT

By providing documentation to form a window on an individual child, a teacher may share insights regarding a child's growth and development with the child's parents and/or with colleagues. The teacher may improve the accuracy of her own view of the child through periodic, systematic examination of individual documentation. Documentation through this window will focus on individually produced items or on evidence of the individual child's participation in the group. Individual products that constitute documentation may include items commonly collected for children's portfolios, such as examples of the child's drawing, writing, constructions, or songs. The benefits of the principle that "the more informed you are, the better able you are to make decisions" (L. G. Katz, personal communication, August 16, 1995) are applicable here.

For example, consider the window on a child named Hope created by prekindergarten teacher Ruth Harkema:

> Hope had great growth in attitude and abilities. This is her snake representation at the beginning of the project on snakes (see Figure 2.1a). Her comment, when asked what she wanted to learn about snakes, was a very firm: "DO NOT OPEN CAGE!" But by the end of the project we saw her smile and eagerly

Figure 2.1a. Hope's first representation reveals limited understanding of the characteristics of the snake.

Figure 2.1b. Hope's final drawing of a snake included patterns and scales, and its shape represented Hope's understanding of how the snake moves.

Figure 2.2. Hope's writing of her story revealed her growing confidence with letters and their sounds.

reach out to touch snakes! This is her final drawing (see Figure 2.1b). Notice the detailed scales and patterns the later drawing exhibits.

Hope blossomed through her persistent participation in every part of the project from painting and drawing at school and the zoo, researching and reporting, touching and feeling snakes, to designing them out of wood and Model Magic. She was no longer afraid of snakes, but delighted in touching them, and confidently dictated in her final journal entry, "We go to the zoo." Her friend interrupted, "How do I write snake?" As I helped Madison isolate the sounds, Hope snatched the marker from my hand, saying, "I do it, too." She drew lines for her own words and proceeded to sound out the rest of her snake story. Although her letters did not always fall on the page in correct order and she needed help with the "g" of "cage," [Hope,] . . . adopted from China and unable to speak English 20 months earlier, [was now able] . . . to write her new language (see Figure 2.2). Hope's curiosity, persistence, and desire to learn and to do everything her classmates did—those "dispositions" created the basis for her growth and development through project work.

With these two paragraphs and samples of Hope's work, Mrs. Harkema has helped us understand a great deal about Hope's knowledge and skills, but just as important, we have learned about her dispositions and her approach to interactions with others. We also see how the combination of these dispositions and engagement in a meaningful project helped her develop rapid mastery of a second language.

Another type of documentation that provides a window on the child's development is the child's self-reflections, which may be collected in audio- or videotape recordings, anecdotal notes, webs or lists made by the individual child, or a child's contributions to webs or lists made by a group. An example of a self-reflection that includes a statement of disposition or feeling was collected in the course of a project conducted in Judy Cagle's preprimary classroom for 3- and 4-year-olds:

Taylor was one of several children using clay and small pieces of mylar to construct small buildings. Taylor is a very verbal child with strong language skills, but he had shown a marked lack of interest in using art materials. However, the Reflections Project really engaged Taylor's interest, and he constructed an elaborate clay church with many entrances and windows. He painted the clay structure orange and cut and carefully glued mylar windows onto his church. Completing his church took Taylor several days. On completion of his construction, Taylor turned to me and said, "Teacher, this is the best thing I've ever done in my whole life!" I thought this statement was especially significant in view of Taylor's earlier avoidance of the art materials.

That day Ms. Cagle noted in her journal Taylor's self-appraisal and newfound satisfaction with his art ability. She made a note to herself to build on Taylor's interest in representing buildings in three dimensions by presenting him with alternative materials for construction. Later that week, she recorded the statement as an anecdotal record in Taylor's portfolio and recorded his self-appraisal on his developmental checklist (Dichtelmiller, Jablon, Dorfman, Marsden, & Meisels, 2001). Since she considered this statement to be such a milestone in his development, Ms. Cagle displayed a photograph of Taylor's church in the hallway.

She wanted Taylor's parents to see the construction he had built in the art area and to recognize that his statement indicated a new positive evaluation of himself as an artist. The item on the developmental checklist that Ms. Cagle supported with her documentation of Taylor's statement was VI A-1 in "The Arts" section of the Work Sampling System: "Uses a variety of art materials for tactile experience and exploration" (Dichtelmiller, Jablon, Marsden, & Meisels, 2001, p. 160).

As shown in this example, observations of a child's development made during the course of a project may take the form of data points on a developmental checklist, or of anecdotal notes or statements on dispositions. Items of work saved for a child's individual portfolio might include photos, tape recordings, and samples or products.

As in the case of Taylor, the teacher selects those items for documentation that indicate significant growth or development and displays those items that reveal growth and that may, at the same time, tell the story of the project. Had Ms. Cagle attempted to document for display the comments of all the children in her class who had chosen to construct buildings with clay, she would have needlessly used time and space and consequently reduced her own efficiency. In addition, had she uniformly displayed all the children's comments, those viewing the display might have overlooked the importance of Taylor's statement. A teacher who documents effectively looks for and displays work that provides evidence of each child's growth and development. On occasion a teacher might create a minidisplay that focuses on the growth of a child who has been particularly engaged in a project. This minidisplay,

then, might be included in the larger display documenting the development of the project.

More typically, however, the teacher publicly documents a project using the work of many children in the class. In this way, all children have work displayed, but all of their work is not displayed at the same time. For example, part of a display of a Rabbit Project might be made up of a writing sample from one child, a drawing sample from another child, and a tape-recorded sample of a song about rabbits created by another. Each sample is selected because of the growth it reveals in the individual child's development, but in their totality, the various samples also tell the story of the project.

A WINDOW ON A LEARNING EXPERIENCE

When the purpose of the documentation is to organize, demonstrate, and display to others the general growth in knowledge, skills, dispositions, and feelings (Chard, 1994) of the children involved in a learning experience, the teacher may select documentation to form another window. The view through this window enables the teacher to share the impact of the project on the children's learning with other teachers, parents, or visitors.

For example, one mother, a local public school board member who viewed a display of children's artwork, started an ongoing conversation with the leaders of an Arts in Action program about how art can positively impact children's socioemotional development. This mother used the documentation as a springboard for her own thinking about advocacy for after-school arts programs in the public elementary school.

Items for documentation might be group products such as songs, writing, constructions, webs, drawings, or paintings. These are often accompanied by narratives written by the teacher, the children, or both together. An excellent example of the creation of a window on a learning experience is present in Mary Ann Gottlieb's narrative of the miniproject that her multiage class, ages 5 and 6, experienced as part of their Water Project. This narrative, along with photographs and samples of the children's work included in a display, made it possible for others to see into the learning experience.

When we first webbed the topic, water, the children thought of many ways we use water at home. Candy suggested we make a house showing how water gets into the house where we use it, and then how water leaves the house. We investigated different kinds of houses, creating and drawing various kinds of homes. Danny was an expert on trailers since he lived in one. He said, "My house doesn't have a basement or upstairs. But we have a yard and a place to play."

We decided to construct a single-family home and studied Mrs. Beneke's dollhouse for additional information. After drawing that house, we made a list of materials we needed for construction. We measured the dollhouse and began collecting paper boxes. Charles said that taping the boxes together would be "ugly." Michael suggested that we "hot glue" the boxes together and offered to bring his mother's glue gun. Ms. Gottlieb glued the boxes, but they did not remain stable. Finally we tried brads and were satisfied with the results.

Janay traced the roof of the dollhouse onto the cardboard, did the cutting, assisted in mixing the paint ("You need to add more white . . . more . . . OK.") so that it matched the dollhouse, and painted the roof.

We collected paper towel tubes to use for the pipes. However, once they were assembled into lengths, the tubes proved to be too large for indoor piping. Another discussion resulted in Demetrus suggesting that we use pencils. "I'll tape them together along the edge," he said. He used his scissors to score and then cut them into proper sizes. Bigger pencils were used for the waste-water pipes. By using different colored pencils, Michael said that "you can tell which pipes have clean water and which pipes carry dirty water." He was careful to place the plumbing fixtures in places where the pipes ran.

After seeing and representing a real water meter, Carl made a water meter for outside the house. His knowledge of how meters look enabled him to select appropriate materials and work independently.

Furniture was made with "found items." Many children participated in its construction. Stephen and Charles worked together to build the bedroom furniture. Tiara and Andrea made the washer and dryer. Michael and Justin H. tried several materials before finally constructing the bathtub.

The house is not finished. Justin H. plans to make drain pipes leading away from the house. The pictures, mirrors, and most of the curtains are yet to be constructed and hung. The appliances and plumbing fixtures are complete.

Panels of mounted documentation, books for parents, notes of teacher discussions with other staff, teacher journals, and project journals are useful types of documentation for providing this view of the learning experience.

One value of documentation is the ability it gives us to share the importance and thought that goes into learning experiences that may not produce patently impressive products. The younger the child, the more likely this is to be the case. For example, a 3-year-old boy named Aiden loved to engage in active play with trucks and cars. He had no art samples in his portfolio, so Maggie Beneke planned an activity aimed at increasing his participation in art activities by incorporating motion and trucks into the art area. Her documentation of what happened when she implemented this lesson provides an insider's view of this learning experience.

Rayha and Trey began by rolling their cars back and forth through paint that had been squirted onto paper taped over the surface of the empty water table. When Aiden arrived, he joined them, and picked up a car tentatively. As the children discussed the different lines, colors, and sounds their cars were making, they began zooming their cars around with more motion. Aiden was making zigzag lines and Rayha was making straight lines. The three children inspected how the colors changed as they drove their trucks and cars through them at various speeds.

Rayha asked if she could squirt more paint herself. Rayha tested squeezing the bottle lightly as she moved her arms all around to distribute the paint. After seeing how Rayha squeezed the paint, Trey wanted to try. He supported his body against the water table so that he could have a better grip on the bottle of paint. Although I guided his hands as he squeezed, Trey was very proud to hold the paint himself. This sparked Aiden's curiosity, who also tried out the role of "paint squeezer."

Rayha soon became interested in the tape that was holding the paper to the water table and determined that it was time for a fresh sheet of white paper. The children each took a side of a piece of new paper and helped tape it down to the table. They explored how to smooth the paper down over the hard surface of the water table before taping so the trucks would roll smoothly. They inspected the smoothness with their hands and taped the paper to the sides. I cut the remaining edges off with scissors. Once again, the children began comparing the tire tracks their vehicles were making and shooting the paint from one side of the table to the other.

When the second piece of paper was ready to be removed, the children knew how to unhook it from the table, because they had helped me tape it down. They took the pieces of tape off themselves and I carried the paper over to hang. The children had observed me when I got the first two pieces of paper, and this time retrieved a third big piece of paper by themselves. When I returned from hanging the paper, they were trimming the edges with child-sized scissors. We distributed tape, repositioned the paper, and the children began painting again. Rayha, who was quickly becoming the director of the activity, told Aiden that wiping his hands on his shirt was "not a good idea" (see Figure 2.3).

When the third piece of paper became really wet, I asked the kids if they'd like to make a print. I took another sheet of paper, and the four of us laid it across the already taped-down piece. We pressed the clean paper down with our hands and then lifted it up covered with some of the wet paint, and looked for the lines they had made with their vehicles.

The next day we did the activity again, and this time Evan, who would often observe rather than participate in social activities in the classroom, joined us. He really opened up! He was zooming his cars around fast and crashing into other children's cars (see Figure 2.4).

Aiden, Trey, and Rayha helped show Evan how to make different lines, colors, and textures with their vehicles. Rayha demonstrated how to squirt the paint all around. When Evan announced that the paper was ripping, Trey began to remove the tape. But in the meantime, Rayha had gotten another big piece of paper, to make a print. This time they had a shared understanding of how to make a print and were more in control of the paper. When we lifted the paper off together, they were proud and delighted.

Rayha was an instigator in this activity as she evaluated the process of squirting, taping, cutting, and printing. But each child contributed to the collaborative effort by choosing which vehicles to use, deciding to add certain colors of paint, investigating the motion and lines of their vehicles, examining the quality of the paper, and working together to tape and make prints.

This documentation reveals the learning that took place for each of the 3-year-old children involved. Aiden became interested in working in the art area and voluntarily returned to this activity on the second day. Trey, who has limited use of the left side of his body, was able to compensate for his physical disability and was a full and eager participant in the activity. We see that Rayha showed initiative and practiced her leadership skills, and that Evan socialized and played. We also see that the children showed the disposition to work as a team and that they were able to work together to figure out how they could engage in this project without the teacher's assistance. Beyond the accomplishments of each

Figure 2.3. Rayha encourages Aiden as he tentatively removes the tape and paper from the water table.

Figure 2.4. The four children worked enthusiastically, driving their cars to make patterns on the paper.

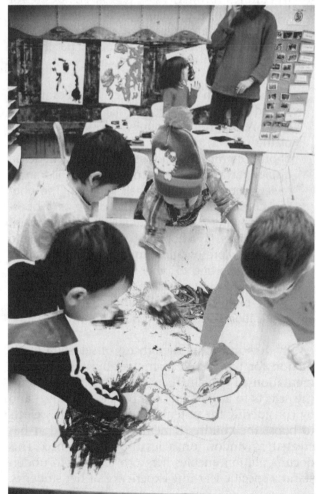

of the children, this window on a learning experience reveals the process the teacher went through to make this a positive, meaningful learning experience for each child involved. The addition of photographs to this documentation can help to open the window even further.

Documenting to provide a window on a learning experience using a narrative of the project also enables the teachers to model a useful process for children. Teachers can explain their purpose in selecting items for documentation and the ways they choose to display and write about them. They can solicit the children's ideas about what should be included in the narrative of the project. The children can then incorporate this knowledge of the process in creating their own documentation of their individual and group projects to share with other children and adults, thereby deepening their understanding of the project, their place within it, and the relationship of the project to those outside the classroom who will read the documentation. Creating their own documentation helps children to "construct an identity and find a place within . . . [their] culture" (Bruner, 1996, p. 42). The desire for such a transfer of the documentation process from adult to child is apparent in a summary of project documentation by Gail Gordon, a preprimary teacher:

> Documentation of our project activities is displayed in the hallway for parents, teachers, administrators, and the community to view. The history of the project, displayed with a summary sheet, photos, comments, and work samples will be on display for a while to encourage the children to review and reflect upon their learning. The photos, constructions, and artwork serve as a boost to the children's memory, enabling them to revisit the activities. I am hoping that they will be able to use these representations to report the activities to others. Reporting to other students, parents, and visitors will help them deepen their understanding of the project topic and demonstrate their communication skills and enthusiasm for project work.

By demonstrating the process of selecting information for the project narrative, by writing documentation to explain the significance of the items she selects to accompany the project narrative, and by considering the potential of the items she selects to boost the children's memories, Ms. Gordon has created a window on a learning experience. This documentation enables her, as a teacher, to understand a specific learning experience of her students.

Furthermore, the documentation can be shared with others. She has also modeled a process for children to emulate.

A WINDOW ON TEACHER SELF-REFLECTION

A teacher may create this third type of window, a window for teacher self-reflection, when her purpose is to reflect on her role in the learning experience of the children up until that point in time and to evaluate and revise her role based on that reflection. She may use documentation such as entries in her daily journal, observations and suggestions from colleagues, and feedback from parents and the children themselves to evaluate her effectiveness in guiding the children through a project. She may revisit a web in which she has "forecasted" (S. C. Chard, personal communication, August 15, 1995) project activities as part of her planning process and compared the activities on the web with the type and quantity of activities that were actually generated by the project. She may also assess the amount of involvement by the individual children in the class as recorded and dated on the web.

The documentation the teacher brings together for this purpose allows him to reflect on and improve the quality of his own judgment of the development of the individual children in his class and the class as a whole as they engage in project work. The more accurately a teacher can "read" a child's knowledge, skills, dispositions, and feelings (S. C. Chard, personal communication, August 15, 1995), the more able he is both to gauge the child's zone of proximal development and to provoke growth in the child by tapping the child's intrinsic motivation. Once the teacher has an accurate picture of each individual in his class, he can assess the effectiveness of his teaching to the group and the individual child. He can teach "these" children, instead of "the" children. The essence of good teaching is judgment based on good information. Good information for teaching the class as a whole comes from the teacher's reflections over time on the individual children in his class as they engage in learning experiences. Reflecting on his teaching enables him to make decisions, such as what materials to provide and what situations to set up to simultaneously engage all children in learning. In a sense, he judges the zone of proximal development of the group as a whole. When teachers teach as a team, they can enrich one another's view of the proximal development of the group by sharing these reflections with the others.

When beginning a project with the children, a teacher can anticipate the need for documentation for each aspect of the project. As the project develops, the teacher may refer back to this documentation to monitor the need for changes in methods. Gail Gordon's self-reflection as entered in her teacher journal on the Baby Project is a case in point:

> Project teaching is as engaging for the teachers as for the students, and as it emerges it becomes necessary to make decisions about selecting materials, evaluating progress, and timing learning experiences. Our project is still in process. Some children may be interested in constructing a baby swing for our baby area. We are going to decide together to extend or to culminate activities. I look forward to children reporting their learning to parents and friends.

And, finally, as the project is completed, this window allows the teacher to gain insight by which to improve the effectiveness of her methods and to plan for further professional development. As she continues in her journal, Ms. Gordon reflects on the experience she and her assistant have had as part of the project:

> We are growing in our abilities to slow down and listen to the interests and developmental needs of the children. We are learning to be more flexible in lesson planning and more willing to schedule large blocks of uninterrupted time. We are learning to create space in the classroom for project materials and children's work-in-process. Children and teachers are valuing work more by keeping it at school to continue and refine. We understand more fully the importance of allowing children to work out solutions to problems they may encounter. We realize that we need to revisit topics to study them in more depth.

Over time, documentation for self-reflection provides the vehicle for the teacher to improve the accuracy and efficiency of the documentation she provides for the window on a child's development and the window on a learning experience. Consequently, the view through the window for teacher self-reflection has perhaps the greatest potential impact of the three.

CHAPTER 3

The Documentation Web: Providing a Map for Documentation

web: —5. A complex, interconnected structure or arrangement.
—*American Heritage Dictionary* (2000)

The world can doubtless never be well known by theory: practice is absolutely necessary; but surely it is of great use to a young man, before he sets out for that country, full of mazes, windings, and turnings, to have at least a general map of it, made by some experienced traveler.
—Lord Chesterfield (1694–1773). Letter, August 30, 1749

Most teachers in this age of accountability have some familiarity with documenting children's learning. They may use a developmental checklist required in a specific educational program, or they may use anecdotal notes to provide information for parents. They may systematically collect some children's work, such as self-portraits, at the beginning and end of the year. Teachers may not, however, be fully aware of how many options are available for assessing and demonstrating children's learning.

DIFFERENT WAYS TO DOCUMENT

There are as many different ways to document children's learning as there are ways that children learn. Howard Gardner's (1993, 1999, 2000) theory of multiple intelligences has helped teachers to recognize that there are more valid ways of learning than the traditional school focus on the development of verbal/language and logical/mathematical thinking. Attention should also be paid to children's musical, visual/spatial, body/kinesthetic, interpersonal, and intrapersonal intelligences. This is especially true for the young child, as demonstrated by the following anecdote:

When returning from a field trip to the zoo, most of the children were able to contribute to a class list of what they saw except for one little boy. Af-

ter the discussion, however, he went to the block area and created a detailed block structure showing the habitats for each animal, the zookeepers' work area, the parking and admission areas, and even the restrooms! The teacher wrote an anecdotal note recording the words the boy had used when describing the parts of his block zoo, the congruence of the layout with the actual zoo environment, and the accuracy of his comments about what happens in the zoo.

If only verbal evidence collected in the group experience had been considered, the teacher, and others, might have concluded incorrectly that the child did not gain much from the field trip experience. Because the child was encouraged to represent his understanding in the way he was most comfortable and the teacher was open and and ready to collect this evidence of learning, a more accurate understanding of the impact of the learning experience on the child was gained. Traditional ways of measuring learning often do not enable the teacher to look at other intelligences or ways of learning such as Gardner describes.

When we were first working with teachers as they started to document the many ways that children demonstrate learning, we began to collect different types of documentation. Initially, we just made a list to serve as a reference for the teachers. We quickly, however, changed to using a web as a graphic organizer. The technique of webbing has developed from the expression of radiant thinking as a mind map. The thinker is focused on a central image, and the main themes of the subject radiate from that central image like branches. Webbing is a common strategy of organizing knowledge during project work with children. The use of webbing is a way to determine children's knowledge before they begin a study and to follow the growth of that knowledge throughout a project (Helm & Katz, 2001).

Sylvia Chard (1994) describes the process of developing a web:

The process of making a topic web enables the teacher to use his or her own general knowledge of the topic as a starting point for planning the project. Each individual person has very similar but slightly differently organized mind maps of any given topic. When the teacher starts with her own mind map or web she becomes more interested in the topic and curious about her own knowledge. She can also more easily evaluate the ideas which children offer and incorporate them appropriately into the planning. (p. 33)

As teachers documented children's learning using topic webs and we became acquainted with the concept of mind mapping, we naturally began to document our own learning about the process of documentation by drawing a web. The first web of types of documentation was developed for the staff of the Valeska Hinton Early Childhood Education Center. The purpose was to assist teachers in expanding their concepts of how they might collect evidence of children's learning and to support their developing skills in documentation. This web then became a map for discussion and experimentation by the teachers at other schools.

UNDERSTANDING THE DOCUMENTATION WEB

Our web grew and changed as teachers shared projects and the ways in which they collected and communicated about the learning that occurred, and as they developed ways to present documentation from different points of view. The web shown in Figure 3.1 groups the variety of ways of gathering evidence about children's learning around the central topic of types of documentation. Radiating out from the web are five clusters: individual portfolios, narratives, observations of progress and performance, child self-reflections, and products (individual or group). Each of these types of documentation can provide a way to view children's work.

This web is not an exhaustive list of all possible types of documentation. There are as many different

Figure 3.1. Web showing types of documentation.

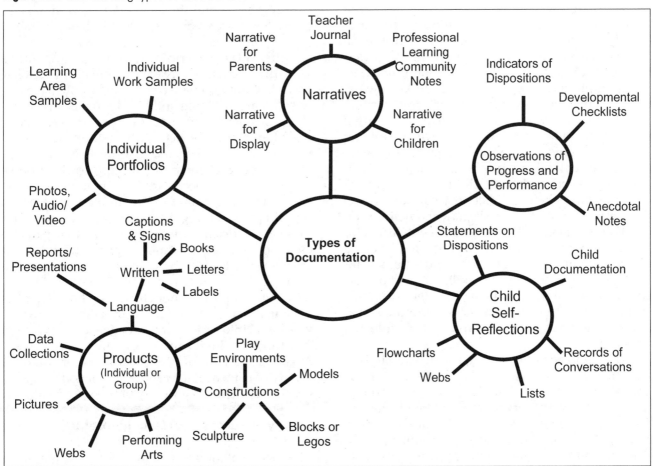

ways to document learning as there are ways that active, engaged children try to make sense of their world. The web is also not meant to be an exclusive classification system for evidence of children's learning. Just as a teacher can design a specific learning experience that will stimulate a variety of areas of a child's development, one sample of a child's work may be considered as more than one type of documentation. For example, an anecdotal note about a child's first attempt to write a word on a drawing about a project could become part of an individual portfolio or it could become part of a project history book that is a narrative about the project. The web stimulates discussion about documentation by providing a vocabulary and a structure for teachers to communicate with one another about documentation and decision making.

USING THE WEB TO INCREASE VARIATION

The documentation web can remind teachers of the variety of ways to document. Documentation is most effective when teachers vary their documentation to match the learning experiences of the children and to meet the needs of the audiences for whom the documentation is intended. The more familiar a teacher becomes with the variety of types of documentation, the more options the teacher has to select the most appropriate one. For example, a teacher who wanted to know what a child knew about a project topic might think about collecting the child's drawings and written work about the project. After reviewing the types of documentation, the teacher might also decide to have the child participate in constructing a new, revised web about what the child knows about the topic, or have the child dictate a narrative to accompany a photographic display about the project. Using a variety of ways to document also helps the teacher to get accurate information about a particular child. For example, a child who has not devloped extensive language skills may not be able to dictate a narrative but may be able to draw a picture or construct a block play environment that reveals the depth of understanding the child has about the topic.

This approach of gathering a variety of kinds of evidence of children's learning and thinking is more compatible with today's understanding of and emphasis on the variability in how children think and learn, as explained earlier. It is also more compatible with what we know about how adults process evidence and communication messages (Helm & Helm, 2006).

Points of View

As we shared the concept of webbing with teachers, a reflective experience was designed to accompany the introduction of the documentation web. A large bag was placed on a table in the center of the room. In the bag was a small wooden chair with a high back. On the chair was a doll named Nessa. Teachers sat in a large circle around the edge of the room. As the bag was removed, revealing Nessa and the chair, the teachers drew a picture of exactly what they saw (see Figure 3.2). After they had completed their drawings, members of the group walked around the room and viewed one another's drawings and compared them.

The variations were extensive. In the first place, sketches varied depending on where the artist was sitting in the room. Some pictures showed only the back of the chair and no doll. Some showed the side of the chair with just the tip of Nessa's hand showing. Some showed all of Nessa. These variations were caused by the position, or viewing point, of each artist. Then there were other variations that were even more revealing. Some drawings were very large and some very small. Some had extensive detail, and some were mere sketches. Some artists drew Nessa and the chair, and a few drew only Nessa. Some artists drew Nessa, the chair, the table, or even the other artists drawing Nessa.

After this experience with a change in point of view, the teachers discussed the similarities between their drawing experience and how people have different views of a child and his experience in school. Variations were again discussed, but this time regarding differences in the perception of learning, school, the role of the teacher, and so forth. This experience focused the teachers on the need to consider other viewpoints, to expect variations in how different people would interpret information about a child, how they would bring their own point of view to the experience. Teachers began to realize that parents, children, colleagues, administrators, and members of the community at large might be looking at the learning that occurred in their classrooms in very different ways. Even though the teacher may plan documentation to provide a specific window or view of a child or learning experience, the viewer's point of view limits and/or expands what is seen. An understanding of the necessity of providing a variety of evidence of learning and of communicating that evidence in a variety of ways emerged.

Variety in Purposes of Documentation

Documentation is used for a variety of purposes. It is helpful to keep in mind how documentation

Figure 3.2. Teachers view and draw the doll, Nessa, while seated in a circle. Their drawings reveal the different perspectives of their positions. This experience leads to a discussion of different points of view regarding children and how this affects the use of documentation.

might be used when deciding what type of documentation would be best to collect. For example, in a school or program where standardized tests are the primary method of showing children's achievement, displaying samples of student work and sharing student accomplishments through photos can refocus the community on other evidence of student learning, often showing positive results. A work product can capture the impact of specific learning experiences in ways that no test scores can. Evidence of learning using checklists based on national standards and systematic collections of children's work can bring credibility to a learning experience. Certain types of documentation are especially powerful, easier to understand, or more appealing to specific audiences. By collecting a variety of types of documentation, educators are able to be more flexible and efficient in their use of documentation.

Figure 3.3 provides a summary of the purposes of documentation discussed in Chapter 1 and ways in which different types of documentation can be useful for these different purposes and audiences (as discussed in Helm & Helm, 2006).

Each type of documentation shown in our documentation web (in Figure 3.1) is discussed separately in Chapters 4 through 8 of this book. Each chapter focuses on how a particular type looks in real classrooms. Samples of documentation from projects and other classroom activities show how the specific type of documentation can be integrated with teaching and how teachers can use it to determine teaching strategies and demonstrate children's learning.

Figure 3.3. Documentation is used for many different purposes.

Purposes of Documentation	Goal	How It Is Collected	Types of Documentation	Shared With
Guiding Instruction	Assists teacher in responding, planning next experience, materials	Ongoing with immediate reflection	Work samples, observations and observational notes, learning community notes, digital photographs	Professional learning communities, colleagues, sometimes individual parents
Assessment	Document knowledge, skills and dispositions of individual children for assessment	Ongoing, curriculum embedded	Work samples collected into portfolios, observations, photographs and video recordings	Parents and administration
Studying Pedagogy	Provides insight into the teaching and learning processes, source of professional growth	Ongoing, reflection is usually after the experience	Work samples, photographs and video recordings, transcribed tapes, anecdotal notes, dialogue, teacher journals	Professional learning communities, colleagues, parents, professionals outside of the school
Communication with Others	To communicate with others about what is happening in educational programs	All types of documentation are reviewed and selected	Selected work samples, photographs and video recordings, portions of transcribed tapes, notes, dialogues All types of documentation can be shared	Parents, other professionals and community

CHAPTER 4

Narratives: Telling the Story

narrate: —*tr.* To tell (a story, for example) in speech in writing. —*intr.* To give an account of events.
—*American Heritage Dictionary* (2000)

Narratives that tell the story of a learning experience such as a project can be used to provide documentation for all three windows: the window on a child's development, the window on a learning experience, and the window for teacher self-reflection. They can take the form of stories for and by children, records of conversations that a teacher has with other teachers, teacher journals, narratives for parents in the form of books and letters, or visual displays.

THE STORY

Stories are a powerful way to help others understand an event or an experience that a person has had. Many learning experiences, especially projects, are, by their nature, good stories. As Sylvia Chard (1994) states, "In a sense, like a good story, the project can be described as having a beginning, a middle and an end, each memorable in its own way" (p. 40). The telling of this story by the teachers or children can provide powerful evidence of the development of skills and knowledge. An example of a narrative is the teacher journal notes of Anna Brown that were used as a narrative of the Reflections Project displayed in the hallway near her classroom:

March 7: Again, I asked the children to tell me what they knew about reflections and our second attempt at webbing turned into a brainstorming session from which a couple of jobs were generated. [For example, Katie suggested:] "Make a rainbow in a mirror."

March 8: Katie started to work on their project. She held a prism and a flashlight before the mirror. There was no rainbow, and so she elicited the support of her classmates in gathering together

our collection of small flashlights. They simultaneously shined them into the mirror. Her logic was that if you shined the lights encased in an assortment of rainbow colors on a mirror, the color of the flashlights' plastic casings would somehow become infused with the light and cast a spectrum of colors onto the mirror.

March 9: Katie and Jequila worked on her project. First, they tried the flashlight and a prism; and when that did not yield the effects that they were after, Katie decided to exchange the prism for a quart of water. There was a small rainbow in the mirror; however, this did not satisfy them. Jequila collected an assortment of colored blocks and colored links. They experimented [with] placing them over the water and with lining them up in front of the mirror.

Andrew made a rainbow (drawing) and gave it to Katie to use in her project. They held the rainbow in front of the mirror, and there was a reflection of a rainbow in the mirror. Although it was not expressed, Katie seemed to be persisting in the belief that she needed the water and the light to generate a rainbow. For the next few minutes, Katie and Jequila experimented with shining the light behind Andrew's picture and with holding it over the quart of water, shining the light over and under it.

March 10: Katie's mother and I talked about her project, and from Linda I learned that Katie had been discussing her plans over dinner. She was also tuning into a science show on PBS for ideas.

This story about Katie's attempt to make a rainbow in a mirror provided insight for the teacher and the parent into Katie's knowledge, skills, and dispositions (window on a child's development). Ms. Brown was able to determine that Katie had some knowledge about light and rainbows and the relationship of water and glass to the making of rainbows. She was able to use this information to determine what materials and experiences she should introduce into the classroom to advance Katie's knowledge. The teacher and parent both noted that Katie had developed a number of problem-solving skills. For example, she knew how to do an experiment, how to get others to think about her problem and offer solutions, and where to find helpful information. Both the teacher and the parent also noted that the story revealed Katie's curiosity and her disposition to learn. The narrative provided evidence for Ms. Brown to confidently mark Katie "proficient" on the Work Sampling developmental checklist item, "Seeks answers to questions through active exploration," in the "Scientific Thinking" domain (Dichtelmiller, Jablon, Dorfman, Marsden, & Meisels, 2001, p. 124)).

Later in the journal, the teacher reflected on this narrative and what she had learned about how children learn.

> The children were engaged in the project on a variety of levels. They asked questions, made observations, experimented, cooperated, and shared. . . . Their work reflects an insightfulness and persistence that I had not seen before in some of our children. . . . If I had it to do all over again, I would listen more, ask more questions, and encourage the children to experiment more. I would relax more and remember that there's nothing more important than my time with the children. There's a groove of understanding that the thoughts of children flow through; I would try to find a way of moving in that groove more often than I do.

Anna Brown later shared her insights with her colleagues during a discussion of the progress of the Reflections Project.

Children enjoy telling the story of their projects. The narratives that children produce take on many forms, such as dictated stories, pictures that show the progress of the project, and even complete books. For some children, preparing their own narrative of the project is the way that they end the story. Ten days after Katie conducted her experiments, she felt motivated to finish her part of the Reflections Project by recording the experience in drawings and words.

> *March 20:* I asked Katie if she's finished with getting a rainbow to reflect into a mirror. She tells me that she is. Later, while I am working on paperwork, she indicates that she wants to work on it again. She works out a plan and shares it with me. Her plan seems to be a history of the work she did on her part of the project (see Figure 4.1.).

Figure 4.1. Katie's pictorial summary of her participation in the project.

Katie 3/20/95

A rainbow in the mirror.

If you draw a rainbow and put it in front of the mirror It will make a rainbow.

This is the rainbow.

ᒥᗷᥱᛕᑊᗷᑊ This is what I wrote about the rainbow.

These are the hearts that you see in the rainbow.

COLLECTING STORIES

Narratives are a valuable way to document learning. Parts of the narrative of a project are usually written over a period of time, thus making change and growth in knowledge, skills, and dispositions evident. Narratives can capture the interest of a variety of audiences. Stories interest people because of their unknown endings. Another advantage of using stories to document projects is that stories help parents and other adults understand the way that children construct their own learning through making sense and meaning of their experiences. There is an added element of surprise and suspense when children are involved in active learning experiences because the outcome of the story is not highly predictable. When Beth Crider-Olcott's class began its project on the puppy Scout, she had not predicted that it would end up as an in-depth study of a veterinarian's office. When stories are shared as they are in the process of evolving, this element of surprise increases adults' interest in the project and encourages their participation and attention.

To capitalize on the evolving nature of the project, teachers sometimes write narratives to accompany hall displays and then continuously update the narrative as children's work proceeds. An example of this type of updated narrative written by teacher Renee Jackson is from the Butterfly Project. The first paragraph was the first narrative that was posted. The second paragraph was a follow-up narrative.

> Green Five is just beginning a study of butterflies. It all began with my trip to Kentucky. The butterflies were already in the fields and gardens. I told the children about seeing them and one thing led to another. We made a web and our study began.

> We have just received some very young caterpillars in the mail. The children are already planning how to record their growth and changes in the next few weeks. We also have children's predictions on how long it will be before they begin to change. It has been an exciting 2 weeks and there is lots more to learn. The children have shown in-depth thinking and creativity.

Children and adults are able to check back with the display to see the progress that the class has made in investigating their topic. This type of narrative is also especially helpful for parents because it enables them to discuss the project with their children.

Narratives written for and by children are also well received. Many children, like Katie, attempt to write their own narrative in pictures or words. These narratives are often bound into a book and made available for children to read and reread. Children enjoy these books telling the story of the completed projects. Teachers send home project history books containing photos and narratives that tell the story of a project in the children's own words. The Mailbag sequence, which follows later in this chapter, comes from a project history book on a project on mail. Directions for making a project history book are provided in Chapter 12.

Children not only enjoy but also learn from these narratives. At the Valeska Hinton Early Childhood Center, we noticed that children learn through hearing these stories and viewing the displays. Even very young children not directly involved in a project have become interested in what other children do. This can have a powerful effect on the children's disposition to learn. This interest can be seen in the following note from parent Nancy Higgins, reflect-

ing on the experience of her 3-year-old daughter, Brigid.

> In her first nine weeks at this school, her class has completed a project on balls. In addition, she has proceeded to describe projects from other classes to us. She has talked about hats and babies, which is her personal favorite.

The Hat Project was done by children in the classroom next door, and the Babies Project had been done by her multiage classroom the year before Brigid entered. Brigid learned about the projects through the oral storytelling of children and through displays and project books from the previous year's work.

DETERMINING CONTENT BY THE AUDIENCE

Many of the narratives given in the examples above are suitable for a variety of audiences: parents, children, and other teachers. However, as in all types of documentation, there are times when the narrative must be tailored to particular audiences (Helm & Helm, 2006). Narratives for children often focus on the story line of the learning experience. They serve a valuable purpose by enabling the children to revisit and reprocess the experience and to see themselves as investigators.

In narratives for parents, teachers may want to include more in-depth information, such as why a topic was selected, what standards were achieved, how a topic fits into an overall curriculum plan, or what decisions the teacher made in the progress of the project. A teacher may choose to point out through a narrative what a particular observation or event tells the teacher about a child's development. When documenting the Mail Project, Kathy Steinheimer provided parents with additional information in the project history book that children took home to read. She indicated the parent information by putting it on colored pages. The parent could read the story in the book to the child and read the colored pages silently simultaneously or at another time. Additional teacher comments for parents were printed in a different type size and font. For example, in the middle of a series of pictures showing a debate between two children about how to make a mailbag, this comment for parents was inserted in bold letters:

> Children need opportunities to discuss and argue. Thus they will gain in their ability to persuade and compromise, two very important social skills.

Similarly, Sallee Beneke's project history book on the Meadow Project also had information targeted for children and for adults. Pages for adults were on the left-hand side of the book and were on paper with a pale flower background. Pages on the right-hand side were for children and were on beige paper. Parents could read the book to their child easily by focusing on the right-hand pages and come back later to study the left-hand pages.

Some narratives may be written for a professional audience. When teachers prepared a display for other teachers about the Water Project, Mary Ann Gottlieb chose to add this narrative to copies of Work Sampling developmental checklists.

> We took a checklist for each age level and highlighted in yellow any of the indicators of development that we were able to observe in the Water Project. This was very informative to us because it showed us that we were providing experiences in all the developmental areas that we were monitoring and had actually stimulated growth in many of them.

Teachers often accomplish this same goal by placing state or district standards in smaller type at the bottom of a page in a history book or on a display so parents or administrators can connect the learning experience described in the narrative with these required standards.

Sometimes it is important for the narrative to be in the children's own words. This is especially appropriate when children are beginning to understand the function of print, are attempting to figure out the reading process by matching letters with spoken words, or are already readers and writers. When very young children speak their opinion, it is respectful of the learning process to record it in writing exactly as the child says it instead of editing it for grammar or spelling. Stacy Berg took this dictation of 3- and 4-year-olds' thoughts on their progress in building a giant walk-in model of an aquarium as part of the Water Project.

> *Daniel:* We been painting. We been hitting on the hammer and slammin the nails with the hammer.
> *Alyssa:* We been making fish. We been drawing. We been hanging them with string and tape.
> *Romelle:* We been cutting fish. We put chicken fence over the project—the wood. We tied fish on with wire string. We painted rocks and colored fish.
> *Alyssa:* The fish look good to me 'cause they're colored.
> *Brittany:* We made fish good.

> *Bryanna:* We put fish in pretty good.
> *Romelle:* The fish. We did a good job on them. Everyone got their fish in the right shape.
> *Alyssa:* The rocks look not good 'cause they're messy.
> *Brittany:* People didn't paint the whole sides of rocks.
> *Bryanna:* We did not make good names on the fish when we wroted our names.
> *Romelle:* The blue paint doesn't look good because it's starting to crackle up.

Defining the audience for whom the documentation is intended and deciding what to include in the narrative for that particular audience are two important documentation skills for teachers. It is neither possible nor desirable to write down or explain everything that happens in the course of a project. As the author Raymond Chandler (1997) says, "A good story cannot be devised; it has to be distilled" (p. 75). To *distill,* according to the *American Heritage Dictionary,* means to separate or extract the essential elements. Like a good storyteller, the teacher must define what is most important to communicate to the intended audience.

As teachers become more skilled at documentation, they will often use wall displays that evolve as the learning experience unfolds in the classroom. To assist viewers in understanding what they are seeing and to provide teachers with a framework for the distilling process, a summary form is often used (see Figure 4.2). The summary briefly tells the essential story elements of the learning experience, similar to a synopsis or a condensed version of a book. Sometimes summaries are displayed using a special frame or color of paper. Placed near the beginning of the display in a prominent location, the summary helps orient the viewer to the learning experience. A sample summary form for a learning experience and for a project can be found in Chapter 13.

TAPPING THE POWER OF NARRATIVES: THE MAILBAG STORY

Narratives, whether they are abbreviated, as on the project summary form and in project history books, or presented to viewers in installments by evolving displays, can be extremely effective in capturing the development of knowledge and skills. Like the other types of documentation described in Chapters 5 through 8, they require the teacher to plan ahead, organize carefully, and be consistent and persistent about documenting. However, narratives require more than just organization. Of all the types of

Figure 4.2. The Project Summary sheet enables viewers of displays to get an overview of the project.

Project Summary

Valeska Hinton Early Childhood Education Center

Teachers Gottlieb and Lockhart

Room B4   **Age Level 5–7 yrs.**   **Time Span March–April**

Title of Focus of the Project

   Water Around the House—We investigated how water travels to and through the house. We became familiar with different ways water is used at home.

History of the Project

   This project emerged naturally from an investigation of snow and ice. After webbing prior knowledge of water, the children webbed water around the house. A large house was constructed to exhibit the plumbing. Laundry facilities were investigated, resulting in another construction activity.

What Did the Children Learn

   Through investigation the children have experienced floating and sinking properties, surface tension, and evaporation. Careers in water treatment and the plumbing trade have been explored. Knowledge has been constructed about the sources of water in the home, appliances using water, and how plumbing fixtures work.

Plans for the Future

   This project will continue as we move into another project about water outdoors—specifically water in the creek. We will explore a creekbed, examine the wildlife and plant life, and construct our own creekbed.

documentation, it is the narrative that is most open to teacher creativity. Storytelling is an art form. A teacher who learns to tell stories well can open the windows and entice others in. Often with young children, narratives take the form of picture stories.

   An example of a well-told picture story is the Mailbag Story, which occurred during the Mail Project in Kathy Steinheimer's prekindergarten classroom. Stories like this can be used to show the value of a learning experience. Ms. Steinheimer not only tells what happened but also shows how in project work learning standards can be achieved, problem-solving skills can be developed, and the strengthening of dispositions such as persistence can be supported. As you look at the photos and read the narrative for the Mailbag Story, we suggest you think about the following questions:

- What academic skills did the children learn as they were making their mailbag?
- What social skills did the children develop as they were making their mailbag?
- What dispositions were strengthened in this learning experience?
- Based on this narrative, did you form a conclusion about the value of this type of learning experience for young children? If so, what conclusion?

- Based on this narrative, did you form an opinion about the skills of this teacher? If so, what conclusion?

Creating a Mailbag

   The Valeska Hinton Center, as described in the Introduction, covers most of a city block and has four color-coded villages. The children did not realize that they would need a mailbag until they started to gather the mail from the villages and saw how much mail there was to gather. Almost all the mail carriers could be seen dropping mail as they walked to the post office (see Figure 4.3). That is when someone said that they needed a mailbag. Thus, the need was recognized and the work began to meet that need.

   The children were exposed to and had access to several reference books pertaining to the mail system. They readily utilized these books to gain information on how to make the items that they needed, such as their mailbag (see Figure 4.4). In addition, the books helped the children understand the mail-sorting process. The children became very independent in their research and often initiated a search for information. This initiative in seeking knowledge is a life skill that will serve the children well throughout their lives.

   The teacher recorded an interaction between Karissa and Tim in the following anecdotal note, which became a Language Core Item for both children. (Core items are part of the authentic assessment system used in the center. The use of core items are explained in Chapter 6.) Karissa and Tim, two 4-year-olds, took on the job of creating a mailbag out of paper (see Figure 4.5). This led to a lengthy interchange

Figure 4.3. Child carrying mail and dropping it.

Figure 4.4.
Children looking at books.

Figure 4.7.
Tim showing Karissa the book.

Figure 4.5.
Two children folding the paper for the bag.

Figure 4.8.
Tim holding the ruler while Karissa draws the line.

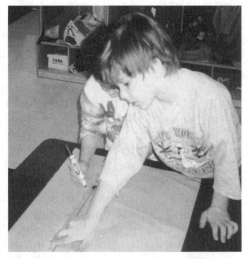

Figure 4.6.
Karissa beginning to cut.

Figure 4.9.
Taping on the handle.

about the handle. Karissa drew a short handle using a picture on the cover of a book as her reference. Tim told her that it had to be bigger. Thus, Karissa drew a handle that was a little longer and wider. Tim told her that the handle was too fat. Karissa insisted that it would work and began cutting (Figure 4.6). Tim tried to convince Karissa that he needed the long strip on the edge of her paper. She did not agree and kept on cutting. Then he showed her the picture on the book cover (see Figure 4.7). Karissa kept on cutting. Next, she tried her handle on for size and discovered that it would not work. Therefore, she asked Tim to draw the handle. She cut out the long and narrow handle that he drew. It tore as she cut it out. However, they still thought that it would work after they cut it out. It did not. I gave them a yard-stick and showed the pair how to draw a straight line with it. They made a long and wide handle for the bag, which they attached to the bag with tape (see Figures 4.8 and 4.9). After a trial run without mail, they were satisfied with their accomplishment.

Thoughts on Observation and Timing

Karissa and Tim benefited from the opportunity to discuss and solve their own problem. They argued with purpose and invested energy in their argument. As their teacher, I observed their actions and discussion carefully. I carefully considered when and if my assistance would be needed. I decided that my assistance was not needed until the end when their narrow, crooked handle tore repeatedly and a little frustration showed on their faces. That is when I taught them how to use a ruler to draw a straight line. They learned this new skill and successfully completed their task. It is very important that adults observe children in order to see when and if their intervention is needed. In addition to timing, the amount of guidance needs to be considered. Children become independent in their thinking only when given opportunities to do so, as Karissa and Tim had here.

The Story Continues

The children created their first mailbag out of paper and tape, but they discovered it would not hold the mail (see Figure 4.10). Then Tim suggested that they try a cardboard box. The mail carriers reported that it was too heavy and that it took two people to carry it (see Figure 4.11). This led to a need for a stronger, lighter material. At my suggestion, the children used fabric to make the final mailbag (see Figure 4.12). This process took several days and involved several children reflecting on their own

Figure 4.10. Delivering the mail with the new bag.

Figure 4.11. Delivering the mail with the box.

Figure 4.12. Kyle cutting (striped sweater).

work as well as the work of others (see Figures 4.13 and 4.14). With each reflection came another solution and greater success (see Figure 4.15).

Reflecting on This Documentation

Did this picture story capture what happened in this classroom? What are your answers to the questions listed earlier?

The elements that make a good story are the same elements that make this powerful documentation. There is a plot, a conflict or struggle that the main characters go through. They are learning to work with others, or discovering the way things are, or learning something about themselves, like needs or feelings. The plot begins, we discover what the challenge is; then things happen, things go right or wrong; and then there is a resolution of the plot and a final statement. The story begins right away with the action, and after the problem is solved, it ends quickly. Most of the story is focused on the action of the children in the process of learning and discovering.

Narratives are powerful documentation because they tell many stories of learning: children learning, teachers learning about teaching, and parents learning about how children learn and how teachers teach.

Figure 4.13. Children tyring to find the bottom of the bag.

Figure 4.14. Tim painting the mailbag.

Figure 4.15. Mailman examining the mailbag.

CHAPTER 5

Observations of Progress and Performance: Watching the Child

observation: —1. an act or instance of observing 2. the gathering of information (as for scientific studies) by noting facts or occurrences 3. a conclusion drawn from observing.
—*Merriam-Webster Dictionary* (2005)

Observing and recording development for a variety of purposes are familiar practices for most early childhood teachers. These practices have commonly been used to report on mastery of discrete skills, to assess children's work in school, or to indicate the frequency, duration, and nature of a behavior at a particular point in time. In general, observations of child development may be recorded as items on a checklist, as anecdotal notes, or as indicators of dispositions. Observation systems, such as the Work Sampling System (Dichtelmiller, Jablon, Dorfman, Marsden, & Meisels, 2001) and the *High/Scope Child Observational Record (COR)* (High/Scope Educational Research Foundation, 2003), have been developed that expand the practical uses of the checklist (Cohen, 1993). These systems enhance the teacher's ability to report on children's progress and performance. According to Dichtelmiller, Jablon, Dorfman, Marsden, and Meisels (2001), "Performance refers to the level of a student's behavior, skills, and accomplishments at a particular point in time," and "progress refers to growth over time" (p. 218).

Observing is an intentional act, and learning to be a good observer takes time, practice, and training. Learning to ask open-ended questions that cause children to think can help teachers uncover valuable information about children's thought processes and feelings. However, this information may be lost if teachers don't practice active listening. Learning takes place in the social environment of the classroom, and a responsive adult is an important component of this environment. Children need enough time to process information if they are to provide thoughtful answers to a teacher's questions. This is called giving children adequate "wait time" (Black, Harrison, Lee, Marshall, & William,

2004, p. 14). Time to talk and a classroom environment that is rich with meaningful things to think and talk about is another key to successful collection of observations.

DEVELOPMENTAL CHECKLISTS

Familiar Uses

Teachers in preschools and child-care centers often use a checklist to report on a child's performance on school "readiness" skills. These checklists include those that are commercially produced as well as those versions produced by teachers themselves. Sometimes checklists are designed by a committee or group of educators who generate items based on their experience with children or by combining items from various checklists. The completed checklists are sometimes sent home with a child, and the parent and teacher may then meet and use the checklist as a basis for discussion about how the child is doing in school. A brief statement regarding the child's overall progress and potential to adapt successfully to the next level of education often accompanies the checklist.

In many kindergarten and first- and second-grade classrooms, school report cards are sent home at regular intervals with letter grades or numerical indicators of performance on skills. Many teachers at these grade levels use a checklist format instead of using traditional letter grades to report on a child's mastery of knowledge and skills in prespecified academic and social areas. As with many preschool versions, a space or a section for brief comments often accompanies the checklist.

Teachers working with children with identified special needs often use criterion-referenced developmental checklists to assess children's development and to determine the Individual Education Plan (IEP). These checklists are called "criterion-referenced" because the decision about how to rate the child's performance is based on a comparison with research-based developmental criteria and not on comparing the child to other children. High-quality criterion-referenced developmental checklists are usually based on normative data and have support data on validity and reliability. In addition, they often provide a more detailed breakdown of the assessed skill into subskills than does the "readiness" checklist.

Expanded Uses

Teachers are expanding the way they use checklists to document the growth and development of skills over a period of time. Rather than focusing only on whether or not a child has mastered a particular skill at a particular point in time, some checklists have been developed that can be used for ongoing observation of children's development. When these developmental checklists are systematically combined with anecdotal records and a child's work samples, they enable a teacher to more reliably identify important learning goals as they emerge and become consistent. These goals might include dispositions and feelings as well as knowledge and skills (Chard, 1994). In this way, a teacher may guide children toward experiences that challenge them, rather than teaching skills they have already mastered or are not ready to attempt.

This use of checklists is consistent with Vygotsky's theory that teaching is most likely to be effective when the teacher identifies the child's zone of proximal development and helps the child achieve mastery (Berk & Winsler, 1995). For example, the checklist component of the Work Sampling System accommodates the use of ongoing observational assessment to inform instruction by providing three choices for each item that correspond to varying levels of development. The three levels defined in the Work Sampling System are as follows:

> *Not Yet* indicates that the skill, knowledge, or behavior has not been demonstrated yet.
> *In Process* indicates that the skill, knowledge, or behavior is emergent, and is not demonstrated consistently.
> *Proficient* indicates that the skill, knowledge, or behavior is firmly within the child's range of performance. (Dichtelmiller, Jablon, Dorfman, Marsden, & Meisels, 2001, p. 42)

The labeled vegetable drawings by 4-year-old Baxter, a second-year student in Beth Crider-Olcott's multiage preprimary room, provide an example of these three levels (see Figure 5.1). On April 26, Ms. Crider-Olcott's students did representational drawings of potatoes as part of an investigation of veg-

Figure 5.1. Baxter's drawing labels.

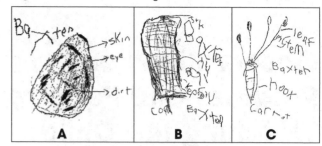

The teacher needed to label this drawing of a potato (A) for Baxter on April 26. Baxter's ability and disposition to label his own vegetable drawing begins to emerge, as seen in his labeling of a drawing (B) of an ear of corn on May 2. Baxter was able to proficiently copy the labels for a subsequent drawing (C).

etables. The children dictated labels for the parts of their drawings to associate teacher Sue Blasco. She labeled the potato drawings for the children who did not have the writing skills to label their own. In the April 26 drawing of a potato, Baxter needed someone else to label his drawing for him. At this point, Ms. Crider-Olcott would have marked the Work Sampling checklist item "Language and Literacy" D-2, "Uses letter-like shapes, symbols, and letters to convey meaning" as "not yet" (Dichtelmiller, Jablon, Dorfman, Marsden, & Meisels, 2001, p. 42; Dichtelmiller, Jablon, Marsden, & Meisels, 2001, p. 58). However, in Baxter's May 2 drawing of corn, letters and letter-like shapes emerged. At this point, Ms. Crider-Olcott knew that instruction in letter formation was within Baxter's zone of development and that he had a strong desire to learn to make letters. She spent some time helping Baxter copy letters, showing him how letters are formed. The May 10 drawing with labels shows that Ms. Crider-Olcott's timely instruction helped Baxter reach a level in a short period of time that could certainly be called "proficient."

Documenting children's progress toward mastery of standards is another expanded use of checklists. Forty-eight states have developed early learning standards (Scott-Little & Martella, 2006). Many of these states, such as Illinois (Illinois State Board of Education, 2001), have developed observational checklists that are aligned with their state's standards for early learning. Schools and districts have also taken the time and effort to align the standards of their state with the observation tool that they are using. Having the standards embedded in their observation tool can increase teachers' confidence that they are focusing their observations on important areas of learning, and it can make a useful basis for discussion among teachers from different classrooms and centers.

Another expanded use of developmental checklists is in coordination of programming for children with special needs. "Use of natural settings, developmentally appropriate practices, and family-centered methods" (Sandall, Hemmeter, Smith, & McLean, 2005, p. 45) have become important features of programming for young children with special needs. Inclusion is more than the physical presence of a child with a disability in the regular classroom. It involves developing a relationship with that child, helping the child become a member of the classroom community, and providing the child with meaningful access to the core curriculum (Fisher & Frey, 2001). Keeping these principles in mind can help teachers improve their observations of *all* the children in their classrooms, not just those with identified disabilities.

Observation of a child in the natural context of the classroom helps a teacher be sensitive to the child's development and support him in engagement in a full range of classroom content, rather than focusing only on areas of developmental delay. Including parents as partners in observation can also help teachers support successful programming for children with special needs.

Many special educators and regular educators collaborate in teaching children with special needs who are included in classrooms with typically developing children, and frequently they team teach. Using the same checklist for all children facilitates coordination of children's IEP goals and objectives. Using the checklist as a basis for discussion helps the parent, special education teacher, and the regular classroom teacher communicate, since they are using the same terms to describe the child's development. IEP goals may then be written using the language of the checklist. Parents appreciate having their child's work documented and discussed in much the same way as that of the other children in the class. When parents are partners in observing the way the child functions in the classroom setting, they are more likely to understand and contribute to the value of activities planned for their child and can better support the child's development at home.

As they observe and interact with children in the natural classroom setting, teachers are able to discover and capitalize on children's interests and develop relationships with children and therefore judge their performance more accurately. For example, observation helped prekindergarten teacher Ruth Harkema note and build on the interest of a 4-year-old boy in her class:

Noah, a boy with autism and sensory integration issues, amazed us with his project work. Because his face rarely displayed change of mood or focus on what we were doing, we were not sure before the project how much he was absorbing. He clearly benefited from the structure inherent in the project approach.

After our trip to the zoo, he attempted to draw a penguin. The occupational therapist had suggested we give him a weighted pencil and put a rice or sand bag on his wrist during art or writing activities. This fell off easily, and so, during the penguin drawing, I tried putting my hand on his wrist, pushing in the opposite direction to his stroke to see if that would help (see Figure 5.2). The results were stunning. His final story dictation with its long catalog of penguin antics at the zoo reinforced how important visual learning opportunities were for Noah (see Figure 5.3).

The progress of children with some disabilities may be very gradual and come in very small increments. Observing and interacting with a child can help a teacher identify progress, plan optimal lessons and changes in the environment, and share progress with parents and colleagues.

Figure 5.2. Ruth Harkema, Noah's teacher, discovered that if she pushed against his hand as he drew, he had better control of his marker.

ANECDOTAL NOTES

Familiar Uses

An *anecdote* can be defined as a "short account of an interesting or humorous incident" (*American Heritage Dictionary*, 2000). Teachers use these "brief, narrative descriptions of specific events" to develop an understanding of "behavior when there are no other means to evaluate it directly" (Gullo, 2005, p. 86). Perhaps the most common systematic use of anecdotal notes occurs when a teacher suspects that a child is experiencing a significant delay in development, particularly in the area of classroom behavior and/or self-help skills. In this situation, the teacher is often asked to document the frequency, duration, and nature of the delay over a period of time. The documentation may be used to make a case for further professional evaluation for the purpose of accessing services for the child. Anecdotal notes are usually a part of this documentation.

Teachers are also familiar with the use of anecdotal notes to communicate with parents. Often a note is written describing an unusual behavior or incident involving a child. A note describing something positive the child has done may be sent home with the intention of building a feeling of esprit de

corps between parents and the teacher. Sometimes humorous anecdotes are included in newsletters for parents from the teacher.

Expanded Uses

As teachers become more aware of the importance of documenting children's development, they are expanding their use of anecdotal notes as a way of providing evidence of development. Anecdotal notes may be used as evidence for a profile of the knowledge, skills, attitudes, and dispositions of the child documented in a checklist. They allow the teacher to bring the child's learning experience to life. They help the teacher create a window that lets the viewer understand not just that the child achieved a certain level of performance, but *how* the child went about it. For example, an anecdote from Jordan's teacher gives us insight into changes in Jordan's disposition to interact with others:

> A shy newcomer to the class, Jordan came quietly to the table several days in succession and carefully studied the zoo penguin photographs. Her drawings show increasing detail and accuracy of shape, and delightfully she began to interact with her classmates.

By observing and noting the increasing detail in Jordan's drawings and her growing ability to interact socially with others, her teacher, Ruth Harkema, provided evidence of Jordan's progress. By supplementing the anecdote with other types of documentation (see Figures 5.4, 5.5, and 5.6), Ms. Harkema has strengthened this evidence.

This anecdotal note can also be used to document early learning benchmarks in art, "Investigates the elements of visual arts"; science, "Gather data about themselves and their surroundings"; and social/emotional development, "Develop relationships with children and adults" (Illinois State Board of Education, Division of Early Childhood, 2002).

Optimal use of anecdotal notes requires that several elements be present. First, the teacher should "know what to look for, how to recognize features of children's learning at different ages, and the criteria to use to evaluate students fairly and reliably" (Dichtelmiller, Jablon, Dorfman, Marsden, & Meisels, 2001, p. 11). When firmly grounded in knowledge of child development and the activities typical of a developmentally appropriate classroom, the teacher can have realistic expectations of a child's development in all areas of the curriculum.

Second, the developmental guidelines used to inform her observations should be in agreement with the teacher's knowledge of child development and

Figure 5.3. Each child told a story about the zoo. Noah's final story, displayed next to his picture, reveals his interest and knowledge about penguins.

> They bite. They swim.
> They can play in the snow.
> They can jump
> in the
> water.
> They like to play and
> go in their houses.
> They walk with two feet.
> They make noise.
> They wear bracelets.
> They can play
> in the
> water.
> They can bounce.
> They can go to sleep.
> They can wake up.
> It bites with a beak.
> They can roll.
> They can walk.
> They can stand up.
> They can grow.
> They can make their
> wings go backwards.
> They're black and white.

Figure 5.4. Jordan made field sketches of penguins on her trip to the zoo.

Figure 5.5. Jordan joins other children to draw and talk.

Figure 5.6. Jordan's final sketch of a penguin is more detailed and accurate.

curriculum. As she makes observations and writes anecdotes as evidence of development, the teacher can reflect on these developmental guidelines.

Third, a teacher should plan for the time and materials needed for observing and recording development. It is helpful to gather together and keep handy the materials used to record and organize observations. The longer one waits to record an observation, the less likely one will record it accurately and the more likely one is to forget to record it at all.

Fourth, a teacher should set up a system for regularly observing and writing anecdotes about a child in all areas of development. Then she will be able to see "how children integrate multiple skills in a meaningful context" (Dichtelmiller, Jablon, Dorfman, Marsden, & Meisels, 2001, p. 120).

When these four elements are in place—(1) knowledge of child development, (2) a checklist that is in agreement with the teacher's knowledge of child development and curriculum, (3) planning for time and materials, and (4) a system for observing and writing anecdotes—a teacher can create an ongoing, individualized profile of the child's knowledge, skills, and behaviors that emphasizes strengths, progress, and sources of concern. When the teacher adds sample products of the child's work in the area mentioned in the anecdotal note, evidence of growth is strengthened. Such a teacher has supporting documentation for planning curriculum to identify the zone of proximal development of each child.

Take, for example, the case of Tyler. In addition to the fact that he was the youngest 3-year-old in Stacy Berg's multiage prekindergarten class at the Valeska Hinton Center, Tyler had not developed receptive language skills as quickly as others his age. This partially accounted for Tyler's inability to stay focused in many class activities. Ms. Berg and several other teachers had decided to develop projects centering around the theme of water. Fish became the focus of the project work in Tyler's room. Ms. Berg noted during the course of this project that a new skill was emerging for Tyler. Referring to her anecdotal notes, which follow, she was able to document Tyler's skill as "in process" on checklist item A-1 in the "Scientific Thinking" section for 3-year-olds: "Uses senses to explore classroom materials and natural phenomena."

In order to study and investigate a real fish, a large red snapper was brought in for the children to explore. While many children were reluctant to touch the fish, all of the children looked at the different parts of the fish and talked about what they saw. Many children had questions which we were able to answer by looking through our many fish resources. Comments about the fish included the following:

Stacy: What does his eye feel like?
Tyler: Water.
Stacy: What is it?
Tyler: A fish.
Stacy: Where do fish live?
Tyler: Water.

In the past during many class experiments and investigations, Tyler would leave the group as the language was too difficult and he could not participate. When the red snapper was brought into the classroom, Tyler voluntarily sat and explored the fish for 20 minutes. With the real object at his fingers, Tyler attempted to participate in the conversation with the other children as he looked at and touched the fish.

Because she recognized that Tyler's participation in the group and comments on the red snapper represented "new behavior" for him, Ms. Berg made special note of it by displaying a photograph of Tyler examining the red snapper in the corridor outside the classroom (see Figure 5.7). She further documented the significance of this picture with the written explanation quoted above. This documentation gave Ms. Berg the opportunity to share an awareness of Tyler's emerging skill with others in the school environment so that they, too, might challenge him at his developmental level. At their next parent-teacher conference, Ms. Berg explained to Tyler's mother that he was making progress in language. Using the example of the red snapper discussion as recorded on the anecdotal note to document this point, she discussed with Tyler's mother strategies she could use at home to help Tyler develop this emerging skill. As in the case of Ms. Berg and Tyler, by looking for and documenting skills as they begin to emerge, a teacher may discover an area ripe for growth and become more effective by involving others who are close to the child. Anecdotal records may also be used to construct a time line documenting the development of a skill from the time a child first uses it, through the stages of development, and on to mastery.

NOTES ON DISPOSITIONS

Observations recorded as anecdotal notes may enhance a teacher's ability to follow the child's emotional response to learning by documenting the development of the child's dispositions to play, to work with others, to read, to research, to like school, and to have a sense of competence. For example, the teacher of 6-year-old Benjamin selected the following quote from the audio recording she had made of the class discussion that day. As he pointed at his drawing (see Figure 5.8), he said:

> This is a spider monkey. Its face is bald, but all the rest has fur on it. It swings on trees and climbs on trees. It suits my attitude. It's in the rain forest. They usually go in the canopy and the midlayer. I like how I did the background.

Figure 5.7. Tyler examines and discusses the red snapper firsthand.

Figure 5.8. Including a copy of Benjamin's painting of the spider monkey with his teacher's anecdotal note and his words provides evidence of his knowledge, skills, and dispositions.

In the anecdotal note she wrote about this statement, she said, "Ben's words show his positive attitude and disposition to reflect on his own work and his comfort with his own personality. He loves details and knows a lot about the rain forest and spider monkeys."

Jessica, a child in Pam Scranton's multiage pre-kindergarten classroom at the Valeska Hinton Early Childhood Education Center, was part of a class exploration of laundromats. Ms. Scranton made the following observations of Jessica's disposition to work with others:

> Jessica has a hard time playing and cooperating in the family living area; she doesn't like to share control of the play sequence. However, during the course of this project, Jessica has been able to share control and work cooperatively with the other children involved. She was able to offer ideas for the list of materials needed and helped collect laundry items, even bringing in materials from home.

An example of a disposition leading to a sense of competence can be found in the documentation of the Water Project work that took place in Mary Ann Gottlieb's room:

> Dustin tried several times to trace around the faucet. He was challenged by the uneven surfaces as he tried to trace. However, he continued to work until finally he placed the faucet off the paper and represented it as he perceived it. Dustin's work has become much neater as the Water Project has progressed. He works less rapidly, using an eraser or starting over in order to make his drawings more representational. He is developing the dispositions of independence and resourcefulness.

As they become familiar with the teacher's use of anecdotes to document their child's learning, parents often contribute anecdotes that reveal the dispositions of their children when outside of the school environment. Such information can help the teacher see whether the growth seen at school is transferring to the home environment. For example, when a class at the Illinois Valley Community College child-care center began their Meadow Project, 3-year-old Brady was inclined to step on the crickets he found. But as the project developed, his mother, Michelle, wrote a note to his teacher to let her know how Brady's attitude toward the insects had changed:

> In our basement there are a lot of crickets. . . . Brady wants to go in the basement every day to find crickets. He tells me, "Mommy, I go get my friend to put in my bed." I have to try to explain why he can't.

THE PROJECT APPROACH AND OBSERVATION

Project work provides an excellent environment for observing child development, since projects are largely child directed and teacher guided. In project work, a child (or a group of children) selects a question to be answered or a problem to be solved and then, with teacher guidance as needed and/or peer assistance, experiments to solve the problem (Helm & Katz, 2001). Since these experiences are child initiated, they provide an opportunity to see children when they are truly engaged, thereby showing their best abilities. It is possible to identify the zone of proximal development for children with a wide range of abilities in the context of project work. In addition, since projects develop over a period of time, they provide opportunities for many observations of the stages of development of children's work or dispositions. Thus, a teacher can construct a very accurate picture of a child's level of development in all domains at a particular point in time and over a period of days, weeks, or even years.

TECHNOLOGY AND OBSERVATION

One of the challenges of observation and authentic assessment is finding the time to record observations and finding an efficient way to organize them. Recent advances in technology have helped many teachers meet this challenge. Take, for example, the pilot Early Childhood Standards Project (ECSP). The project website, https://www.pdaobserve.org/, presents an observation and assessment system that "combines the power of a hand-held personal digital assistant with centralized databases and reporting tools to help teachers create accurate, timely, reliable, valid, and thorough evaluations of student progress" (Illinois Resource Center, 2005). Each teacher has access to a personal password-protected site for her classroom.

The program that was developed for this pilot website allows teachers to record and organize their observations and anecdotal notes from any computer with Internet access. These observations can be linked with items on an observational checklist. Photographs can also be uploaded, attached, stored on the website, and printed as portfolio samples. Observations can be sorted and viewed in many ways. For example, a teacher can view a bar graph that allows her to see the number of observations she has collected by learning area, child, or checklist item.

Teachers who have attended preliminary training on standards, observation, and assessment, are given a Palm personal digital assistant (PDA) and instruction on how to use the PDA to record their observations of young children. Observations can then be entered on the PDA and transferred to the ECSP website at the teacher's convenience by hot-syncing the PDA with the Internet site. Observations are automatically sorted by date and by child. The PDA is small and provides a way to record quick notes that the teacher can expand and develop more fully, after the note is uploaded to the ECSP website.

STAYING FOCUSED

Sometimes, as teachers become involved in a new practice, such as documentation, they lose sight of their original goal, and the practice itself becomes the goal. Documenting that does not lead to evaluation of curriculum and instruction and translate to implementation is of little value. As long as teachers remember that documentation is a tool meant to inform their teaching, their time learning these new skills will have been well spent.

CHAPTER 6

Individual Portfolios: Capturing Children's Competence

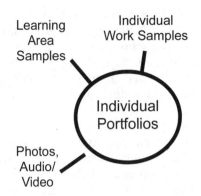

Learning Area Samples

Individual Work Samples

Individual Portfolios

Photos, Audio/ Video

> **Portfolio:** Purposeful collections of work that illustrate children's efforts, progress, and achievements.
> —Meisels et al. (1994)

One type of documentation familiar to teachers is the collection of children's work. For years, teachers have been saving children's work to share with parents and to use at the end of the year to evaluate a child's progress. Teachers often collect children's self-portraits or writing samples. This type of collection has some of the characteristics of a good documentation process. The material collected represents authentic work of the children; that is, it comes from work that children do as part of the ongoing learning process in the classroom. It also is work unique to each child as distinct from the standardized responses on achievement or readiness tests. If the teacher systematically collects the children's work, such as self-portraits in the fall and the following spring, the teacher is also able to document observed growth over time. With an increased emphasis on standards in primary classrooms and in many state-funded prekindergarten programs, authentic assessment systems that meet accountability standards and demonstrate the effectiveness of active, engaged learning strategies require a more systematic approach. Assessment of young children requires *ongoing* collections of their work. These collections, commonly termed *portfolios,* enable teachers and others to document achievement of standards. Even more important, portfolios enable documentation of learning beyond factual knowledge to include problem solving, hypothesizing, predicting, creative thinking, and personal and social development.

UNDERSTANDING THE USE OF PORTFOLIOS

There are many different approaches to systematizing a portfolio collection process. Gullo (2005) discusses a variety of types of portfolios that have been effectively used in early childhood programs. Some programs use a three-folio system with separate portfolios for ongoing work, current work, and permanently kept work (Mills, 1989; Vermont Department of Education, 1988, 1989). Howard Gardner's (1993) work on multiple intelligences has resulted in portfolio systems focusing on individualized characteristics of students that are revealed when children approach problems and do projects. Gardner also uses the term *processfolio,* which is a portfolio in which the student documents personal involvement throughout the process of doing a project, including planning, interim work, and reflections.

As explained in the Introduction, several of the schools highlighted in this book use the Work Sampling System as the primary instrument for assessment. One of the three components of the Work Sampling System is the systematic collection of children's work into a portfolio. According to Meisels and colleagues (1994), "Portfolios capture the evolution of children's competence, providing rich documentation of their classroom experience throughout the year" (p. 13). The purposes of portfolios in the Work Sampling System include the following:

- Capturing the quality of the child's thinking and work
- Showing the child's progress over time
- Involving the child in assessing his or her own work
- Reflecting the types of classroom experiences available to the child
- Assisting teachers with an opportunity to reflect on their expectations of student work
- Giving students, teachers, families, administrators, and other decision makers essential information about student progress and classroom activities. (p. 13)

The Work Sampling System portfolios consist of two types of items: *Core Items* and *Individualized Items.* Core Items reflect a child's work across the whole curriculum as well as the child's growth over time. They document student work in five domains of learning:

Language and Literacy, Mathematical Thinking, Scientific Thinking, Social Studies, and The Arts. Teachers in a school determine which items they want to collect by identifying particular areas of learning within each domain. They collect the same type of item three times a year. For example, the Core Item for Language and Literacy for 3-year-olds is the collection of a sample of a child's conversation. At the end of the year, the teacher will have three samples of the child's conversation spaced throughout the year. This enables the teacher to see growth. A Core Item collection sheet can be kept on each child so that the teacher knows what has been collected for each Core Item. Some Core Items that these schools chose to collect are listed in Table 6.1.

In addition to the Core Items for each domain, teachers also collect Individualized Items. These items represent a significant event, an integrated learning experience from multiple domains, or an area of special interest to a child. Although many of the teachers at these schools had previously collected children's work for portfolios even before the Work Sampling System was adopted for use, they found that the structure of the Work Sampling collection system had distinct advantages. Teachers often do not know what to collect and soon are confronted with a large number of children's work samples and no way to reflect on them in an organized way. Gullo (2005) points out that

> alternative or authentic assessment describes an organizational approach, not a specific procedure. . . . It is an approach to assessment that helps individuals organize and make sense out of some of the various types of informal assessment procedures. (p. 95)

Restricting the collecting to a specified number of learning area samples and individual work samples kept the teacher from being overwhelmed by the collection task. Using the specified Core Items for each learning area helped the teacher focus on each area of a child's development. This moderated the *halo effect*, the tendency for advancement in one area of development to influence the teacher's judgment of development in other areas. Limiting the number of items also made the portfolio more manageable when the teacher needed to review and reflect upon children's progress while writing a summary.

This combination of two separate approaches within one portfolio collection also resolves a paradigm conflict identifed by Paulson and Paulson (1994) of opposite uses of the portfolio. The *positivist paradigm* of the portfolio requires that it be used to infer how much learning has occurred with the meaning of the materials held constant across users, contexts, and purposes. The *constructivist paradigm* of the portfolio assumes that meaning varies across individuals, over time, and with purpose; hence, a summary of development is too complex for description. By collecting learning area portfolio items for all children, which are based on standards, and also collecting individual items, which are evidence of complex, highly individualized learning experiences, both of these paradigms are included in the process.

Dichtelmiller, Jablon, Dorfman, Marsden, and Meisels (2001) recommend that for a collection process to be effective, items should be informative, easy to collect, and reflective of meaningful classroom activities. At Valeska Hinton Early Childhood Education Center and Illinois Valley Community College, the Work Sampling process of systematic collection and observation is used in conjunction

Table 6.1. Work Sampling System domains.

Domain	Sample Core Items*
Language and Literacy	Sample of a conversation (ages 3, 4) Sample of a child's writing (ages 3, 4, and K & 1st) Record of child's retelling of a story (K) Record of a child's understanding of a story from text (1st)
Mathematical Thinking	Record of a child's interest in counting (age 3) Record of child's sorting by one or more attributes (ages 3, 4) Record of child's patterning (age 4) Example of a child using numbers to solve a problem (K & 1st)
Scientific Thinking	Record of a child's recognition of differences and similarities in objects (age 3, 4) Recorded questions asked or comments made about the scientific world (ages 3, 4) Charts and graphs that were used to collect and analyze data (K & 1st)
Social Studies	Record of recognition of own characteristics or those of family through drawings or conversation (ages 3, 4) Recognition of family or community roles (ages 3, 4, and K & 1st) Child-drawn map that indicates child's geographic understanding (1st)
The Arts	Record of child's participation in music, drama, or dance activity (ages 3, 4) Record of child's willingness to try different art media (ages 3, 4) Record of child's attempt to show feelings or tell a story through art (K & 1st) Record of a child's appreciation of the art of others (K & 1st)

* *In the Work Sampling System, each school or district decides which Core Items to collect at each age or grade level. Items are collected at three times: the beginning, middle, and end of the school year. Repeatedly collecting the same items over the year allows growth to be observed.*

with project work. The assembling of a collection of children's work for the portfolio was a natural adjunct to the active, engaged learning experiences of the project approach. When children are investigating a topic of high interest, they produce a significant number of high-quality work samples. Many Core and Individualized Items for the portfolio are collected during the projects.

COLLECTING SPECIFIC LEARNING AREA SAMPLES

Using a Core Item Sheet

Even if a teacher is not using the Work Sampling System, it is helpful to collect the same type of sample for a specific learning area such as writing. This process can be simplified by using a Core Item sheet for the learning area sample, which was developed by staff at the Valeska Hinton Center to simplify the collection of the Core Items in a multiage setting. Figure 6.1 is an example of a blank Core Item sheet. Teachers tape or staple children's work or a photo to the Core Item sheet when they collect it. If they are writing down an anecdotal note to document a Core Item, they may just write directly on the sheet. There is one sheet for each child for each Core Item. The sheets are color coded by domain; for example, Language and Literacy Core Item sheets are all yellow, Social Studies are all blue. Each Core Item sheet has a description of the Core Item that needs to be collected and spaces to check other information that the teacher may wish to record.

At the beginning of each collection period (three times a year), the teacher takes the appropriate Core Item sheets that will be needed for all the members of the class, places their names on the appropriate sheets according to their age level, then stacks them by Core Item. While collecting children's work, anecdotal notes, photos of work, or photos of children exhibiting skills, the teacher quickly puts it onto the appropriate Core Item sheet and files it in the child's portfolio or stacks it to be filed later. As time passes, the stack of empty Core Item sheets becomes smaller; there will be fewer and fewer Core Item sheets left to complete. The Core Item sheet reminds the teacher what needs to be collected on each child. When all the empty Core Item sheets are gone, all the necessary items have been collected. This method also makes it easier for teachers when they review the portfolio. Because the sheets are color coded, they can quickly find all the samples that relate to a particular domain simply by finding the appropriate color. For example, in reflecting on a child's growth in Language and Literacy, the teacher can pull out all the Core Items that are on yellow sheets of paper. Because the dates and other information are in the same place on each sheet, it is also easy to locate the date and put the sheets in order to assess progress.

As classrooms became involved in projects, a side benefit of the Core Item sheets was discovered. They became an efficient way for a teacher to display children's work on a particular project. When used as display items, they facilitated the presentation of the learning that had occurred during the project. Having the Core Item listed on each sheet with an accompanying explanation of the significance of the item in the development of the child provided a ready-made "narrative" to cue parents and others into the learning experience. They also demonstrated how project work coordinated with the center's curriculum and assessment system and facilitated discussion of children's work with parents and other professionals.

The two Core Item sheets in Figures 6.2 and 6.3 were collected during the Blue Village's Water Project. Both were used for project displays in addition to being placed in children's individual portfolios. Each teacher used the Core Item sheet in a slightly different way to meet the documentation needs. Pam Scranton collected 4-year-old Veldez's work sample of emergent writing (Figure 6.2) from his play with the water treatment plant that the children had built with blocks. It is a good sample of letter shapes that he had written to facilitate his play. She quickly marked with checks in boxes that this was a new behavior for Veldez and that it was spontaneous. It will be helpful to her later on as she reviews and reflects on his progress for the summary report. She stapled the sample to the Core Item sheet and attached a quick portfolio item Post-it that she had written to remember the significance of the sample. The description of the Core Item on

Figure 6.1. The Core Item sheet enables the teacher to easily collect and record information.

Name		Valeska Hinton Early Childhood Education Center
Language and Literacy #2 for 3 Year Olds Work Sampling System Core Item		

☐ Fall	Date _____	
☐ Winter	☐ Emerging Behavior	☐ Spontaneous
☐ Spring	☐ Proficient	☐ Teacher Initiated

Core Item # 2: **Record of a child's writing** At the three year old level, writing attempts are not conventional. Scribbling and telling someone that it is writing or scribbling letter-like marks are beginning writing attempts. The samples show a beginning understanding of the use of words for communication.

the sheet provided a cue to others as to why the sample was important. It also informed those who might not have background knowledge about the typical development of writing skills.

When teacher Mary Ann Gottlieb collected the Mathematical Thinking Core Item (Figure 6.3) by 5-year-old Tisha, she used the Core Item sheet a little differently. She took a picture as a record of Tisha's counting with one-to-one correspondence. She later typed her description of the event directly onto the sheet and added the picture. This was an efficient way to document a skill that did not produce a product like the previous example.

The example that appears below is a Core Item collected from the Baby Project by teacher Gail Gordon. The first paragraph is the description of the Core Item that was printed on the top of the sheet. Ms. Gordon wrote the second paragraph describing the child's behavior directly on the Core Item sheet.

Scientific Thinking #1 for 4-Year-Olds

Core Item #1: Record of questions asked and comments made. Child verbalizes wonder about the scientific world by asking questions or making comments such as, "What's inside of . . .", "How does [something] work", "What happens when . . ."

After reading the book *Baby* by Fran Manushkin, Quanisha asked, "How do babies get food when they are still in their momma's stomach?" We thought about who would know the answer to that question. She decided maybe her doctor, and maybe we could ask him. She also said, "Babies cry in there."

When Rachel Bystry collected the following Core Item during her classroom's Ball Project, she wrote an anecdotal note about what she had observed on the playground. She had simply recorded this observation on a Post-it note designed for Work Sampling collection and checked the appropriate domain:

> Briana dumped bag of balls out on the ground and lined them up from smallest to largest . . . seven balls.

She then stuck this note onto the appropriate Core Item sheet.

This technique enabled Ms. Bystry to capture the information before she forgot the event. Sometimes a Core Item will be expanded to provide more information after the teacher has had time to reflect

Figure 6.2. This Core Item sheet includes a sample of a child's work and a teacher's anecdotal notes.

Figure 6.3. This Core Item sheet has a photo attached to show the child's participation in graphing.

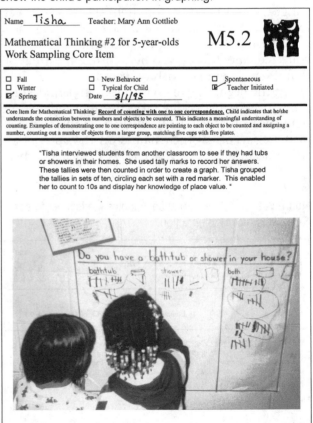

on the observation. This is the Core Item that Ms. Bystry finally inserted into Briana's portfolio:

> During outside time, Briana dumped a bag of balls out onto the ground. She was playing by herself and proceeded to line the balls up in order from the smallest to the largest. There was a total of seven balls. She began lining the balls up and switching them one by one. She would switch a couple of balls, step back and look to see if they were just as she wanted them. Briana was engaged in this activity for 15 to 20 minutes.

Teachers have noted that the more interested the children are in the project topic, the better the quality of the Core and Individualized Items. Children are motivated to try new skills and to risk asking for knowledge when they are involved in a project. During project work, the Core Items collected are more often spontaneous than teacher initiated. This results in identification of more "emergent" or "in process" behavior. And the teacher, being better able to assess where the children are, can plan additional learning activities.

Learning Areas or Core Items Over Time

When items from the same learning area are collected over a period of time, such as throughout preschool or across several grade levels, the development in that area can be striking. This can be seen in a series of portfolio items from Discovery Preschool. Teacher Pam Scranton has documented the development of Luke in learning how to write:

> Luke begins his 3-year-old year at Discovery Preschool. He is a typical 3-year-old. Luke is very interested in playing with all the new materials and keeps busy figuring out how to be a friend, share, and listen during large-group times. Since journals have been introduced, Luke spends most of small-group time exploring the writing tools and the different ways they look on his paper. Luke is clearly in the scribble stage of writing—he knows that writing is his speech written down and can assign meaning to his scribbles (see Figure 6.4).
>
> A few months later, Luke is in the next stage of writing development. In this portfolio sample (see Figure 6.5), he is making letterlike shapes in

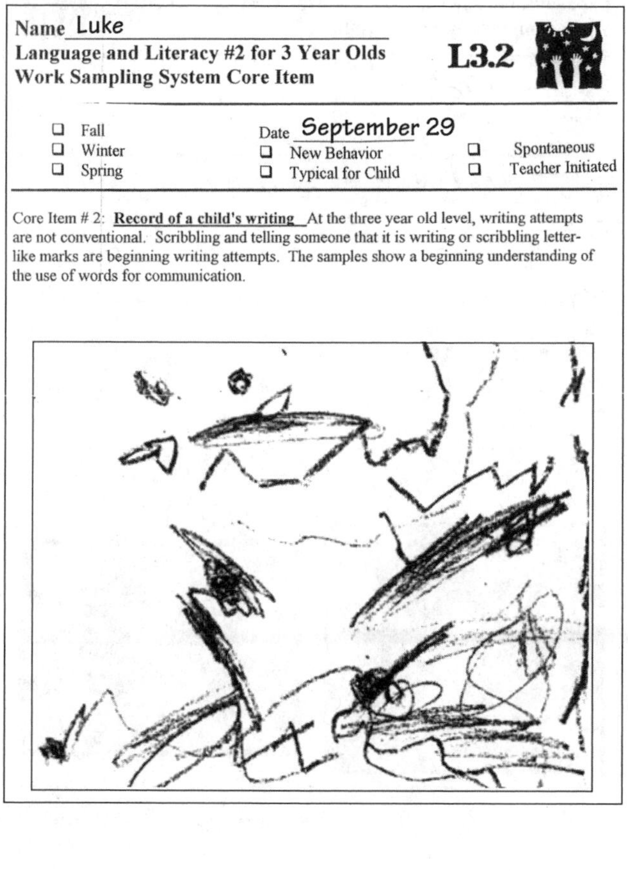

Figure 6.4. Luke's writing portfolio item shows scribbling. The description on the sheet provides parents with an idea of what to expect at this age.

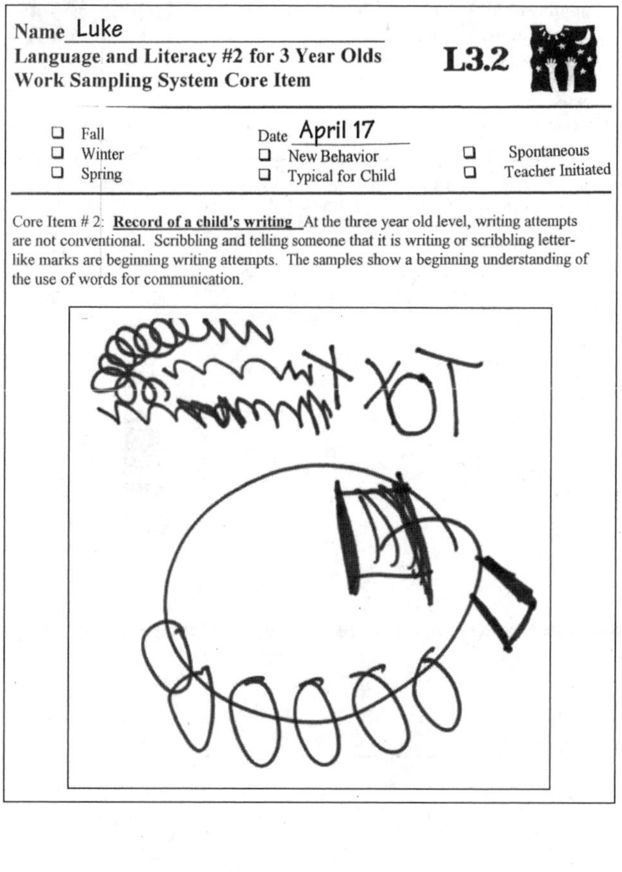

Name Luke
Language and Literacy #2 for 3 Year Olds
Work Sampling System Core Item **L3.2**

☐ Fall   Date **September 29**
☐ Winter   ☐ New Behavior   ☐ Spontaneous
☐ Spring   ☐ Typical for Child ☐ Teacher Initiated

Core Item # 2: **Record of a child's writing** At the three year old level, writing attempts are not conventional. Scribbling and telling someone that it is writing or scribbling letterlike marks are beginning writing attempts. The samples show a beginning understanding of the use of words for communication.

Figure 6.5. Pam took the following dictation from Luke about this sample: "I made some T's 'cause my picture is a tractor!"

Name Luke
Language and Literacy #2 for 3 Year Olds
Work Sampling System Core Item **L3.2**

☐ Fall   Date **April 17**
☐ Winter   ☐ New Behavior   ☐ Spontaneous
☐ Spring   ☐ Typical for Child ☐ Teacher Initiated

Core Item # 2: **Record of a child's writing** At the three year old level, writing attempts are not conventional. Scribbling and telling someone that it is writing or scribbling letterlike marks are beginning writing attempts. The samples show a beginning understanding of the use of words for communication.

his journal. Luke is beginning to identify some sounds, but is still very unsure of the letter formations.

Luke is now 4 years old and growing in his ability to make sense of the written word. In this portfolio sample, Luke demonstrates some understanding of sounds and letters. On this page in his journal (see Figure 6.6) he has drawn a picture of something that happened during outside time and attempts to label his drawing. It says "dirt." Luke can identify the beginning sound in the word dirt. He then chose random letters that he knows how to make to finish his word.

Luke is in his second year of preschool. During the Construction Project, Luke became very interested in constructing the tractors he had investigated on the field site visit. Many of the older children are busy labeling their own constructions and displaying them for the culminating event—a project night. Following the lead of an older child, Luke makes his very first attempt at developmental spelling (see Figure 6.7).

This sequence shows Luke's progression in learning to write in preschool. As parents leave Discovery Preschool, they receive the portfolios to take home. The explanations on the Core Item sheets enable them to remember why the work samples are meaningful and contribute to the parents' and the child's image of the child as a competent learner.

As children grow in their skills, the portfolio items become more and more complex. Children become involved in thinking about their own work and evaluating it. Figure 6.8 shows how Oscar, a first grader in a dual language program in West Liberty, Iowa, is mastering the task of writing. He also reveals his dispositions towards reading, writing, and school.

COLLECTING INDIVIDUAL WORK SAMPLES

In addition to Core Items, Individualized Items are also collected for each child. Individualized Items are described in the Work Sampling System (Meisels et al., 1994) as follows:

Figure 6.6. "It says 'dirt.'" Luke can identify the beginning sound in the word "dirt." He then chose random letters that he knows how to make to finish his word.

Name Luke
Language and Literacy #2 for 4 Year Olds
Work Sampling System Core Item   L4.2

☐ Fall   Date October 6
☐ Winter   ☐ New Behavior   ☐ Spontaneous
☐ Spring   ☐ Typical for Child ☐ Teacher Initiated

Core Item #2 : **Record of a child's writing.** At the four year old level, writing attempts are not conventional. Scribbling and telling someone that it is writing or scribbling letter-like marks are beginning writing attempts. Rows of squiggles may imitate print. The samples show a beginning understanding of the use of words for communication.

Figure 6.7. Luke presented this writing to his teacher and said, "Look, Mrs. Scranton! I wroted backhoe loader!"

Name Luke
Language and Literacy #2 for 4 Year Olds
Work Sampling System Core Item   L4.2

☐ Fall   Date May 8
☐ Winter   ☐ New Behavior   ☐ Spontaneous
☐ Spring   ☐ Typical for Child ☐ Teacher Initiated

Core Item #2 : **Record of a child's writing.** At the four year old level, writing attempts are not conventional. Scribbling and telling someone that it is writing or scribbling letter-like marks are beginning writing attempts. Rows of squiggles may imitate print. The samples show a beginning understanding of the use of words for communication.

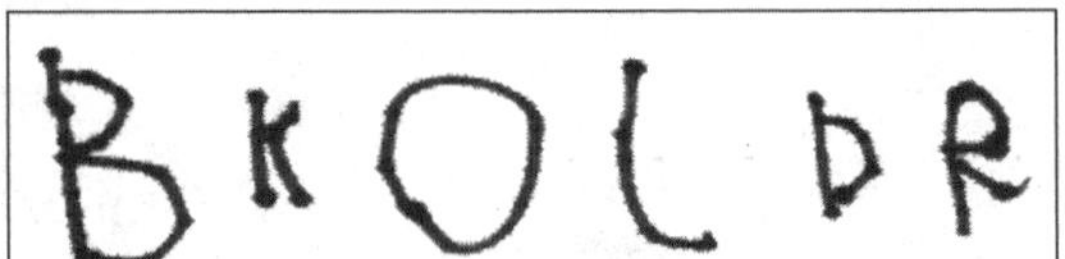

"Backhoe Loader"

These items display students' unique characteristics, learning styles, and strengths as well as their integration of skills and knowledge from several domains. A minimum of five Individualized Items is selected each collection period. Individualized Items can represent a significant event, such as the first finger painting of a child who has always avoided messy activities, or a book report on which the student worked particularly hard. (p. 16)

An example of individuality that can be seen in collected work samples is the very different ways in which two 4-year-olds in Michelle Didesch's classroom approached representing a firefighter's hat as part of the Hat Project. Ms. Didesch took the following notes on yellow legal pads that she keeps in her classroom for such use.

Mary and Chris decided to make a fireman hat after firefighters visited our classroom. Chris put the hat on a piece of paper and traced around it. He drew what he saw on the underside on one side. Then he drew what he saw on the top side on the other side of his paper. He included the head straps which had holes in them, the creases (lines) on the top, and the writing on the front (see Figure 6.9). Mary looked at the shape of the hat, drew it, and cut it out. Then she added a strap so it could fit on her head (see Figure 6.10).

Individualized Items may also be work samples that reflect an integration of learning from multiple domains. Children often work together to produce a product. On an Individualized Item sheet Monica Borrowman described the writing samples she collected from 4-year-olds in the block area (see Figure 6.11). This sample shows some significant skills on the part of the children. The cooperation and sharing of the task indicates their level of personal social development, while the work with letters and sounds indicates their level of understanding of literacy.

Often children will become intensely interested in a topic or a particular phenomena that they are observing or studying. They may study it in great depth or at a level of complexity that is not anticipated by the teacher. Work samples and observations of this in-depth study are also collected in the portfolio as Individualized Items. Two Individualized Items were collected from 4-year-old Korey by teacher Judy Cagle during the Reflections Project. When the teacher provided mirrors and paper shapes for experimentation, Korey produced the work shown in Figure 6.12. Korey observed reflections in water both in natural surroundings and in books. Ms. Cagle asked if he would like to draw a picture of water reflections, and he made the

picture "Tree Reflected in Water" (see Figure 6.13). Korey continued to work with this concept, eventually becoming able to make a drawing in which he would correctly look at a shape and determine where the line of symmetry would fall.

OTHER PORTFOLIO ITEMS

Teachers have found that it is often more effective and efficient to use electronic media, such as tape recordings, videotapes, and photographs, to document

Figure 6.8. Oscar, a first grader, not only shows his writing skills but also what he thinks about his own reading and writing.

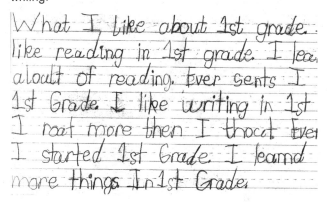

Figure 6.9. Chris's approach to drawing the hat was to draw the front, turn the paper over and draw the back.

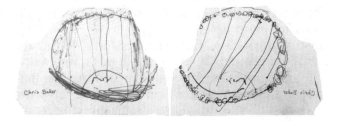

Figure 6.10. Mary drew the parts of the hat, then cut them out to make a hat.

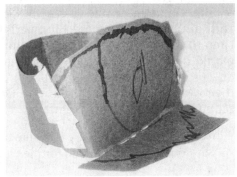

Figure 6.11. This Individualized Portfolio Item documents integrated learning.

Figure 6.12. The first Individualized Portfolio Item shows Korey's exploration of a topic.

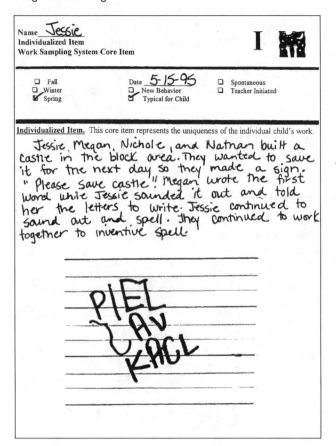

children's learning. A video can capture movement, children's expression, and light. Videos and photos enable the "collection" of large structures and play environments that children create.

These types of documentation also enable children to revisit experiences and provide a basis for discussing the project experiences and reflecting on what was learned. Children can, in this way, provide their own documentation of experiences. Children can use photographs of field trips to refresh their memory. Photos and videos also enable children to focus on a particular item or aspect of an experience that they may not have noticed when they were on site. Children can be taught to operate cameras and take photos to record information they need later. In Chapter 12, readers can see how photos are placed on a planning board for review at the end of a project. An example of children documenting their own research is shown in Gail Gordon's project narrative of the Baby Project.

We went to see the baby furniture so that maybe we could build something for the baby area in our room. We discussed jobs before we left. Ms. Gordon wrote the plans on her clipboard (see Figure 6.14). Then we read the note together and each child copied his word (job) on their clipboard. Ms. Gordon reviewed how to use the camera. Each child took a photo of his item. While they were waiting for their turn, they drew their item on their clipboard (see Figures 6.15 and 6.16).

Tape recorders also make documentation easier and more efficient. Collecting questions and answers on a tape recorder enables the teacher to reflect on them later and to focus on more than one child. Placing a tape recorder on a table where children are working also enables the teacher to assist other children while still capturing valuable documentation of learning.

All of the types of documentation used for collecting individual portfolios enable the teacher to better assess the child's learning and to plan additional experiences based on that assessment. By storing the collected work samples, observations, and electronic media in an individual portfolio for each child in-

Figure 6.13. In this picture Korey integrated his knowledge into this representation of a pond.

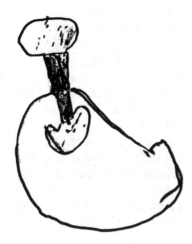

Figure 6.14. The teacher recorded the plans for the trip to the sibling care room.

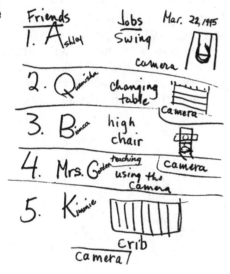

Figure 6.15. Children sketching what they are observing on the field trip.

Figure 6.16. A child's sketch of a high chair.

stead of in a class collection, the teacher is naturally focused on each child's development. The teacher is assisted in focusing on the whole child rather than on development in one academic area by having the portfolio organized so that a specific number of items are collected from each domain. The teacher periodically reviews the children's work in combination with a developmental checklist. This carefully planned, systematic collection provides excellent documentation for making educational decisions and provides a window on a child's development.

ELECTRONIC PORTFOLIOS

Many teachers and programs are now experimenting with electronic portfolios, which enable the easy integration of audio, video, graphics, and text. All of the types of documentation in the documentation web can be captured in an electronic portfolio through photographs, teacher notes, real work samples, and scanned or photographed work samples. Instead of storing these in a file folder or notebook, they are stored on a floppy disk, Zip disk, CD, or website. Although electronic portfolios are possible in prekindergarten and kindergarten, they are more often used in the later years of early childhood, the primary grades, when children can participate in the recording and collection process.

Electronic portfolios enable the use of hypertext links to organize the material, connecting evidence with appropriate outcomes, goals, or standards. Helen Barrett (2005) describes these portfolios as "containers" that can enhance the portfolio collection process. Electronic portfolios may be stored on a school or national website or on a teacher's computer. They may be shared in parent/teacher conferences, viewed by parents at home over the Internet on a password-accessible site, or copied and given to parents at the close of a school year.

Barrett (2005) describes the following enhancements to portfolios that come from technology: archiving, linking of work to thinking, storytelling, collaborating, and publishing. For example, an electronic portfolio can contain a video clip of a child pretend-reading in the fall, and in the spring show the child actually reading simple text. An electronic portfolio can capture not only the block representation of the zoo that a group of children made but also their excited explanation of the parts of the construction, including their use of new vocabulary words and new concepts about the classification of animals. In addition, the clip of the group can be easily duplicated and become a part of each child's portfolio.

There are many electronic portfolio services available that provide complete archiving and software support for electronic portfolios. Some of these link directly to assessment systems for aggregating and reporting data. There are also software products that teachers can purchase and use on-site for electronic portfolios. The more technologically adept teacher has many options: adaptation of standard multimedia software by means of directions on the Internet; hypermedia card formats, such as Hyper-Studio or Superlink; presentation software, such as PowerPoint; web or network compatible hypermedia, such as Macromedia Dreamweaver or Netscape Compose. Even programs that are more familiar, such as Microsoft Word, can be used for electronic portfolio development.

As with all technology enhancements, the teacher will need to decide if the enhancements justify the time required to utilize the technology. Is it worth the extra time it takes to scan or photograph a piece of work, type in the standard achieved, and link an audio file? Or can the same goal be achieved by simply stapling the artwork to a piece of paper that has been previously prepared with the standard listed and an explanation for parents? This is when the importance of having a clear understanding of the purpose and the audience for the portfolio is valuable. The value of making portfolios electronic will depend on the age of the children, the purpose of the portfolio, and the audience.

CHAPTER 7

Individual and Group Products: Seeing Is Believing

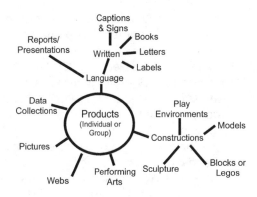

Individual and group products, the manifestations of children's learning, are perhaps the most obvious and familiar way that teachers document growth. There is considerable potential inherent in products for teachers to reflect on their teaching and to share with others their insights into the growth of children's knowledge, skills, abilities, and dispositions as indicated by the products. Teachers who take advantage of this potential can examine the growth revealed in both the end product and in the process of production.

Writing and art samples are commonly collected by adults as proof of children's learning. However, teachers may find it helpful to broaden the variety of samples they consider. Pictures, webs, performances, constructions, collections of data, and samples of oral and written language are additional products that provide significant opportunities for documentation. Occasionally these products speak for themselves, but generally they are more useful when selected for a particular purpose and accompanied by thoughtful written documentation explaining their significance.

In displays of group work, rather than displaying all of one type of work by all the children in the class, the teacher may find it helpful to display only those products that provide a window on a learning experience, a window on a child's development through participation in the group learning experience, or a window for teacher self-reflection. Considering each of these windows or purposes for documentation will guide teacher decision making.

PICTURES

"Any and all forms of purposeful visual expressions, beginning with controlled scribbling" can be defined as "picture making" (Mayesky, 1990, p. 165). While picture making is usually a part of the curriculum in most American early childhood programs, considering children's pictures in terms of their potential for documentation may help the teacher create views through the three windows. Teachers may find it helpful to document and evaluate pictures in new or additional ways. They might ask themselves:

- What was the meaning of the work for the child?
- What integration of knowledge and skills did the picture show?
- Was the child attempting to represent something, or was the child using drawing symbolically?
- Did the child engage in problem solving in the production of the picture?
- Did the child revisit an earlier picture or attempt to revisit the picture of another child?
- Does the picture show movement toward mastery of any learning standards?

A demonstration of the criteria implied in the above questions emerged in a series of paintings created in Sallee Beneke's prekindergarten classroom:

During December and January our class of 3-, 4-, and 5-year-olds studied water. We often place a picture of something that is related to our current topic of study at the top of the easel so that children can use it as a basis for discussion with other children, or to remind them of the topic or theme in the classroom. In the second week of December we displayed a picture from a calendar of a mama duck and her babies sitting on a log by water. This simple addition to the environment sparked a powerful learning experience that impacted children with a wide range of ages and abilities.

This chain reaction began when 5-year-old Nicole painted a representation of the log, and then began to paint the mama duck, beginning with her feet. Nicole's friend Alex, another 5-year-old in the class, was impressed with Nicole's effort, and she too wanted to try and paint the mama duck on the log. Alex worked on her painting for some time, and by the end of the first morning, she had painted the mama and all five baby ducks (see Figure 7.1a). Her painting made a big impression on 3-year-old Peyton, who looked up from the snack table, pointed to Alex's painting, and said, "Hey, that's really good!" Other children looked at Alex's painting and shared in Peyton's admiration during snack.

The following day, we asked Alex if she would like to work on her painting some more. She said she would like that, so we put Alex's painting back up on the easel and asked her if she noticed anything new. We talked about the reflections of the mama duck and her babies in the water. Alex was intrigued by the challenge of thinking about and painting the reflections. We were amazed by the accuracy of her work! Bethany, another 5-year-old, watched Alex work and talked with her about what she was doing (see Figure 7.1b). When Alex was finished, Bethany announced that she would like to paint the ducks. Bethany's painting reflects a sense of symmetry and pattern that we often see in her work. She has a style that makes it easy to identify her work (see Figure 7.1c). Watching these older girls work on their paintings inspired several of the younger children to paint their own versions of the duck picture (see Figure 7.1d). Three-year-old Peyton's version included the log and the mama duck's foot—those same items she had discussed with Nicole the previous day (see Figure 7.1e).

Because we were documenting this experience and not just looking at the product, we were able to see the opportunity to extend the experience. We brought many small mirrors into the classroom and placed them in several of the learning centers. Alex's interest in and experiments with reflections continued to develop, and other children picked it up. We also recognized the children's general interest in ducks, so we began to hatch a set of baby mallards. On the morning that the baby ducks hatched, Alex and her friends held several small mirrors up to the side of the aquarium, and when I asked them what they were doing, they said, "We want to see if they can see their own reflections!" (see Figure 7.1f).

Attempting to paint the ducks was a child-initiated chain reaction. This was unlike a more typical painting or drawing experience that we value, in which individual children experiment with art materials and use them in an imaginative and playful way to "pretend" on paper. Documentation of the experience enables us to capture this component of the experience. This was

a child-initiated attempt to capture the features they saw in the photograph that were interesting to them and interpret them on their own paper.

This extended documentation (photographing, taking notes, discussing) is often what enables a product to be useful for documentation of standards. Each of the children who participated brought their own interests and abilities to the task, and many of the Illinois Early Learning Standards were met. Alex was most deeply involved, so it's interesting to look at the range of standards that she achieved during this task (see Figure 7.2). For teachers who want to document standards through products of children's learning, it can be helpful to keep a list of standards readily available and then examine that list while documenting and also while examining the documentation and reflecting on it with others.

Although not all products provide documentation of the quantity of standards that were met in Alex's painting, products of child-initiated learning typically represent multiple standards. Classrooms where teachers focus on developing rich, meaningful, child-initiated learning experiences are more likely to produce products that meet multiple standards than are classrooms where teacher-initiated activities are directed at meeting a particular standard. The key to successfully documenting early learning standards is to develop an awareness of what the standards are and how they might be manifested in classrooms. This technique can be used with all the different types of individual and group products described in this chapter.

Representational Pictures

Children use representational drawing as a way of recording the features they deem important about a person, place, or thing. In describing this type of drawing, Victor Lowenfeld (1987) stated that children in the preschematic stage are no longer scribbling:

Although the drawings themselves may not look particularly different to the adult, to the child this stage of development is very important. Now he is consciously making forms that have some relationship to the world around him. This conscious creation of form is the beginning of graphic communication. . . . In scribbling, the child was mainly involved in a kinesthetic activity, but now he is involved with the establishment of a relationship with what he intends to represent. This gives him a great feeling of satisfaction.

These new drawings are important not only for the child but for the parent or teacher, who now has

(Text continues on page 55)

Figure 7.1a. Five-year-old Alex was inspired by the photograph on the easel to paint the mama duck and all five ducklings.

Figure 7.1b. Alex adds the ducks' reflections and then describes elements of her painting to Bethany.

Figure 7.1c. Bethany decides to make her own painting of the ducks.

Figure 7.1d. Several younger children then made their own interpretations of the photograph of the ducks.

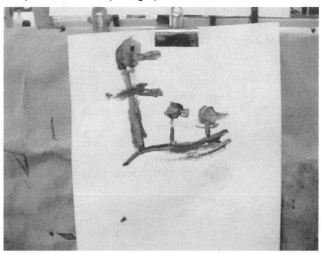

Figure 7.1e. Three-year-old Peyton's version included the log and the mama duck's foot.

Figure 7.1f. The children hold mirrors up to the glass to see if the ducks can see their own reflections.

Figure 7.2. Alex met many standards as a result of painting, discussing her painting, and exploring reflections.

Illinois Early Learning Standards		Evidence in Duck Painting Experience
Language Arts		
3.C.EC	Use drawing and writing skills to convey meaning and information.	Painted duck and ducklings on log.
4.A.EC	Listen with understanding and respond to directions and conversations.	Conversed with other children and teachers about her painting and the reflections.
4.B.EC	Communicate needs, ideas, and thoughts.	Discussed how she painted the ducklings' reflections.
5.A.EC	Seek answers to questions through active exploration.	Experimented with the concept of reflection.
5.B.EC	Relate prior knowledge to new information.	Revisited her earlier painting and reexamined the calendar picture of ducks.
5.C.EC	Communicate information with others.	Explained to other children how she painted the reflections.
Mathematics		
6.A.ECa	Use concepts that include number recognition, counting, and one-to-one correspondence.	Established one-to-one correspondence between the ducks in the calendar picture, the ducks on the log, and the ducks' reflections.
6.A.ECb	Count with understanding and recognize "how many" in sets of objects.	Counted the individual and total sets of ducks and ducklings (on log, in reflection, total).
8.A.EC	Sort and classify objects by a variety of properties.	Sorted reflections by size and direction they faced. Classified as ducks and reflections.
8.B.ECa	Recognize, duplicate, and extend simple patterns, such as sequences of sounds, shapes, and colors.	Patterns in the markings on the ducks were replicated.
8.B.ECb	Begin to order objects in series or rows.	Ordered ducks in rows.
8.D.EC	Describe qualitative change, such as measuring to see who is growing taller.	Said, "The mother duck is taller than the babies."
11.A.ECb	Uses senses to explore and observe materials and natural phenomena.	Experimented with mirrors.
12.A.ECa	Investigate and categorize living things in the environment.	Discussed why the mama and baby ducks were on the log.
18.B.EC	Understand that each of us belongs to a family and recognize that families vary.	Described the ducks as a family.
Fine Arts		
25.A.ECd	Investigate the elements of the visual arts.	Working with paint at the easel. Exploring principles of pattern and rhythm.
25.B.EC	Describe or respond to their own creative work or the creative work of others.	Discussed similarities, differences between the paintings. Discussed her strategies.
Social/Emotional Development		
31.A.ECb	Exhibit persistence and creativity in seeking solutions to problems.	Returned to painting and solved problem of reflections.
31.A.ECd	Show some initiative and independence in actions.	Was a leader in this child-initiated activity.
32.A.ECc	Show empathy and caring for others.	Willingly discussed how she painted the ducks and their reflections.
32.A.ECd	Use the classroom environment purposefully and respectfully	Used the calendar picture of ducklings as a thought jogger.
32.B.ECb	Share materials and experiences and take turns.	Shared her expertise and took turns at the easel.
32.B.ECd	Develop relationships with children and adults.	Acted as a mentor to younger children, and responded to invitation to try painting reflection offered by adults.

a tangible record of the child's thinking process. This gives the adult a concrete object he can see and discuss with the child, and it also provides clues about what is important in the child's life and how he is beginning to organize his relationship with his environment. (pp. 153–157)

An example of thinking about children's artwork as representational can be found in the following reflection from Sallee Beneke's journal. This reflection was used to document a portion of the mural that was produced by her multiage preschool class as part of their Meadow Project.

Today I set up the overhead projector in the hallway and tacked the partially finished mural to the wall. I had used the copy machine to create transparencies of the children's meadow and insect drawings, and children were invited to choose, project, and trace the drawings of their choice onto the mural. Chase, who has shown little interest in drawing, came out to see what was going on. Emma was adding her daisies to the mural. He watched as I moved the transparency around on the overhead and scooted the projector in and out to and from the wall, asking Emma where she wanted the daisies to be on the picture. He watched Emma trace her daisies and was excited by the process. Soon he said, "I want to draw on there!" so I gave him a transparency and told him to go to the project area and draw something from the meadow. Emma left and I walked over to see what he was doing. He was slowly drawing a circle. It was not a relaxed, smooth line. He was working so hard at it that some parts weren't curved. We went back to the projector, and I asked him where he wanted his drawing to be placed on the picture. He pointed to the side of Emma's flower and said, "Right here. It's an egg sac." Jacob was watching, and I asked him if he'd like to put one of his drawings on the picture. He had several. He chose a drawing that he had earlier called a beetle. It had six legs. When I asked him where he wanted to place it, he said, "On Chase's egg sac. It's a spider." I said, "But yesterday you told me it was a beetle because it had six legs." Chase agreed with Jacob that it was a spider. I said, "Well, I'll make it go on the egg sac, but I'm not sure it's a spider." Jacob transferred the beetle picture onto the mural, looked at it, and then said, "I know! Just a minute." He ran into the room and came out with several of the plastic creatures from the sand table. He found the beetle and counted its legs. He took the plastic spider with him to the mural and added a leg onto each side of the beetle. "There," he said. "Now it's really a spider." Chase watched closely throughout this process and would point out his egg sac and the spider to anyone who came by. This was a very exciting part of my day. I could almost feel the learning in the air. This was my first observation of Chase using and naming representational drawing, and both Chase and Jacob demonstrated that they were integrating knowledge about the meadow. Jacob and Chase both demonstrated a disposition to work together, and Jacob showed his ability to do research and self-correct.

As noted in the journal entry, children's knowledge and skills are reflected in several ways in this example. By displaying this journal entry and the drawings of Chase, Emma, and Jacob alongside the mural, all three windows are opened. As the reader follows Chase and Jacob through the process of combining their contributions to the mural, a view is created on the individual development and dispositions of the children. Similarly, by displaying this journal entry with the mural, a window on the value of the production of the mural as a learning experience is created. Other teachers who read this entry while examining the mural may use it to reflect on their own teaching and documentation skills.

An example of representational drawing at the primary level can be found in the Bradford first-grade Water Project. Teacher Kim Fisher describes the learning experience that led up to Kyle's drawing of a water tower (shown in Figure 7.3):

Once the idea for the field trip was discussed, we began thinking of things that we would like to find out on the field trip. After quite a bit of discussion, the children compiled a list of questions. At this point, we talked about the need for each person to be responsible for finding out some information at the field site, so that when we got back, we could put everyone's information together and learn a lot. The children volunteered to ask the questions on the list. Each wanted to find the answers to their own questions and, usually, someone else wanted to help them. We wrote names by each question so we could remember who was responsible for what.

As in the case of Kyle and his drawing of the water tower, displaying a narrative explaining the circumstances leading up to the drawing, along with the drawing, serves to heighten the viewer's awareness of the importance of the picture and draw the viewer's attention to the child's knowledge as revealed in the detail of the picture.

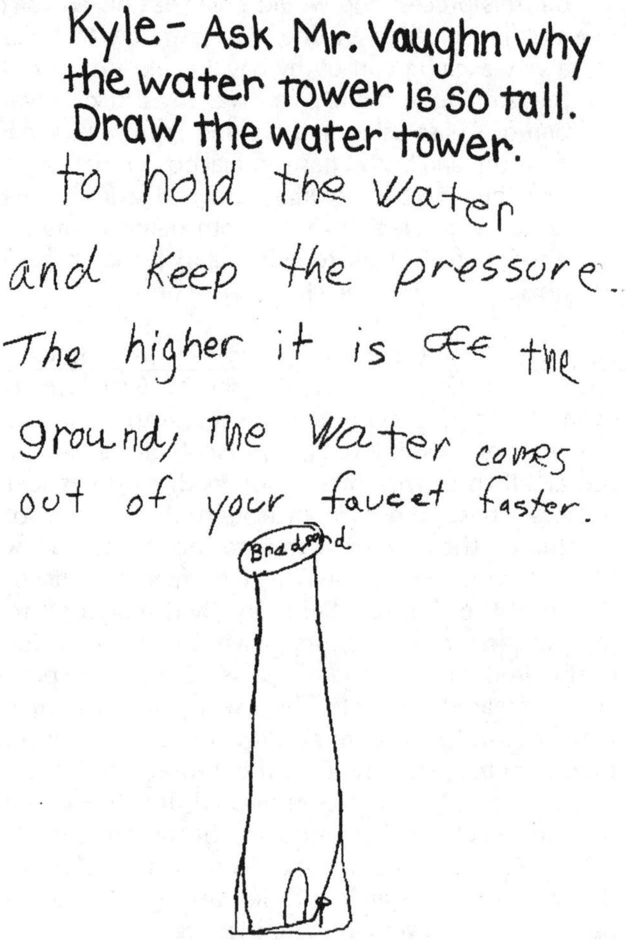

Figure 7.3. Kyle's drawing and text provide information about the water tower to share with his class.

Kyle - Ask Mr. Vaughn why the water tower is so tall. Draw the water tower.

to hold the Water and keep the pressure. The higher it is off the ground, the Water comes out of your faucet faster.

Bradford

Figure 7.4. The growth in 5-year-old Marla's knowledge of butterflies can be seen in the difference in detail between her 9/24 and 10/1 drawings.

9/24   10/1

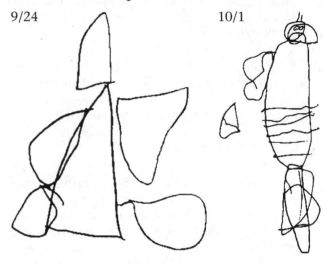

Time 1 and Time 2 Pictures

Teachers can create strong documentation of growth in knowledge and skills by displaying pictures in which the child has revisited an earlier topic or by displaying a picture to which the child has directly returned to do editing. Such a display is sometimes called a display of Time 1 and Time 2 drawings. For example, consider two drawings of a butterfly by 5-year-old Marla (see Figure 7.4). In Marla's Time 1 picture on September 24, the butterfly has only two sections to its body. It has four wings, a body, and a head. However, by October 1 (Time 2) Marla has learned so much about butterflies that she is able to represent them in much more detail. She has communicated her knowledge of the antennae, eyes, three body parts, four wings, and six legs (drawn as lines across the abdomen). By sharing or displaying these two drawings as a

set, the teacher can open a window on a child's development by providing strong documentation of Marla's growth over time.

When a narrative account is added to the display to explain the context within which the Time 1 and Time 2 drawings were produced, all three windows are opened. For example, in the Bradford first grade when Jordan created two different drawings of a fence (see Figure 7.5), her teacher recorded this account:

Another thing the children enjoyed doing was making sketches. One day, while waiting for their project to dry, Jordan brought a sketch of the swimming pool fence and Brittany brought a sketch of the water tower to show me. After admiring their sketches, I asked if possibly they would like to look at the photographs of the fence and water tower on display at the back bulletin board. I suggested they might find even more details to add to their pictures. After looking at the photographs, they asked to take the photos to their desks. After a while, they brought second sketches to me that incorporated the details from the photographs.

Jordan's Time 1 and Time 2 drawings, along with the journal of her teacher, provide a window on Jordan's development, a window on the learning experience within which this kind of growth can take place, and a window for teachers to reflect on their own classroom-management techniques and use of reference materials and drawing in the

Figure 7.5. Drawings of a swimming pool fence by Jordan. She drew the top picture from memory; the use of reference pictures helped her to show great improvement in the bottom drawing.

Figure 7.6. Bethany used a combination of representational drawing and symbols to represent the wheel and its motion.

classroom. This method of redoing a task does not always have to repeat the exact same task. An example of slightly varying a task but still providing evidence of growth is the series of vegetable pictures shown in Chapter 5 (refer to Figure 5.1).

Symbolic Pictures

Sometimes children draw to symbolize something rather than represent it. Maps and diagrams are an instance of this. Or they may use symbolic drawing to depict something that is not visible to the eye or is an abstract concept. The *American Heritage Dictionary* (2000) defines *symbolism* as "the practice of representing things by means of symbols or of attributing symbolic meanings or significance to objects, events, or relationships." *Symbols* themselves are defined as "something that represents something else by association, resemblance, or convention." For example, 4-year-old Bethany combined representational and symbolic drawing to express her ideas about a wheel as she made a field sketch in the Automotive Lab at the community college where her child-care center was located (Clearinghouse on Early Education and Parenting, 2004). When Bethany was asked by Jeff, a visitor, to explain

her drawing (see Figure 7.6), her teacher Sallee Beneke recorded their dialogue:

> *Bethany:* (points at center of drawing) That is the middle, and that (draws finger across wheel) is part of the wheel. And that's (points at the center of the drawing) a little picture that goes in the middle. And that's (draws finger across curved lines on the left side of the drawing) so they would know that it's moving. And that's (points to arrow on left side of drawing) so they would know what direction it is going. It's not going up (pointing at place on the left side of the page where she's covered over an arrow with her pencil) and I drawed it going up, so I did it that way.
> *Jeff:* What do you call it?
> *Sallee:* Which one is it that you're drawing, Bethany?
> *Bethany:* (pointing to wheel on a car that is up on a lift) That wheel. (pauses) It looks like it's turning.

In her drawing, Bethany represented what she could see when she looked at the wheel and also symbolized information about the wheel that she could not see. For example, she used the curved lines and the arrow to indicate the motion and direction she imagined the wheel might take.

The work of Ashley, a first grader in Ms. Fisher's class, demonstrates the use of symbolic drawing at the elementary level. During a field trip to visit the Bradford water tower, Ashley's assignment was to "Ask how water gets to school." Ashley symbolized her knowledge by drawing the school and the water tower, and then connecting the two locations with pipes (see Figure 7.7). However, Ashley has never seen these pipes. She only knew of their existence from the explanation given by the water tower caretaker. Like representational art, symbolic art is a product that can be used to open a window on the development of an individual child. Ashley's drawing revealed her understanding of the way water enters and leaves buildings.

Children can use symbolic drawing to represent their knowledge of relationships in space. After a field trip to the grocery store, children in Val Timmes's multiage primary class created floor plans to use in the construction of a grocery store in their classroom. They symbolized the location of shelves and aisles with the use of simple lines. Their intent was not to represent them as they really looked, but rather to symbolize them in order to show their location (see Figure 7.8). By displaying these floor plans along with a narrative describing the events that led up to the drawing, the teacher can create a window on a learning experience as well as a window on a child's development.

Children sometimes use symbolic drawing to represent things that are abstract concepts to them. Kim Fisher's first-grade class generated a list of questions that they had about water. The children were then asked to select a question and develop a hypothesis to answer it. Jordan selected the question, "How do you get waves to move in the water?" and she prepared a drawing to explain her hypothesis, which was "The wind." In her drawing, Jordan used a line to symbolize the force of the wind (see Figure 7.9).

WRITTEN LANGUAGE PRODUCTS

Traditionally, children's written work is displayed or sent home from school to inform parents of their child's progress in reading, writing, math, and science. However, in some cases, these products may be photocopied worksheets or pages from a commercially produced workbook that contain limited explanation of the significance of the child's work or the circumstances in which it was produced. These products are commonly used in American primary schools to document children's learning.

Figure 7.7. Ashley's drawing shows her understanding of the way the pipes take water from the water tower to the school.

Figure 7.8. A first grader's floor plan for the class grocery store uses lines and spaces to symbolize placement of the various departments and aisles.

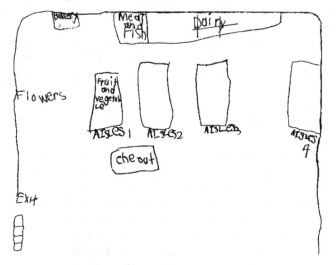

To provide richer views through the three windows, teachers may find it helpful to consider using other written language products, including child-made captions, signs, labels, graphs, charts, books, and letters.

Labels, Captions, and Signs

As children begin to develop an understanding of print, they often add labels to their pictures. For

Figure 7.9. First grader Jordan used a diagonal line to symbolize the wind pushing against the water to form waves.

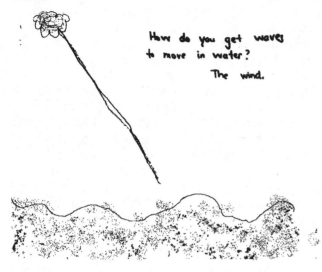

Figure 7.10. Kindergartner Dillon made a word bubble to give the reader insight into the meaning of his drawing.

Figure 7.11. "Our Bunny Warren," a sign 3-year-old Jacob created to label a rabbit warren he constructed as part of a project.

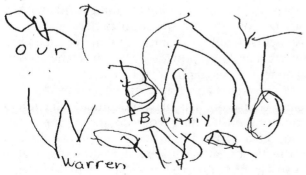

instance, Dillon, a student in Sallee Beneke's kindergarten class, sketched one of two baby pigs that visited the classroom. He indicated that this was the larger of the two pigs by writing, "Big fat pig" alongside his drawing (see Figure 7.10). Children will label objects in play environments, constructions, diagrams, and other items of interest in their environment.

Captions provide them with another way of conveying information. For example, in Kathy Steinheimer's preschool class, when examining photographs from learning experiences, the children will dictate what is happening in the photo, adding information from their own point of view.

Signs are often made by children for the purpose of identifying objects, places, or events. For example, a child might make a sign to identify a play area, such as "The Bakery." Children also make signs to communicate with others, such as posters to advertise a schoolwide canned food drive. Making signs helps children understand the function of literacy skills.

When labels, captions, and signs are collected for documentation, it is helpful for the teacher to provide additional information about the process that the child used to produce these literacy samples. For example, as part of their investigation of rabbits, the children of the Illinois Valley Community College (IVCC) Early Childhood Center constructed a rabbit warren. Jacob (3.11; i.e., 3 years, 11 months) made a sign for the front of the warren (see Figure 7.11). By looking at the sign itself, the viewer can tell that the child is learning many of the conventions of print, such as forming letters, combining letters and spaces, sizing letters evenly, and orienting letters left-to-right. It is unclear, however, how much of this knowledge and skill is Jacob's and how much teacher input and direction took place. It is also unclear whether Jacob was motivated to write this sign or whether it was a teacher-imposed task. However, when student teacher Ellen Bejster documented the process that took place as Jacob wrote the sign, windows were created on three views:

> We began a rabbit warren, made out of boxes, during choice time on Wednesday, November 13. A small group of children were working on the project, measuring and drawing where they wanted the rabbit holes to be cut. . . . On Wednesday, November 20, . . . I asked Jacob if he wanted to write the sign for the warren, and he said, "Yes, I will do it." I wanted to know how well he could print. I gave him white construction paper and a marker

and said, "Let's write 'Our Bunny Warren.'" He asked, "How do you spell that?" I began to tell him the letters and showed him where on the paper to start his first word. Jacob knew how to write an "o." I showed him how to make a "u" and so forth on another piece of paper, and he copied each letter I made, one letter at a time. We went through each word in this manner, and he separated the words on his own. Jacob also knew how to make the letter "a" in warren without my help. Chase (4.9), Lewis (3.6), and Amanda (4.4) watched as Jacob made the sign and then we taped it to the warren.

Looking back I could have let more problem solving go on by letting him decide what our sign should say. I feel it was good to work on one letter at a time rather than my writing the whole thing out and letting him copy it. In this way I found he knew there were separations between words and that he did know the letters "o" and "a." I assume he knew this because these letters are in his name.

Ms. Bejster has thus made us aware of the learning experience that motivated Jacob to produce his sign, the amount of teacher support necessary for him to produce the sign, and her reflecting process on the learning that took place. The significance of Jacob's sign and his growth in using written language was enhanced by the addition of Ms. Bejster's documentation.

Graphs and Charts

Young children often participate eagerly in the production of charts and graphs. The products of children's charting and graphing often provide a window on the learning of the group as a whole, as well as that of individual children. For instance, several large graphs were generated by the first-grade students of Rachel Bystry at Lincoln School in Princeton, Illinois. Ms. Bystry documented the learning of her class as they engaged in an investigation of apples that ultimately led to the construction of an apple store. As part of their investigation, the children generated questions about apples and used them to survey their parents and other children in their K–4 school. They asked their parents such questions as, "Do you like apple butter?" "Do you like apple pie?" They asked the other children in their K–4 building, "Which kind of apple do you like best?" The children summarized their findings in large graphs and charts, which they displayed in their classroom. For example, one group of children tallied their parents' responses to the question, "Do you like apple pie?" Then they used the number of

parents who voted to determine how many "slices" to make in a pie chart and colored wedges that corresonded to either the "yes" or "no" vote for each parent. Likewise, several children in Ms. Bystry's class were able to create their own bar graphs to show the results of a survey on apples. Here again, the teacher's documentation increases the significance of the product to the viewer. Ms. Bystry's documentation helps us understand that these first graders were able to read a graph and to understand the experience that prompted them to create their own graphs. She began the learning experience by showing the children a graph, explaining that it represented the answers to their survey question, providing some clues to the information conveyed by the graph, and then challenging them to figure out the rest of the information conveyed:

> The question was "What color apple do you like best?" Ten [of the people surveyed] said red; five, green; and five, yellow. I told them [the children] that 20 people had participated, but the number of people who chose each color was not on the graph. I then asked them if they could figure out how many people had chosen red. There were a couple guesses that were way off, then one boy took a big gasp and said, "I know." Then he told me that 10 had chosen red. I asked him to explain how he had come to that answer. He explained it to the class, and several more hands went up to tell how many had chosen red and green. I was very surprised they were able to understand and read graphs, so I told them I wanted them to try and make their own graphs. They broke up into their teams of five, and I gave each group their own original question. None of the groups had the same question as I had represented, and none had the same question as another group. Every group was able to accurately represent their data in graph form! Two made pie charts and two made bar graphs (see Figure 7.12).

In situations like this, a teacher can effectively display the graphs and charts along with the survey questions that were used to gather the data. By displaying the portion of her journal quoted above, this teacher could provide insight into the accomplishment these graphs represent.

Some charts and graphs are created by children in the course of their play and provide documentation of their learning. For example, Tommy (4.4) produced a chart while working in the writing area of the IVCC Early Childhood Center (see Figure 7.13). He had observed the teacher make several

Figure 7.12. Pie chart and bar graph by first graders show the result of two surveys.

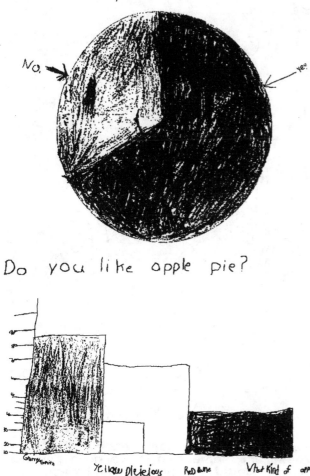

Do you like apple pie?

Figure 7.13. A chart spontaneously produced in the writing area by a 4-year-old child.

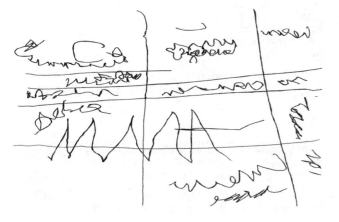

charts and graphs and then spontaneously began to produce his own imitations. Tommy's teacher displayed his chart along with documentation suggesting that the viewer notice the use of both horizontal and vertical drawing, the purposeful variation in size of print, and the use of "white space."

Letters

Children's letters are another opportunity to document children's growth in literacy and their knowledge of the conventions of print. For example, 5-year-old Kelsey asked her teacher to help her write a letter to her sister Erin. As Kelsey added thoughts to the letter, it grew until it was several pages in length. The teacher used this letter to provide a window on the development of Kelsey's emergent writing, a Core Item in Kelsey's portfolio. A part of the teacher's documentation of the significance of Kelsey's letter went as follows:

> I wrote out the words for Kelsey to copy. A comparison of the following sample of Kelsey's letter with the model I made for her reveals that she is accustomed to using capital "e" and "g" and makes her letters all the same height. She did not include any punctuation, probably because she did not take note of it. Kelsey is aware that words are grouped in a left-to-right progression on lines, but she seems unsure about how many words to include on a line; both "this" and "move" are on a line all by themselves, but the other three lines of her letter contain two to five words (see Figure 7.14).

The teacher filed Kelsey's letter in her portfolio as a writing sample. She might also have been able to create a window on the development of an individual child by displaying a page or two from Kelsey's letter, along with the sample of the teacher's own handwritten example and documentation telling the story of the letter and its significance. Such a display might be used by teachers or other adults to inform their own understanding of the development of writing in children.

Letters written by groups of children can also be used as documentation. Rachel Bystry's first-grade class formed committees to take care of the different jobs involved in creating an apple store. The committees included marketing, advertising, decorating, and construction. These committees produced many kinds of group writing. For example, the members of the advertisement committee wrote their own individual letters and then combined them to form a computer-written letter to parents

Figure 7.14. Five-year-old Kelsey dictated this letter to her teacher (top) and then copied it (bottom).

I have to tell you this news. Ted is going to move after Christmas.

I have to tell you
this
news Ted is going to
move
after Christmas

to ask for donations (see Figure 7.15). The teacher might make effective use of these products by creating a display in which the preliminary letters by several of the individual children are displayed along with the final group letter. The teacher could also display an explanation of the process the children went through to integrate their letters into one.

Books

Helping children produce their own books as a group or as individuals has become increasingly common as early childhood teachers have come to value providing children with opportunities to use emergent writing in meaningful context. These books provide not only an indication of the level of the child's developing literacy skills, but also a window into the child's knowledge, ideas, and dispositions. Including the ages of the children involved, the context or learning experience within which the book was written, and any pertinent teacher reflections can be a useful accompaniment to documentation of such products.

Figure 7.15. A rough draft by two members of the first-grade advertisement committee (top) and the full committee's final letter (bottom).

Dear Parents,
we are maiking a apple stor
These are some things we need for our
store. Could you please send them in.
Please start sending them in on Monday.
It will be open for open house. We will
let you know when we are having our
specials.
green paint
red paint
boxes all sizes
5 resrigerator boxe s'
shelves
rug to wipe feet
wood straps
recipes for
apple donuts
apple bonuts
apple bread
caramel apples
aple pie

From,
advertisement committees

As part of their investigation of rabbits, preschoolers in Sallee Beneke's multiage prekindergarten class wrote a book about the ways in which the class rabbit and turtle were the same and different. Ms. Beneke reflected on the book-writing experience:

I wanted the children to think in more detail about the rabbit, so I decided to present the possibility of a Venn diagram at circle time. I laid out a circle of yellow yarn to stand for Sweetie (the rabbit) and a circle of red yarn to stand for Franklin (the turtle). I explained that the area in the middle where they overlapped was a place for us to put those things that we knew were the same for both Franklin and Sweetie. Then, as each piece of knowledge was brought forth, I wrote it on a Post-it, along with a quick symbol for the idea, and asked the children where the Post-it should go on the diagram. As the diagram filled, it occurred to me that the same thoughts would make a great book. I said, "Hey! Does anybody want to work on making a book out of these ideas during choice time? If you do, I will help you." Mary Kate, Jacob, Marissa, Emma, and Amanda all came to work on the book at choice time. Each of them had definite ideas about which page (Post-it) they would like to make. I wrote out the words on the page, and they provided the illustrations. Later in the day some of the children moved back to the diagram and copied words from the Post-its directly onto the diagram. Mary Kate copied three of the Post-its. This was the first time I observed Lewis attempting to copy letters. I had to assist him "hand-over-hand." He was very pleased that he had written on the diagram just like Emma and Mary Kate. The next step may be to see if any of the children would like to revisit the book and write their own words this time.

In this case, the documentation explains the significance of the process that led to the final product. The teacher might use the children's book, along with a narrative somewhat like the sample above, to explain the growth and problem solving that took place during the production of the book. A copy of this book and the narrative could be included in each child's portfolio, and a display of the same material would open a window on a learning experience for adult visitors and colleagues.

VERBAL LANGUAGE PRODUCTS

Children's verbalizations about a topic can provide insight into their knowledge, skills, and disposition to learn. In the past, early childhood teachers often documented a child's ability to recite memorized materials such as nursery rhymes, fingerplays, and chants. As with written language, teachers may find it helpful to expand the types of verbal products they document, thereby providing a richer view through the three windows. Other verbal products might include hypotheses or opinions, stories, discussions, or questions.

Hypotheses

During projects, investigations, and other active learning experiences, children often formulate their own hypotheses. For example, Robert, a student in Dot Schuler's second-grade class, read his journal entry on bluffs and the comments Ms. Schuler had written on his entry to his classmates. He then challenged the other second graders to speculate about the nature of bluffs. Ms. Schuler found that she could learn a lot about her class and their ability to integrate knowledge and form opinions or ideas about events, objects, or phenomena. She recorded the following discussion about the children's speculation about the geographic concept of a bluff:

> Robert wrote in his journal about a bluff. He read it to the class, as well as my question, "What is a bluff?" Here are the responses he got.
> 1. A big old rock, and dirt and rocks and leaves on it. (Ross)
> 2. Rock. (Matt)
> 3. A half of a mountain. (Scott)
> 4. Shells pushed up against each other for thousands of years (that's what my dad told me). (Sarah)
> 5. A worm in a rock for thousands of years. (Brittani)
> 6. Lava explodes and makes hard rocks. (Troy)

In this sequence, Ms. Schuler found out not only what individual children didn't know about bluffs; she also found out what other related concepts these individual children have about rocks and rock formation and how they are integrating these concepts.

Discussions and Questions

Discussions and questions are also valuable verbal language products. During a project on insects, children in Sallee Beneke's multiage preschool group planned to build a representation of a giant cocoon with a variety of materials, including blue paper. By recording a conversation among this group as they planned the construction of the giant cocoon, Ms. Beneke found evidence of their developing knowledge of measurement in inches.

Teacher: Now, how much blue do you want?
Marla: Twenty inches, I think.

Teacher: Twenty inches. OK, let's measure. Let's start with this piece. Do you know what 20 looks like? See that's 20 right there [points to 20 on the yardstick]. OK, and there's 10. Look here, this is 20 inches from here [points to end of yardstick] to here [points to the 20]. Is that enough?

Marla: Yeah, 20 inches.

Teacher: So you only want this much, from here [points to beginning of paper] to here [points to 20 as it lines up on the paper].

Emma: Actually, from there to here [points to other end of yardstick].

Teacher: Ohhh, that would be 36 inches.

A verbal language sample like this would be a good item for the portfolio of each child involved, and it could create a window on teacher self-reflection if used to provide the catalyst for discussion in a staff meeting on teaching technique. When displayed in the same area as the end product the children were creating during the recording of the conversation, the sample could open a window on a learning experience.

Documentation of both small-group and large-group discussions revealed an important learning experience for Kim Fisher's first-grade class after a field trip. As part of their Water Project (mentioned earlier in this chapter), Mr. Vaughn, from Bradford city maintenance, gave the children a tour of the town water tower, pump room building, and reservoir.

> The following day I met with small groups of children in the hallway and discussed the information they brought back from the trip as well as what they would like to show about what they learned. We discussed art, writing, drama, construction, and mathematical possibilities. As the children came up with ideas, we wrote down the idea as well as the materials that they might need. We met again as a whole class to discuss materials that the children could try to bring in. Over the course of the discussions, there were some disagreements about information that the children collected, as well as several new questions. Several children thought Mr. Vaughn had said that there were snakes in the reservoir. Since this is drinking water, they were very concerned. Lillie is a next-door neighbor to Mr. Vaughn, so she set up an appointment with him and interviewed him in regard to the students' questions, then returned to class with the answers:

> - *How does the gas get out of the water in the reservoir?*
>   The water hits the metal plates, sprays into the air, and the gas leeches out of the water.
> - *What if someone fell in the reservoir?*
>   No one is allowed near the reservoir. That is why it is surrounded by a tall fence with barbed wire at the top. If someone did fall in, we have to try to reach in and get them out or call for help.
> - *Why do we drink the reservoir water if there are snakes in it and how does it get clean?*
>   The reservoir water is clean already because it comes from an underground well that is tested to make sure that the water is clean. There are no snakes in the reservoir water. (It was the pool water that the snakes could get into.)

Ms. Fisher has created a window on a learning experience by documenting the process through which she was able to listen to and evaluate the direction of the project work for both individuals and the class as a whole in developing their investigations. She has shown how through discussion she was able to help small groups of students decide on projects that reflected their interests, and she was able to capitalize on disagreements and questions to extend students' problem-solving skills and knowledge of the topic. She has demonstrated the value of children's verbal language products by recording and documenting them in context. She has shown how valuable it can be for teachers to listen to discussion and to use disagreement to promote problem solving and investigation.

Presentations

With assistance from parents and teachers, even 3-year-olds can give reports. For example, after reading a book about guinea pigs with her mother, 3-year-old Sara stood up and reported, "They are not pigs" (see Figure 7.16). Her friend Maddie's report was a little longer. Maddie reported:

- A mommy has 2, 3, 4, or 6 babies at one time.
- Baby guinea pigs drink milk from their mommy's bosoms just like you did.
- They have 2 bosoms just like your mommy, so two can drink at one time.

Figure 7.16. Sara read about pigs with her mother and then gave a report on them at school.

WEBS AND LISTS

A list can be a useful grouping of related information and can reveal much about the knowledge, skills, and dispositions of those who write it. When the process of preparing the list is also documented, the value of the list is enhanced. For example, as part of the project Who Measures What in the Neighborhood, the children in University Primary School made a list of the school's neighbors, what they measured, and how they measured. For example, one of the school's neighbors was the Fire Service Institute. Here is the list of what they measured and why:

Outside fire truck cab:

Hoses and nozzles: They need big circumference hoses for big fires.
Ladder: They need to get the right size ladder for the height of the building.
Water gauge: Controls how much water comes out.
Smoke detector: Measures the clean air.

Inside fire truck cab:

Gas gauge: Tells how much gas is in the tank.
Speedometer: Tells how fast the truck is going.
Odometer: How many miles it's gone.

When the students explained their lists, they shared how the measuring tools worked and why the people they saw used them. The teachers noted that when the students shared their list they felt confident that they had answered their research questions, "How do measuring tools measure?" and "Why do people measure?"

Webs are also products that can be used to document children's learning. Webs can serve as a way to group small lists. They make it possible for children to visualize the relationship between categories and subcategories. They help children visualize a point in a meaningful context. For example, several small groups from Sallee Beneke's class took walks through the meadow behind their preschool to make observations. As each group returned from their walk, the teacher read the items recorded on the web by the previous group, and they were able to compare what they had seen with the observations of the previous group and make additions to the web. One group saw a large spider with black and yellow on its back, and they added this information to the spider section of the web (see Figure 7.17).

Webs can be adapted in several ways to reflect growth in the children's knowledge. For example, when Kim Fisher led a first-grade class in their investigation of water, she found that color coding the items on the web that were added later helped her keep track of additional ideas:

> Concluding that we knew quite a bit about water, we made a classroom web of everything that the children could think of about water. The original web was written in black. As our study of water continued, the children thought of other things that could have been added to the web, and those ideas were added in orange.

A display contrasting the knowledge represented on a web done at the beginning of the project and the web done at the end of the project can make a strong statement about knowledge gained over the course of a learning experience. Many teachers use either webs that represent children's knowledge at different stages of a project or final webs as featured elements of displays about learning experiences. For example, prekindergarten teacher Megan Horwath used a final web in her documentation display on the Bus Project conducted by her mixed-age class (see Figure 7.18).

Figure 7.17. As small groups of children returned from walks in the meadow, they added their observations to this web.

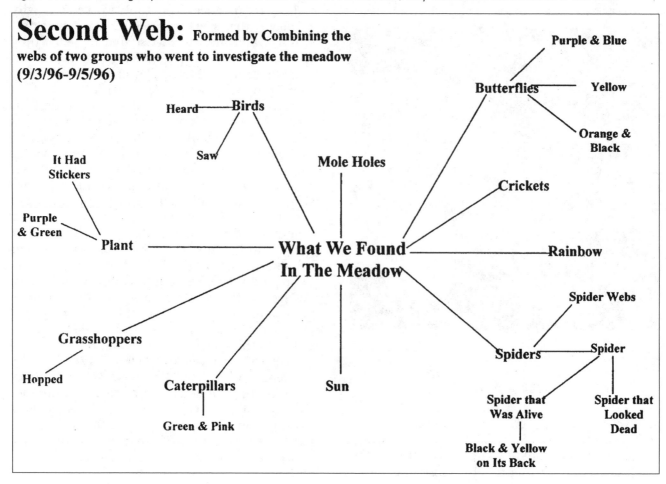

Second Web: Formed by Combining the

webs of two groups who went to investigate the meadow
(9/3/96-9/5/96)

Purple & Blue

Butterflies — Yellow

Heard — Birds

Orange & Black

Saw

Mole Holes

Crickets

It Had Stickers

Purple & Green

Plant

What We Found In The Meadow

Rainbow

Spider Webs

Grasshoppers

Spiders — Spider

Hopped

Caterpillars

Sun

Spider that Was Alive

Spider that Looked Dead

Green & Pink

Black & Yellow on Its Back

PERFORMING ARTS

Music

Although difficult to convey in writing, it is important to note that music and movement are also significant products of children's learning. This journal entry from her teacher documents that as 4-year-old Kendra became increasingly engaged in the Meadow Project, she began to sing about it:

Early this morning Kendra, who was sifting rubber insects out of the sand at the sand table, began to sing about the meadow! It was really something! I had soft jazz piano music playing on the CD player, and I was working in the writing area when I heard her start. It was really kind of a beautiful, soulful kind of warble, a little like a blues piece. It really didn't seem as if it could come out of such a small body. I turned on the tape recorder and asked Mindy to take it over close to Kendra, but the only word I could make out was "meadow." There may not have been any other words. It seemed to be purely a revelation of Kendra's feelings. What was also interesting was that soon other children around the room began to sing. It was almost like hearing birds gradually awakening and joining in, in the early morning. One thing is for certain: Kendra was definitely a leader in this. She knew how to express her feelings about the meadow in music, and the others imitated her. My interpretation of this phenomenon is that with their singing, the children revealed their positive feelings about the beauty of the meadow.

The tape recording of this musical product provides documentation of Kendra's disposition to sing, her disposition toward the meadow, and her ability to lead. Teachers can record samples of music such as the one described above and can use them to provide

Figure 7.18. A school bus web is a central element of Megan Horwath's display.

Figure 7.19. Children moved their bodies creatively as they went swimming in "silver spaghetti."

a window on the development of an individual child or a window for teacher self-reflection, if the tape is shared with colleagues. A teacher might also provide the child with an opportunity for self-reflection by playing the music for the child.

As in Kendra's song, it seems that children often make up songs to reflect their engagement with a material. The singing and the playing are part of a way of doing art that is playful and experimental. In Kendra's case it was the materials in the sand table. Similarly, Rayha, a child in Yvonne Liu-Constant's room at the Eliot-Pearson Children's School, composed and sang a song about markers one morning as she worked at the easel. In a singsong voice she sang, "Big marker, little marker," with rhythm and variation in tone as she rhythmically moved her marker in circular motions on the paper.

Movement

As with music, it is difficult to record movement, other than by anecdotal record, videotape, or frozen moments in time that are recorded in photographs. Nevertheless, particular topics lend themselves to imitation by movement, and in the course of this movement children often demonstrate knowledge about the nature of the subject they are imitating. For example, Kendra, who showed her disposition toward the meadow in her singing, showed her knowledge of butterflies through her movement. Kendra darted back and forth as she ran and would frequently lower herself to the ground to "suck the nectar," then she would

be up and running again. She would run faster when other children called out, "Look out. There's a bird!" Kendra's movements revealed her understanding that butterflies suck nectar from flowers and that birds eat butterflies. Her movements also revealed the degree to which she had mastered skills in gross motor development, such as agility, speed, balance, and coordination, and her disposition to use them for her own purposes.

Three-year-old children at the Eliot-Pearson Children's School explored a material with their whole bodies, and this led to creative movement (see Figure 7.19). Long strips of mylar were introduced in a laundry basket as "silver spaghetti" in a "giant strainer." The children tossed, spun, and plopped their bodies in the spaghetti. They took turns covering each other and their teacher with the shiny strips. They lined the pieces up and made a path to cross the room.

Performances

Children's performances document knowledge, skills, and dispositions. When children are studying a topic, they often will plan a performance, such as a play, dance recital, or puppet show, to share what they have learned. Sometimes children will be inspired to create a performance when they see others perform. The children's performance will often reveal what they found interesting and what they understood about the original performance. For example, after 9-year-old Julian demonstrated shadow puppets to a group of primary students in the Arts in Action program at Tufts University (see Figure 7.20), they enthusiastically created their own puppets. According to one of their teachers, Maggie Beneke, making the shadow puppets was challenging but very motivating because of what they'd seen. The children invented a range of puppet forms with movable parts similar to those observed in the performance (see Figure 7.21). Several children decided to perform improvised puppet shows for the group.

CONSTRUCTIONS

For the purposes of this book, *constructions* can be defined as three-dimensional representations created by children. Children can represent their learning through many kinds of constructions. Three types of constructions that will be described here are play environments, sculpture, and constructions using blocks or building toys.

Play Environments

Play environments are a wonderful source of evidence of children's learning. Here again, a great deal can be learned by observing the problem solving and social interaction that takes place in the process of construction, by examining the end product, and by watching the children as they play in the construction. In creating their own play environments, children replicate what they are aware of and what they consider to be important. The detail that they add to their constructions often provides evidence of the depth of their understanding.

For example, small mixed-age groups composed of prekindergarten, kindergarten, and first-grade children worked together on the construction of a hospital at the Valeska Hinton Center. The groups had made a field trip to the hospital, and each group was in charge of bringing back field sketches of a particular department. In the following days, the groups used their field sketches to construct the various departments they had visited. An elevator, waiting room, gift shop, patient room, X-ray department, and obstetrics department were all constructed and then joined together to turn the wide school hallway into a large "hospital." The details that these children included in their constructions were documentation of the knowledge they had gained. For example, in Figure 7.22 we see the "patient room," which includes an adjustable bed, tray, remote control, IV bag, get-well card, and water pitcher, as well as the "X-ray department" in action. Note the X-ray machine in the background,

which was constructed by one team of children. They have shown their knowledge in the dials, tubes, "electrical connection," and sign that says "X-ray machine."

The construction of a play environment can pose many problems for children. They must work in three dimensions and must decide which materials will work best for them as they move from the planning stage through final construction. In referring to the physical properties of different media as they relate to a child's decision making, George Forman (1994) explains that "a transformation in the medium that a child can easily produce is an affordance. Each affordance provides the child with a method to express an idea by transforming the medium" (p. 42). As young children develop a construction, they must deal with the affordances of the materials they have initially selected to use in communicating their ideas. Children often want the construction not only to *look* real but also to *function* like the real thing. And high-level problem solving takes place as they attempt to make their ideas work. For example, children in Sallee Beneke's kindergarten class wanted to make a grain bin. As the group discussed their vision (see Figure 7.23), one boy suggested that they should develop an auger that would carry corn to the top of the bin. This led to development of several prototypes and ultimately to the invention of a functioning conveyor belt that made use of a handle and crank.

As the Lincoln School first graders constructed their apple store, they had to solve many problems, including the "problem of the shelves." Teacher Rachel Bystry observed and described the problem-solving process and the learning that ultimately took place as follows:

When we started to build our apple store, several boys got excited about building shelves out of cardboard that had been brought in by parents. They cut several long pieces, painted them green, and started taping them together. The first shelf they built had two sides and a top, but it wouldn't stay up. The boys were frustrated, but they knew that we were having an engineer come and visit, and they believed he could help. The engineer was brought in to talk to the children about planning before building. They asked him how to build shelves out of cardboard, and he really didn't have a specific answer, but he told the children that triangles were very strong structures. That afternoon the boys got back together, took their shelves apart, and started over. They rebuilt the shelves using triangles to support the top (see Figure 7.24). They also stacked the shelves two high. They

Figure 7.20. Nine-year-old Julian put on a performance with shadow puppets that inspired the children in the Arts in Action program to create their own puppets and performances.

Figure 7.21. Primary-aged children made shadow puppets to put on their performances.

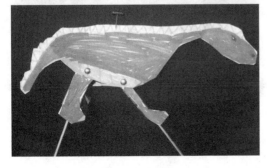

Figure 7.22. Children created this patient room and the radiology department as part of the Hospital Project.

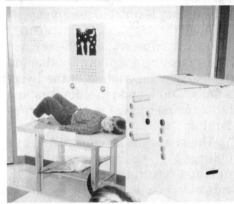

Figure 7.23. Children brainstormed a list of work that needed to be done on the grain bin. The addition of an auger was suggested. This led to problem solving and experimentation.

Figure 7.24. These first graders tackled the problem of building shelves out of cardboard for their apple store.

looked great, and the boys were excited about their structure. The next day they started placing some of the apple merchandise on the shelves, and they kept collapsing. I then noticed the boys taking the shelves apart and asked why. Zack, one of the builders, said, "The triangles worked better, but you can't build shelves out of cardboard. You need wood or metal or something stronger."

This group of boys ultimately built their shelves out of wood, but in the process of experimentation they learned a lot about the affordances of cardboard and the physical ability of various shapes to support weight. They learned to use an expert as a resource, and they displayed great persistence in the course of their experimentation. The teacher documented this by creating a wall display that included photographs and a description of the hypothesizing, experimentation, and reflection that took place. This display could be used to open all three windows on learning.

The grocery store constructed by Val Timmes's multiage K–1 class grew out of an investigation of fruits and vegetables. Their construction was elaborate and included many reproductions of food items as well as furnishings. As the children played in the grocery store, they revealed their knowledge of the function and roles of store employees, the use of the store equipment, and the variety and categories of food and other products. For example, children stocked shelves, ran groceries over a "scanner," and sacked groceries. As the children paid for their groceries and received change, they demonstrated their knowledge of currency and numeracy (see Figure 7.25).

Sculpture

Sculpture is defined as the "art or practice of shaping three-dimensional figures or forms" (*American Heritage Dictionary*, 2000). Children construct sculptures with a variety of materials, such as clay, paper, wire, wood, and cardboard. But whatever materials the child chooses to use, the child's experience or inexperience with the medium must be taken into account and included in the use of the child's sculpture as documentation of learning. For example, 5-year-old Marla, in Sallee Beneke's mixed-age prekindergarten class, was able to include several details in her drawing of a butterfly (refer to Figure 7.4). But in Marla's first experience with clay, when she chose to create a butterfly, the result was extremely simple, a body and two wings. Given additional experiences with clay, Marla was able to

create a clay butterfly with head, thorax, abdomen, four wings, six legs, antennae, and eyes. As Marla revisited the topic in this medium, her knowledge began to emerge.

Small three-dimensional sculptures from materials other than clay might include representations made from paper, cardboard, wire, or any combination of the three. Pictured in Figure 7.26 is a lobster constructed from paper, cardboard, masking tape, a toilet paper roll, and pipe cleaners. It was created by two children in Val Timmes's class for their grocery store. In the play environment, the lobster was kept inside a glass aquarium. The children had observed and sketched the lobsters in the tank on their field trip to the grocery store. The sculpture reveals the children's knowledge of lobster anatomy. For example, they have included antennae but not eye stalks.

Combining other media with clay or claylike materials can provide children with more opportunity to express themselves. For example, as part of a project on farms, children in Karla Konieczki's

Figure 7.25. Children in a multiage K–1 classroom play in the classroom grocery store they have constructed.

Figure 7.26. A small team of children constructed lobsters for a classroom grocery store project.

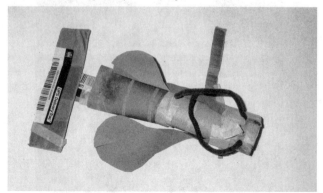

prekindergarten class in LaSalle, Illinois, used a combination of paper and clay figures to create a three-dimensional farm scene (see Figure 7.27). In this scene, two-dimensional farmers rode tractors, while nearby, tiny yellow beaks poked out of white three-dimensional eggs.

Children at the University Primary School in Champaign, Illinois, conducted an in-depth project on machines. Small groups of children made in-depth ministudies on machines that were of interest to them, and many elaborate constructions resulted. For example, a group of children invented a two-sided Dell computer (see Figure 7.28).

Large sculptures are sometimes created by one or more children. For example, one of the culminating activities in the Meadow Project at the IVCC Early Childhood Center was the construction of what the children called "The Giant Butterfly." The length of the body was greater than 6 feet, while the wing span was greater than 8 feet. In the process of creating this butterfly, the children used many skills and solved many problems. This anecdote from Sallee Beneke's journal provides an example:

> The chicken wire form for the head was shaped separately from the larger piece, which was to become the abdomen and thorax. When the time came to join the head to the body, one of the three children working on the sculpture that day wanted to center the head on the top of the body. Jacob (3.11) insisted that the head belonged on the end of the body by the thorax, and finally made his point when he went to the table and got a book with a picture of a butterfly to support his position.

From her observation of the children as they solved this problem, the teacher could tell that Jacob understood the relation of the body parts of the butterfly and that he was able to use reference materials. His disposition to convince the other child with factual information rather than force was also documented in this example. The teacher could use this example to open all three windows.

Blocks and Building Toys

Observation of block play and block structure provides early childhood teachers with an understanding of children's knowledge of math and physics concepts. Block structures can also represent children's knowledge of a topic. Children often bring other materials into the sculpture to add interest or detail to their representation. For example, three

boys in Pam Scranton's multiage preprimary class at the Valeska Hinton Center became interested in constructing a model of a water treatment plant. Their class had looked at reference materials, interviewed an expert, and done preliminary sketches. The boys worked on their construction over a period of days and incorporated found objects, such as egg carton cups, milk jug lids, and paper towel tubes, to represent parts of their model. The completed construction included a parking lot, control panel, and treatment pools (see Figure 7.29). The boys labeled many of the parts of their construction, so the end product provided evidence not only of the knowledge they had gained about water treatment but also of their writing skills.

Figure 7.27. Children used both paper and clay to create a three-dimensional farm scene.

Figure 7.28. Primary-aged children used their imaginations to invent a two-sided Dell computer.

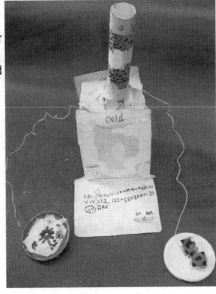

As part of the Machine Project, two boys from the University Primary School at the University of Illinois investigated cranes. After making a field trip to see a real crane in action, they invented and constructed a "Triple Crane" that was designed to lift three things at one time (see Figures 7.30 and 7.31).

Children show us in many ways that they are learning. They produce verbal and written language, pictures, webs, music, and a variety of constructions in which they represent their ideas, thoughts, and feelings. Teachers can take advan-

tage of this wide array of products to assess the development of their knowledge, skills, abilities, and dispositions. In looking at the products of children's learning, it is important that we examine and document not only the end product but also the problem solving and learning that took place in the process of production. Thoughtful documentation of the products of children's learning can open a window on a child's development, a window on a learning experience, and a window on teacher self-reflection.

Figure 7.29. A small group of 3- and 4-year-old boys constructed this water treatment plant of blocks, revealing their understanding of the water treatment process.

Figure 7.30. This crane, created with building toys, documents not only children's understanding of how cranes work but also problem solving and creative thinking.

Figure 7.31. The children also wrote about their crane, which can be used for documenting literacy development.

This is a tripeel crane. it holds 2 itam on ech string!! martin and matthew 1/25/06

it has one swich that hold it in Place!

CHAPTER 8

Self-Reflections of Children: Thinking About Thinking

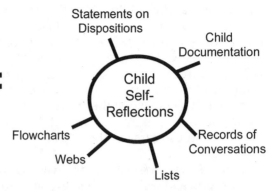

Child self-reflections are statements children make that indicate their awareness of their own knowledge or feelings. These statements can provide a record of the child's emotional and/or intellectual involvement in a project. A record of children's words can be handwritten, audiotaped, or videotaped, and can serve a variety of purposes. The form in which the self-reflection is presented is best determined in relation to the window the teacher hopes to open by using it as documentation.

REFLECTING ON THEIR OWN WORDS

Just as it is sometimes helpful to teachers to reflect on their own teaching by reading their journal entries, watching themselves on videotape, or listening to a tape recording of their interactions with children, it is sometimes helpful to children to reflect on their own words. Children are interested in examining their own ideas as they have previously expressed them. An astute teacher will notice and record statements children make that might provoke new or continued interest in a learning experience if reintroduced at a later time. For example, as the children in Sallee Beneke's prekindergarten class met to plan a construction that would show what they were learning about butterflies, she was able to refer back to an earlier statement by Marissa:

> *Teacher:* Marissa, you told me Monday that you thought we should make a "giant cocoon." Do you still think that's a good idea?
> *Marissa:* Oh yes!
> *Teacher:* Well, would you like to tell everybody else what you were thinking on this?
> *Marissa:* Oh, yes. Well, I was thinking that we could build a really, really big cocoon.
> *Teacher:* What do the rest of you think?
> [Many statements of agreement and further contributions of ideas followed. A list of materials necessary to construct the cocoon was generated by the children.]

By referring back to Marissa's earlier statement, the teacher showed respect for the thinking of children and maintained a sense among the children that they were in control of their own learning. Marissa was given the choice of agreeing with or rejecting her earlier suggestion (to build a giant cocoon). Because she had this choice, she had the opportunity to reflect on, or think critically about, her own idea. The other children were free to agree or disagree with Marissa's idea, which provided them, too, with an additional opportunity to engage in influencing the course of the learning experience.

Teachers who are selective in collecting children's own statements or words and presenting them to the children can guide the course of the learning experience without predetermining it. They can do this by listening with a critical ear to the children's words and by recording and presenting in verbal form those statements that, in their judgment, hold the most potential to maintain child interest in the project and present the most possibilities for extending or deepening the richness of the learning experience. For this purpose teachers will often collect and store short statements or even whole conversations that seem to have potential, even though they may not know exactly how they will use them in the future.

STATEMENTS ABOUT DISPOSITIONS

As discussed in Chapter 1, children's words often reveal their dispositions toward themselves or others. Statements made by a child that reveal his or her "habits of mind and action" (Katz & Chard, 2000, p. 26) often begin with the word "I." Examples would be statements such as "I really like my school," "I was there first," or "I will get you a Kleenex."

A teacher who is interested in collecting self-reflections of dispositions can make a conscious effort to develop the habit of listening for "I"-statements. A collection of these kinds of statements can provide a record of a child's developing character.

For example, as the children in Sallee Beneke's class prepared to paint a giant papier-mâché butterfly that they had constructed, she asked for volunteers to create "plans" for the color scheme of the butterfly. The three volunteers were given simple paper silhouettes of a butterfly shape and asked to bring them to the teacher when they were decorated. The volunteers were free to use any of the materials available in the art area in their "plan."

> Jacob (3.11) came out into the hall with his butterfly plan and said, "I'm going to paint part of this butterfly pink." I said, "But, Jacob, there's no pink on your plan." Jacob said, "OK, I'll fix it." He went back to the art table and returned in a little bit with a piece of pink tissue paper glued onto the middle of his plan. He said, "Now I am ready to paint." He was surprised when I said, "Jacob, we don't have any pink paint." Then he suggested that we make some. The children got so interested in the pink paint that soon we had to bring a gallon of white paint into the project area so that the children could mix white with each of the colors. Jacob surveyed the excitement and declared, "I think I must be a genius to think of this!"

This teacher was able to add this statement to Jacob's portfolio to provide a window on a growing disposition to have confidence in his own intelligence and ability to solve problems. She also created a window on a learning experience by creating a display near the completed giant butterfly featuring Jacob's statement and pictures of the children mixing the paint. The display provided the viewer with insight into the sense of control over their own work that the children felt and so helped to show the source of the sustained persistence and dedication that could lead 3- and 4-year-old children to create and complete such a complex and beautiful construction.

In making this display, the teacher has provided a window on the relationship of dispositions to a learning experience not just for those outside the learning experience to see in, but also for the use of those directly involved to reflect on their own experience. Children are often the most frequent viewers of this type of documentation. They use the display to revisit and reflect on moments or experiences that have meaning for them. The documented statements allow children to ask adults to join them in discussing these moments, which sometimes leads to a discussion between adult and child, adult and children, or child and child as to which dispositions helped the children in their work. A variation on such a display might be to copy and reduce it and include it in a scrapbook format.

Very young children or children with limited expressive language may not be able to verbally express their dispositions, but may express their dispositions through actions and nonverbal expressions. For example, 3-year-old Trey, who was introduced in Chapter 2, understands receptive language and speaks in one- or two-word phrases although he has a hearing loss in his left ear. Trey is also challenged in motor activities because of limited motor control over his left side. He wears leg braces to help his leg muscle development and coordination. His teachers describe him as a happy, social child who interacts freely with his peers at the Eliot-Pearson Children's School. They shared the following example of his disposition to persist in learning a task that is difficult for him.

> Riding the tricycle at outside time has been a priority for Trey for most of the year. Although it wasn't necessarily a goal of his teachers or parents, Trey was determined to ride the tricycle. In the beginning, it was motivated by the social aspect of riding. Trey wanted to be with the rest of the children zooming around on various tricycles and scooters. He would get a teacher to help him get the tricycle out of the shed and sit on the tricycle attempting to simulate the pedaling movement.
>
> Shortly after winter break, a new classroom volunteer took a special interest in Trey's goal. She worked with him outside and helped him figure out how to move the pedals. However, he still needed her help to get started. Now Trey was also motivated by the challenge of pedaling because he saw how the pedals worked. After about 2 months of work, the volunteer had to leave her placement in the classroom. This left Trey without his regular tricycle support. On the 1st day without the volunteer, Trey went and got the tricycle himself, sat down, and started pedaling. This is a picture of Trey riding on his own for the first time (see Figure 8.1).
>
> When Trey saw the picture of himself accomplishing his goal of pedaling on the tricycle, he expressed a clear sense of pride. He looked at the picture, took a big breath, raised his shoulders, and put his hand on his chest. His face was beaming. He touched the picture and said, "Trey. Bike," and looked back at me with a smile.

Trey's response to the photograph of himself pedaling a trike reveals his pride in his accomplishment and his disposition to use body language to help communicate his dispositions. This example demonstrates how helpful it can be to document positive dispositions for very young children or children with limited verbal ability.

Figure 8.1. Trey was proud and happy that he could ride his tricycle independently.

RECORDS OF CONVERSATION

When children are interested in a learning experience, vocabulary and concepts from the experience spontaneously begin to enter their conversations. For example, 6-year-old Kylie's statements to a visitor about preparations for the class apple store revealed her involvement with the learning experience:

"Well, our apple store is fun, but it's a lot of work," she said, sighing. "Of course the boys have been doing the heavy work because they *think* they are stronger than the girls." She rolled her eyes. "The girls have been making lists about what kind of things we want to sell in our store. I like green apples," she said.

These comments, as described by the visitor, reflect both the child's interest and intellectual involvement with the apple store project. A teacher can draw a great deal from a statement like this and can document the fact that the child understands the nature of the work that will need to be done and is actively engaged in planning and decision making in the work. The statement demonstrates that the child feels a sense of ownership in and responsibility for the project. Social interactions are taking place in the course of the project, and the child sees herself as part of a team effort. Although she questions the boys' claim to strength, an assumption that work should naturally be divided along gender lines is also implied in her statement. The documentation of this statement has opened a window for the teacher to see that children in her classroom are dividing tasks according to gender stereotypes of strengths and abilities. Research has indicated

that the teacher needs to challenge such bias with an active/activist approach (Derman-Sparks, 1989). Documentation of children's self-reflections not only enable the teacher to see bias problems, but also can enable the teacher to monitor changes in understanding and practice.

Kylie's self-reflection also provides evidence that she feels challenged by the project but that the challenge is within her zone of proximal development and that she is gaining content knowledge. In other words, the teacher can provide a window on a child's development that documents not only the child's knowledge but also her ability to integrate it with other skills and apply it in a setting that requires problem solving (construction of the apple store).

A perceptive teacher may lead a child to reveal the extent of his or her knowledge through self-reflection. Lee Makovichuk, a teacher in Edmonton, Canada, recorded such a conversation with 5-year-old Richard as he constructed a bird feeder:

At the carpentry area Mike and Alysson join in, eager to help with the construction of the bird feeder. Verbal exchanges happen as the children look at and choose the appropriate materials. I become an observer, as tools are organized, materials decided on, and the work begins.

Richard pauses. "I think I'm the boss."

"Oh, how's that?" I ask.

Richard responds, "Well, I have the plans and I know what needs to be done, so I think I could be the boss."

"So you're the foreman," I reply.

Richard pauses. "No, I'm the Threeman."

As I process this information, Richard notices Alysson has left the work site. "No, I'm the Twoman," he says.

"Okay, Twoman, what do I do?" I ask.

Richard directs me to hold a piece of wood on a piece of linoleum as he traces it. Mike suggests he is to cut the linoleum and produces scissors. Together Richard and Mike struggle with the scissors and linoleum, then decide to use a saw. They place the linoleum in the vise; Mike holds the linoleum while Richard saws it. Together we continue to work, nailing the linoleum onto the piece of wood. Once this task is complete, Mike leaves in the direction of the snack table.

I ask, "Twoman, what's the next step on your plan?"

Richard replies, "I'm not the Twoman anymore, I'm the Oneman."

Confused, I ask, "What makes you the Oneman?"

Richard explains, "Well you see . . . I only have one person now."

"I see two—you and me," I respond.

"Well, I can't work for myself so I count only you," Richard replies.

Understanding is confirmed. I understand Oneman Richard. Smiling, we continue our work.

I choose to support Richard's thinking in regard to quantifying objects (people) and subtraction of real objects. Later, in a subtle approach, perhaps with a story or visitor, we will clarify job titles. . . . I really feel the understanding of quantifying real objects was the task at hand; had I corrected his misunderstanding, I would have missed the opportunity to witness the level of his understanding of quantification.

Self-reflections of engagement with a learning experience can be documented for the child's portfolio or can be effectively displayed by mounting them along with photographs of the child participating in the work. Viewing such documentation may stimulate the child to think reflectively about her participation in the learning experience and may provoke the child to become more deeply involved.

Self-reflections are often spontaneous and occur during playful exchanges with classmates. Anne Haas Dyson (1990) has explained that it is important for us to recognize that play is a prime time for children to develop symbolic thinking:

> As they do in storytelling, in their play children transform emotionally significant experiences in order to express and interpret them, to give outer form to their inner worlds. . . . Thus, play is a "canvas" in which young children can symbolize ideas and feelings through gestures and speech. As children grow as symbolic players and social beings, they paint the canvas of play collaboratively with their friends.
>
> Drawing combined with talk can quite literally become a canvas for children's shared dramas. . . . Researchers who study children's graphic symbolism stress the interaction between children and their own products. Children examine their marks, see further possibilities in them, and then attempt to express new ideas (Golomb, 1988). In centers and classrooms, though, the dialogue between children and their papers can include other people, as children's skill as collaborative storytellers and players infuses their drawing. (p. 54)

For example, Maggie Beneke described the conversation of a group of boys who were each using paint to create imaginary monsters.

Alex began this activity unsure about what he would make. As he and the other boys talked, a dramatic creature emerged in response to their reflections on his work. He began working on an unidentified creature painting, and several children discussed the work-in-process:

"Mine is a good guy, not a bad guy. Mine is trying to save the world and yours is trying to take over the world."—Benjamin (age 6)

After this comment, Alex began to make his lines drippier.

"Ew . . . he's drooling. He'll spit on you!"
—Stefano (age 6)

"He looks more evil with the eyebrows."
—Zacharia (age 7), as Alex added in bright red eyebrows.

When we met at the end of class to look at everyone's work, Alex explained, "It's the wall monster!"

It was exciting to see Alex's original imaginary idea of a "building monster" carry over into his 2-D painting and change into a "wall monster" based on the conversation (see Figure 8.2).

GROWTH IN KNOWLEDGE AND SKILLS

Sometimes when children explain their drawings, we see that they have really created a flowchart that shows the sequence of a series of events. Child self-reflections on these drawings reveal an understanding of the sequence. For example, while Sallee Beneke's prekindergarten class waited for their mal-

Figure 8.2.
Alex's decision to name his painting "The Wall Monster" reflected the verbal engagement he had with his peers while playing.

lard ducklings to hatch, they studied and discussed what was happening inside the eggs. Children frequently sat by the incubator and looked at nonfiction books that showed how a baby bird grows inside the egg. Bethany summarized what she knew about the process in a drawing (see Figure 8.3):

> First the baby is inside (pointing at the figure on the far right). Then the baby is starting to hatch (pointing at the second figure from the right). Then the head hatched (pointing at the second egg from the left.) Then the whole baby's out (pointing at the figure on the far left.)

Bethany's comments and drawing revealed that, even though she could not physically see inside the egg, she understood that the duckling was developing inside the egg and would have to peck its way out. The right-to-left progression of the sequence indicated that she did not yet have a left-to-right orientation.

The statements children make as they present their thoughts for addition to a group or individual list or web also often provide the teacher with a rich sampling of self-reflections. These are self-reflections because they require children to reflect on their own knowledge of a topic, recognize that it is knowledge that they have gained, and then express it so that it may become part of a web or a list. For example, at both the beginning and the end of a project, the teacher often records the children's level of knowledge of the topic under investigation. When compared, the differences in content revealed in the statements recorded on the two webs will reflect growth in the children's knowledge over the course of the project.

While individual statements could certainly be used to create a window on the development of each of the individual children involved, a collection of a set of statements made as a group generates a web or list can be very useful in creating a window on a learning experience. Effective teachers often display a selection of such statements along with the web or list that was the primary product of the children's work. This type of display documents the kinds of thought processes and problem solving that resulted in the product.

Many audiences benefit from a view through this window and may focus on different aspects of it, depending on their point of view. While visitors to the classroom might see the value in the approach to teaching that the teacher is using, a parent might see the contribution of his or her child to the learning experience. For example, Bonnie Grusk, a parent of twin girls, Mary and Emma, in the IVCC early childhood program, wrote the following note after reading the documentation of the Meadow Project. The documentation featured Emma's self-reflections, which were recorded as she worked as part of a small team.

> The feelings I have had about the progress the girls have made in getting along and working together were reinforced when I read about the children working in teams. They are experiencing what it means to be part of a community; and what better time to learn about getting along and about the importance of cooperation than at the age of 3 and 4. Mary and Emma have always been a team of sorts; when you're a twin I believe that just comes with the territory. It is a different type of team now; they listen to each other and really take into consideration what the other has said and/or may be feeling.

By documenting the child's self-reflection, the teacher was able to provide the parent with a window on a child's development that the teacher had observed in the classroom. In turn, this provided an impetus for the parent to think about the child at home and to share her observations with the teacher.

Teachers viewing the same display might read the documentation and use it to think about how this child's self-reflection reveals how the experience encouraged growth in working together. This would be especially meaningful if the teacher would add the parent's thoughts to the display. When children read self-reflections of other children, they are encouraged to reflect on their part in the learning experience. When two or more children view this type of display, they can discuss and critique the work of the group and gain insight that will help them to be more productive in the future.

Figure 8.3. Bethany created a flowchart that shows the development of a baby bird from egg to chick. The chart reads from right to left.

Then the whole baby's out.   Then the head hatched.   Then the baby is starting to hatch.   First the baby is inside.

When the viewers of such documentation are nonreaders or early readers, it is particularly helpful to display photographs taken of the children as they shared their ideas. Photographs take the children back to the moment of the learning experience and put print displays, such as lists and webs, into context. Once the list or web has been read to the children, along with the self-reflections that are displayed, they will likely remember the experience, and spontaneous discussing and critiquing of the work will take place, as it would with older children who read.

An outcome of this type of documentation, then, may be that children become interested in revisiting the experience that is documented and improving on their earlier work. By documenting their statements, the teacher can provoke the interest of the children in expanding on and extending earlier work.

LISTENING TO DOCUMENT STANDARDS

Children's self-reflections often reveal their mastery of standards. Teachers can note and document this mastery, if they are aware of the standards and keep them in mind as they interact with children. For example, 4-year-old Kendra made a series of drawings that reflected her interest in thistles. By looking at her drawings, her teacher could see some of the learning that had taken place. However, her reflections on her work revealed understanding that would not otherwise have been noted by her teacher, Sallee Beneke.

> Our class took a field trip to a nearby meadow to observe the insects in their natural habitat. When we arrived, I spread out the blanket, gave the children their clipboards and pencils and watched as they observed the creatures in the meadow. Several varieties of large colorful butterflies were attracted to the large purple thistles. I asked the children what they would like to draw. To my surprise, several of them wanted to draw thistles. I was particularly impressed with the accuracy of Kendra's drawing (see Figure 8.4).
>
> The next day, I put out fresh thistles with pencils and drawing paper. After a couple of days had passed, I decided it might extend the children's interest in this in-depth study if color was added to the table. I added a set of oil pastels, a new medium for the children. They mainly rubbed the pastel back and forth to see how it worked (see Figure 8.5).
>
> After a few days, however, they began to use the colors in a more purposeful way. I was delighted when I saw that Kendra had made a beautiful drawing of a thistle with colored flowers, leaves

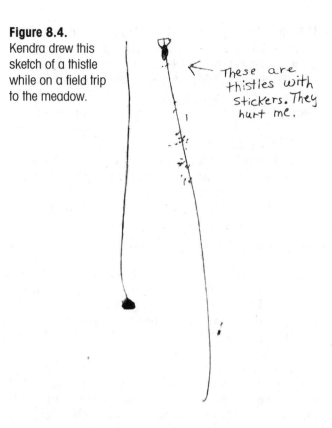

Figure 8.4. Kendra drew this sketch of a thistle while on a field trip to the meadow.

These are thistles with stickers. They hurt me.

Figure 8.5. Kendra experimented with oil pastels by making lines and rubbing them on the paper.

and grass. I was about to ask her if I could save that picture for her portfolio, when she placed her hand on the paper and traced around it. I was internally bemoaning the fact that she had ruined her beautiful drawing when I noticed that she said, "Look, I got lots of bleedings from the stickers." I saw that she had drawn tiny red spots on her fingers and droplets of blood sprinkling down from one side of the thistle (see Figure 8.6). I realized that she had used the new medium not only to show how the plant looked but also to express how it felt to touch it! I realized that it's important to talk with children about their work and really listen to what they say.

If her teacher had not listened to and jotted down Kendra's words and looked closely at her work, she might not have noticed the learning that was evidenced in this interaction. Figure 8.7 shows that 14 early learning standards were met in this experience. Seven of these were documented in response to Kendra's self-reflection on her work. Kendra's teacher was struck with the sequence of development in the three drawings and with the power of

Figure 8.6. After a few days of experience, Kendra could use the oil pastels to express her thoughts and feelings. Notice the dots on her fingers and the drips of blood trickling off the side of the thistle.

"Look, I got lots of bleedings from the stickers."

Kendra's self-reflection to add insight into the learning represented in the drawings, so she displayed the series of drawings and comments on the wall in the art area. Kendra brought her mother to see them and explained them. In essence, she was reflecting on her own self-reflection! These drawings were later used as samples in Kendra's portfolio.

Another example of a conversation which provided evidence of standards is the conversation between 4-year-old Gavin and his teacher when Gavin pretended a calculator was a scale and used it to weigh eggs. He would identify a number on the keypad and then write the number to record the weight of the egg. This enabled the teacher to document both accurate concepts and misconceptions.

> *Gavin:* Let's see how much this egg is.
> *Teacher:* Oh, let's weigh them.
> *Gavin:* Yeah, it's a velociraptor egg.
> *Teacher:* Okay, what does it say? How much does it weigh?
> *Gavin:* It's a 1.
> *Teacher:* How will we remember how much each weighed?
> *Gavin:* I don't know.
> *Teacher:* Should we write it down?
> *Gavin:* Yes, this one is 2. This one is 3.
> *Teacher:* What will happen?
> *Gavin:* It will crack open and the velociraptor will get out. Do you know what meat eater is?
> *Teacher:* Yes.
> *Gavin:* It means they are very mean.
> *Teacher:* Did you measure all them?
> *Gavin:* Well, yeah, but these are cracked.
> *Teacher:* Shouldn't we measure them, too?
> *Gavin:* Yeah, cracked ones are all a 5. This one is little. It's a 6. Where's the 6? Is this a 6 or 8?
> *Teacher:* You're right. It's a 6.
> *Gavin:* Okay. We'll keep it to show the others.

Gavin's teacher used what she learned from this conversation as documentation for a portfolio sample (see Figure 8.8) that she generated on the Early Childhood Standards Project website (Illinois Resource Center, 2005) described in Chapter 5. A record of the conversation and the paper he used to record his numbers were attached (see Figures 8.8 and 8.9).

Four early learning standards were met in the course of Gavin's play, but without his words, the teacher might not have recognized the knowledge and skills that he was using. By identifying the numbers on the keypad, Gavin showed a beginning understanding of number and quantity. As he pretended to weigh the eggs, Gavin revealed

Figure 8.7. Seven of the 14 early learning standards that were met during this experience would not have been documented without Kendra's self-reflection.

Illinois Early Learning Standards		Evidence in Thistle Experience
Language Arts		
1.B.ECa	Predict what will happen next using pictures and content for guides.	Kendra made a picture predicting what would happen if a hand touched the thistle.
3.A.EC	Dictate stories and experiences.	Kendra told the story of what was happening to her hand.
3.C.EC	Use drawing and writing skills to convey meaning and information.	Kendra conveyed the meaning of her interaction with the thistles using art media.
4.A.EC	Listen with understanding and respond to directions and conversations.	Kendra discussed the thistles and her drawings.
4.B.EC	Communicate needs, ideas, and thoughts.	Kendra explained the ideas in her picture.
5.A.EC	Seek answers to questions through active exploration.	When in the meadow, Kendra touched many of the plants that she wanted to draw.
5.C.EC	Communicate information with others.	Kendra used more than one media to communicate her ideas with others.
Mathematics		
6.A.ECa	Use concepts that include number recognition, counting, and one-to-one correspondence.	Kendra drew a hand with the correct number of fingers and added a corresponding number of "bleedings."
Science		
11.A.ECa	Uses senses to explore and observe materials and natural phenomena.	Kendra used the senses of touch and sight to examine and study the thistles.
11.A.ECb	Collect, describe, and record information.	The third drawing summarized what she had learned about thistles.
13.A.EC	Begin to understand basic safety practices.	Kendra learned why touching some plants, such as thistles, should be avoided.
Physical Development		
19.B.EC	Coordinate movements to perform complex tasks.	Kendra demonstrated fine motor control of the pencil and the oil pastels.
Fine Arts		
25.A.ECd	Investigate the elements of the visual arts.	Kendra explored using a new media, oil pastels.
25.B.EC	Describe or respond to their own creative work or the creative work of others.	Kendra described what was happening in the picture for the teacher to record.

an understanding of what it means to participate in measuring activities. When he made the determination that all the cracked eggs were "a 5," he showed an ability to sort objects into subgroups that vary by one or two attributes. By writing the numbers down as he named them, Gavin demonstrated a beginning ability to collect data and make records.

CHILD DOCUMENTATION

As teachers document children's learning, children often model on this behavior and begin to document their own learning. For instance, if a child knows that his teacher is collecting writing samples, he may begin to bring her samples of writing when he thinks he has done a really good job. This self-reflection on

Figure 8.8 Gavin's teacher used the learning reflected in his conversation about weighing eggs to create a sample for his portfolio.

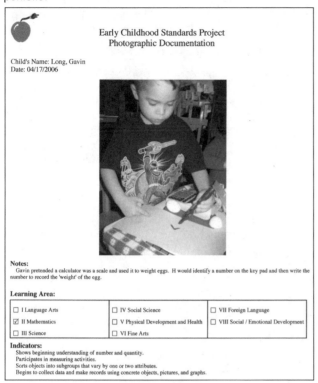

Figure 8.9. Gavin made this record to show how much the eggs weighed.

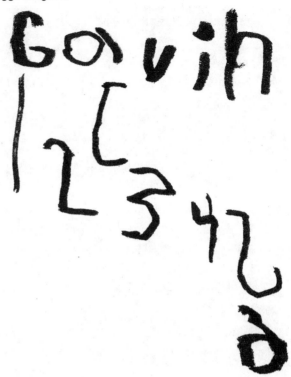

their own work helps prekindergarten as well as elementary children understand what the next step is in the development of a particular skill, and it helps them set goals for themselves. Teachers can support the children's disposition to reflect on their own work in several ways.

Having a special place to store their best samples of work can support children in reflection. Some teachers use storage boxes designed for magazines with the child's name and picture on the side for this purpose. The tops of these boxes are cut at an angle, so that children can see a section of the work that they have stored in the box. Others provide children with a special folder or cubby.

Encouraging children to participate in the selection of pieces to document the learning of the class as a whole is another way that teachers can support self-reflection. Some teachers have a special bulletin board or space set aside on a wall where they keep a visual record of the current learning experiences in their classroom. Often

this is located at the class circle or meeting area. This way, the group can discuss what should be included, and they can talk about why a particular item should be used.

Holding events where children explain the activities of the class to others is another way that children document their learning. For example, a culminating event is typically held at the end of a project (Helm & Katz, 2001). Often, guests are invited to the classroom to hear and see what has been learned. As children decide what will be important for others to see and hear about, they reflect on what has been learned.

As children talk, we find out many things about them. Statements of self-reflection are of particular interest because they provide insight into the child's dispositions and engagement in the learning experience. Selections of these statements can be used to provide others with a window on a child's development and a window on a learning experience as a whole.

PART II
Documentation in Action

CHAPTER 9

Window Into a Real Classroom: The Movie Theater Project

What does documentation in action look like in Kathy Steinheimer's classroom . . . my real world? Sometimes it looks like me scurrying to unlock a cabinet, grabbing my camera from its top shelf, taking the camera out of its case, discovering the batteries are dead (they die every two days), hastily changing them (I usually keep batteries on hand), rushing back over to a child that I had been observing, and snapping a picture of him copying print for the first time. (Hooray, I didn't miss it!) I set my camera on a cubby (I want to be ready for the next big event) and hastily scribble an anecdotal note about the child's writing. In addition, I begin reflecting on the child's writing experience and possible teaching strategies that will help strengthen his dispositions for writing and take him to the next level. I also make a mental note to talk to our special education resource teacher about the child's writing experience. Several days or weeks later, I download the child's photo onto my computer, print it out, and add it and the accompanying dated anecdotal note (sometimes, I forget the date) to his portfolio's Language Arts work samples. I also refer to the child's writing sample as I write his summary report and share his progress with his family at our family/teacher conference. Finally, I include the child's photo with several others of children writing in a hallway documentation display on writing development, complete with written narratives for the display's viewers. That is what documentation in action often looks like in my world . . . give or take a few anecdotal notes or work samples without children's names or dates. Whatever the case . . . the documenting process and accompanying documentation inform my teaching, provoke my thinking, and drive me forward, as I continuously work to assess my teaching, children's development, and individual interests; to develop teaching strategies; to make curriculum decisions; and to prepare to share the children's learning with others. As I have become more proficient in documentation, I have developed more strategies to help my young students become documenters themselves.

In my world, the children also document their experiences. How do children document and use their documentation? This chapter will help you, among other things, develop a clear understanding of how my children researched, documented, and used their documentation in an in-depth study of a movie theater. Documenting the Movie Theater Project provided opportunities for the children to

- Ask and research questions
- Participate in writing experiences that were meaningful to them
- Observe objects closely while drawing them
- Gather, organize, and draw conclusions from information gathered
- Use their documentation as a reference for model equipment construction and operation
- Reflect on what and how much they had learned
- Share their knowledge with others through documentation panels, just like their teacher

However, before I share with you our Movie Theater Project in action through documentation, I need to explain about the class and introduce my fellow colearners and codocumenters. The movie theater project was completed by my students in Yellow 2 at Valeska Hinton Early Childhood Education Center, a public school in an urban setting in Peoria, Illinois. At the time of the Movie Theater Project, the preprimary class had 10 4-year-olds, eight of whom had entered Yellow 2 as 3-year-olds the previous year (Araceli, Avierre, Ben, Faith, Jerriya, Jyree, Kyler, Michaela, Teiara, and T'Nahleg). There were nine 3-year-olds (Anisa, Christian, Ciera, Corey, Drew, Earriana, Evin, Semaj, and Trea Vion). The students were mainly African American (84%) and from families with low incomes (84% qualified for the free or reduced-price lunch program). Over 50% of the students had Individual Education Plans (IEPs). All of these children with special needs were fully included in my class and played an integral role in the Movie Theater

Project. Seven students with IEPs received speech and language therapy, and three additional students with full IEPs received speech and language therapy, resource services, and physical and/or occupational therapy. Mike Shernak, early childhood special education resource teacher, provided resource services to my students by planning with us and working with our students in the classroom, 75 minutes each morning, 3 to 4 days a week. Carrie Noar, my teacher associate, completed our Yellow 2 teaching team.

We adults joined together to help our young students complete a project, an in-depth study of a local movie theater. Together, adults and children made one team, a team of colearners and codocumenters in action.

THE BIRTH OF THE MOVIE THEATER PROJECT

The Movie Theater Project, as with many projects in my room, emerged from children's play. I observed children make rows of chairs, sit down, and stare at a drawing that Michaela, a 4-year-old, drew and taped onto a door. Semaj, a 3-year-old, stated, "We are watching a movie." He pretended to eat popcorn and looked intently at the drawing. Other children and Mrs. Noar joined the cooperative dramatic play. Ben, a 4-year-old, recited short phrases from a "Scooby Doo" cartoon. Mrs. Noar pretended to be scared when Ben spoke like a ghost. More children entered the "theater" and joined in the pretend play. Similar play occurred the following day, with as many as 12 children participating. Michaela and others drew new movie scenes while narrating the story, made rows of chairs, sat down, and ate imaginary popcorn. I listened to several conversations about the movie currently showing.

I documented the children's play by photographing the children's actions and products with my digital camera. I also wrote down the children's comments and action details onto a class name grid chart attached to a clipboard. As I examined my anecdotal notes and photographs, I assessed the movie theater play and noted the children's intense interest, focused cooperative play, use of imaginary objects, play sequences, and conversations. Based on this assessment, I decided to extend the children's play by asking questions, such as "How do you get popcorn at the movie theater?" Many children shrugged their shoulders. Then Semaj stated, "You buy it." This led to a conversation about what else you can purchase to eat at the theater. The children shouted out popcorn, candy, soda, hot dogs, and milk shakes. In order to extend and deepen their dramatic play, I suggested that the children make these items. I also asked,

"What do you need to do to get popcorn or candy at the theater?" I wanted the children to think about the use of trade (money) to obtain goods and services (concessions), which is an Illinois Early Childhood Performance Indicator. In addition, the use of money and the children's lack of it provided an opportunity for them to create pretend dollars and coins.

Children eagerly shouted out what items they wanted to construct and formed impromptu teams based on interests. The teams researched objects by collecting real ones (i.e., candy and money), constructed objects using the real objects as models (Figure 9.1), made lists of products to be sold (Figure 9.2), and created signage (i.e., types of soda available, price of popcorn). As items were constructed, the children added each to a small table, which became the first concession stand, although no one knew that was the term (Figure 9.3). The children increased their play's depth as they incorporated newly created concession items and money into their play, added new play scenarios such as purchasing food items, and lengthened already established scenarios. Figures 9.4 and 9.5 illustrate this new play level. After observing the children making these products, documenting, and assessing the children's growth in play and maintained interest in the movie theater topic, I began to think that this could be turning into a project.

Figure 9.1. T'Nahleg, a 4-year-old, traced around a dollar bill, while Jyree, another 4-year-old, added numbers, print, and a presidential portrait to his dollar. Handling and drawing real objects while observing them increased my children's abilities to gather information through observations.

Figure 9.2. Michaela wrote a drink list. She copied words from soft drink cans and bottles. Michaela taped her list onto the front edge of the concession stand table. The children referred to the list when "purchasing" a drink.

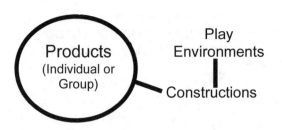

Products
(Individual or
Group)

Play
Environments

Constructions

RAW DOCUMENTATION
GUIDES DECISION MAKING

Narratives

Professional
Learning
Community
Notes

Does the movie the-ater topic have the makings of a project? Is the movie theater a project topic wor-thy of our time and effort? I reviewed my raw documentation (i.e., pho-tographs, anecdotal notes, and children's products), curriculum goals, and assessment guidelines in or-der to answer this question. In addition, I reflected on the almost daily conversations Mrs. Noar, Mr. Shernak, and I had about the children's work.

This reviewing and reflecting process helped me assess several key factors in determining whether or not to begin a project on movie theaters. First, I as-sessed the children's interest in the topic. My hastily scribbled anecdotal notes and photographs revealed to me that 10 to 12 children participated in focused dramatic "movie theater" play over a 2-week period. The children conversed enthusiastically about the topic, constructed new props, and added details to their play scenarios. In addition, new participants were drawn to the play as its depth increased. The children's interest and passion for the topic was sig-nificant enough to warrant further investigation. Second, I considered whether or not the topic was relevant to the children's world. All of my students had been to a movie theater; from the photographs I could see that many role-played what they had experienced; and most told me information about the topic. The children had enough prior knowl-edge to build on, and movie theaters were a part of their world. Third, I assessed whether or not there was enough information that the children did not know to warrant further investigation. I observed and documented many key holes in my students' knowledge during their movie theater play. For ex-ample, the children did not include tickets in their play and did not know how the popcorn was made or how the movie was projected onto the screen. Fourth, I considered whether or not I could use the topic to meet most of my curriculum goals. Would a movie theater project provide opportunities for my students to perform research, solve problems, work as a team, strengthen observation skills by creating observation drawings, increase their vo-cabulary, engage in meaningful writing experienc-es, use mathematical thinking, experiment, build constructions, strengthen dispositions for learning, and increase their dramatic play skills? The strate-gies I used to extend the children's dramatic play had already produced several of these curriculum

Figure 9.3. Semaj used a scoop from the sensory table to fill bags with popcorn (bits of paper). Araceli found plastic cups in the table toys area and lined them up above the drink list. The children stood back, assessed their work, and declared the concession stand open.

Figure 9.4. Araceli gave Jyree a bag of popcorn after he paid $5. The children quickly realized they had to create play dollars before attempting a purchase at the concession stand. Some children ran out of money after multiple purchases, and quickly went back to the art or writing area to create more money.

Figure 9.5. Mrs. Noar pretended to be scared as Earriana described what was happening in the scary movie showing on the pretend screen. Earriana and Michaela's faces show the intensity of the play, while Mrs. Noar's facial expression illustrates the role of the adult as a coparticipant in dramatic play.

goals, as documented in several photos and products collected. For example, as shown in Figure 9.6, while creating a candy wrapper, Trea Vion, although he was only 3 years old, demonstrated his ability to meet several of Peoria Public Schools' 4-year-old grade level expectations, including (1) I can understand that print and symbols carry a message; (2) I can identify some letters including those in my first name; (3) I can use scribbles, letterlike shapes, and letters in writing; and (4) I can begin to copy letters and words. Finally, I reflected on my own interest in the topic. I am a colearner with the children, who needs some prior knowledge and interest in the project topic. I was excited about the movie theater topic. I could envision the many possibilities to strengthen the children's dispositions for learning while meeting our curriculum goals. For example, Figure 9.7 illustrates the Illinois Early Learning Standards covered during the Movie Theater Project.

After reviewing my documentation and assessing all the factors discussed above, I concluded that the movie theater project was a go. We held a class meeting, and I asked the children if they would like to build their own movie theater. They responded with an enthusiastic "Yes!" I chose the goal of building a movie theater because it gave purpose and meaning to the children's investigation and work. The children kept this goal before us throughout this 4-month project. For example, Jyree, age 4, would come up to me at breakfast time and ask, "What do we need to do on the movie project today?" or state, "I need to finish the movie machine panel today."

Figure 9.6. Trea Vion observed a package of candy while re-creating it using paper and markers. He carefully copied in a line from left to right the print found on the wrapper. He identified and labeled several letters as he wrote.

USING DOCUMENTATION TO IDENTIFY PRIOR KNOWLEDGE, MISCONCEPTIONS, AND QUESTIONS

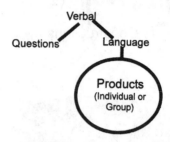

I used my documentation of the children's play, conversations, and a class web to assess what prior knowledge my students had about movie theaters. The children had demonstrated in their play that they knew the theater is filled with rows of chairs and that the movie is shown in front, has a name, and tells a story. I noted the children's misconceptions and holes in knowledge on the topic. During a conversation with several children, I learned that they did not know how tickets were purchased and processed. During a class web experience, my students demonstrated knowledge of movie names (titles), genres (scary and funny), and that there are places at the seats to put drinks so that they will not fall (cup holders). I was pleased that most children listened intently, contributed ideas, and watched information being added to the class web (see Figure 9.8).

We also began to generate a list of questions to investigate. I documented the children's questions by writing them on a large piece of paper and posting it on a wall in our room. Posting our question list in a place accessible to the children allowed us to easily add questions as they arose, reference specific questions, and assess what questions we still needed to answer through further research. This process empowered the children and enabled them to be researchers and codocumenters of their learning.

Semaj, a seasoned questioner, began our question list by asking, "How do they make popcorn?" However, asking questions on a specific topic was difficult for many of my young children. I often used information from a statement to propose a question. For example, when Trea Vion described a cup holder but did not know what it was called, I posed, "What do you call the thing by the chair that holds a drink?" The children wanted answers to their questions and began their investigation with a field experience.

FIELD RESEARCH AND DOCUMENTATION

Using Documentation to Prepare for a Field Experience

While scheduling a field experience with a local movie theater, I arranged to visit the site prior to

Figure 9.7. Illinois Early Learning Standards benchmarks covered by the Movie Theater Project.

Language Arts

1.A.ECa	Understand that pictures and symbols have meaning and that print carries a message.
1.A.ECb	Understand that reading progresses from left to right and top to bottom.
1.A.ECc	Identify labels and signs in the environment.
1.A.ECd	Identify some letters, including those in own name.
1.A.ECe	Make some letter-sound matches.
1.B.ECa	Predict what will happen next using pictures and content for guides.
1.B.ECb	Begin to develop phonological awareness by participating in rhyming activities.
1.B.ECc	Recognize separable and repeating sounds in spoken language.
1.C.ECa	Retell information from a story.
1.C.ECb	Respond to simple questions about reading material.
1.C.ECc	Demonstrate understanding of the literal meaning of stories by making comments.
2.A.EC	Understand that different text forms, such as magazines, notes, lists, letters, and story books, are used for different purposes.
2.B.EC	Show independent interest in reading related activities.
3.A.EC	Use scribbles, approximations of letters, or known letters to represent written language.
3.B.EC	Dictate stories and experiences.
3.C.EC	Use drawing and writing skills to convey meaning and information.
4.A.EC	Listen with understanding and respond to directions and conversations.
4.B.EC	Communicate needs, ideas and thoughts.
5.A.EC	Seek answers to questions through active exploration.
5.B.EC	Relate prior knowledge to new information.
5.C.EC	Communicate information with others.

Mathematics

6.A.ECa	Use concepts that include number recognition, counting and one-to-one correspondence.
6.A.ECb	Count with understanding and recognize "how many" in sets of objects.
6.B.EC	Solve simple mathematical problems.
6.C.ECa	Explore quantity and number.
6.C.ECb	Connect numbers to quantities they represent using physical models and representations.
6.D.EC	Make comparisons of quantities.
7.A.ECa	Demonstrate a beginning understanding of measurement using non-standard units and measurement words.
7.A.ECb	Construct a sense of time through participation in daily activities.
7.B.EC	Show understanding of and use comparative words.
7.C.EC	Incorporate estimating and measuring activities into play.
8.A.EC	Sort and classify objects by a variety of properties.
8.B.ECa	Recognize, duplicate, and extend simple patterns, such as sequences of sounds, shapes, and colors.
8.B.ECb	Begin to order objects in series or rows.
8.C.EC	Participate in situations that involve addition and subtraction using manipulatives.
8.D.EC	Describe qualitative change, such as measuring to see who is growing taller.
9.A.EC	Recognize geometric shapes and structures in the environment.
9.B.EC	Find and name locations with simple words (i.e, "near").
10.A.ECa	Represent data using concrete objects, pictures, and graphs.
10.A.ECb	Make predictions about what will happen next.
10.B.EC	Gather data about themselves and their surroundings.

Science

11.A.ECa	Uses senses to explore and observe materials and natural phenomena.
11.A.ECb	Collect, describe, and record information.
11.B.ECb	Become familiar with the use of technological devices.
12.A.ECb	Show an awareness of changes that occur in themselves and their environment.
12.C.EC	Make comparisons among objects they have observed.
12.D.EC	Describe the effects of forces in nature (e.g. wind, gravity, and magnetism).
12.E.ECb	Participate in recycling in their environment.
13.A.EC	Begin to understand basic safety practices.
13.B.ECa	Express wonder and ask questions about their world.
13.B.ECb	Begin to be aware of technology and how it affects them.

Social Sciences

14.A.EC	Recognize the reasons for rules.
14.C.EC	Participate in voting as a way of making choices.
14.D.EC	Develop an awareness of the roles of leaders in their environment.
15.A.EC	Identify community workers and the services they provide.
15.D.EC	Begin to understand the use of trade to obtain goods and services.
16.A.EC	Recall information about the immediate past.
17.A.ECa	Locate objects and places in familiar environments.
17.A.ECb	Express beginning geographic thinking.
18.A.EC	Recognize similarities and differences in people.
18.B.EC	Understand that each of us belongs to a family and recognize that families vary.

Physical Development and Health

19.A.ECa	Engage in active play using gross motor skills.
19.A.ECb	Engage in active play using fine motor skills.
19.B.EC	Coordinate movements to perform complex tasks.
19.C.EC	Follow simple safety rules while participating in activities.
24.A.ECa	Use appropriate communication skills when expressing needs, wants, and feelings.
24.A.ECb	Use socially acceptable ways to resolve conflict.

Fine Arts

25.A.ECb	Investigate the elements of drama.
25.A.ECd	Investigate the elements of visual arts.
25.B.EC	Describe or respond to their own creative work or the creative work of others.
26.A.ECb	Participate in drama activities.
26.A.ECd	Participate in the visual arts.
26.B.EC	Use creative arts as an avenue for self-expression.

Social/Emotional Development

31.A.ECa	Describe self using several basic characteristics.
31.A.ECb	Exhibit eagerness and curiosity as a learner.
31.A.ECc	Exhibit persistence and creativity in seeking solutions to problems.
31.A.ECd	Show some initiative and independence in actions.
31.A.ECe	Use appropriate communication skills when expressing needs, wants, and feelings.
32.A.ECa	Begin to understand and follow rules.
32.A.ECb	Manage transitions and begin to adapt to changes in routines.
32.A.ECc	Show empathy and caring for others.
32.A.ECd	Use the classroom environment purposefully and respectfully.
32.B.ECa	Engage in cooperative group play.
32.B.ECb	Begin to share materials and experiences and take turns.
32.B.ECc	Respect the rights of self and others.
32.B.ECd	Develop relationships with children and adults.

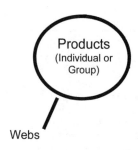

Webs

Figure 9.8. This initial web documents what the children knew about movie theaters at the beginning of our project. I wrote down and categorized the children's ideas during a class discussion and then posted the web in our classroom.

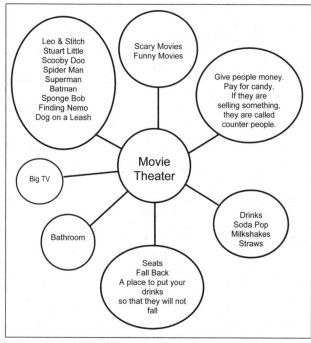

the children's field experience. During the preparation visit, I communicated to the theater manager our field experience's purpose, some of the children's questions from the list, research and documentation techniques my students would utilize, and our expectations for the children's interactions with his staff. It was crucial to let the field experts know that my class had a specific goal— constructing and running a movie theater—and would be asking specific questions, using pretend writing and copying print to record information, and needed time to create observation drawings. Setting the stage with the field experts helped them to realize how powerful young children are and maximized their willingness to share information with our students. In addition, Mr. Shernak and I documented the movie theater facility by photographing and videotaping the theater's environment and equipment with the manager's permission. The photographs and videotape served as documentation resources for revisiting the experience while constructing and operating the theater.

In addition to preparing the field experts for our field experience, I prepared the children to perform

research in the field. The children and I listed items that they wanted to include in their movie theater. I then asked each child to join a research team for a specific item. I met with each two-person team and helped them write two specific questions concerning their item. For example, Drew, a 3-year-old, and Jerriya, a 4-year-old, the soda machine researchers and documenters, asked "How do you make soda?" and "What sizes do you have?" I put each team's questions onto a documentation worksheet and added a section for drawing their specific item. I placed each team's documentation worksheet, along with some extra paper for drawing and writing, onto a clipboard. I met with each team again right before the field trip. We reviewed their documentation worksheet, and I reminded them that their research and documentation would be used to help construct and operate a specific piece of equipment. The children practiced asking their questions. I also stressed to each team the need to write and draw (document) what they discovered during the field experience. In addition, I shared my expectations for the field experience with the class and reminded the children of the investigation's purpose.

Finally, I prepared the chaperones for the field experience. I shared our research and documentation procedures, including ways the adults could help their assigned teams gather and record information. I stressed my expectations for the children's participation in the process, which helped the adults become facilitators and encouragers, while ensuring that the children did the actual research and documentation.

Performing Field Research and Documentation

Upon our arrival at the movie theater, the manager gave us a complete tour of the building, including the projection room, storage rooms, and concession area. He described each area's function and demonstrated how to operate equipment. In addition, as a result of our discussion prior to the field experience, the manager let the children examine and touch many objects (see Figure 9.9). After the whole-group tour, the teams and their chaperones went to their assigned areas. Each team asked their prepared questions, used pretend writing and/or copied print to record information, and completed observation drawings. I observed and photographed children engaged in focused, active research. Each team documented specific details in their drawings, writings, and verbalizations as the movie theater's staff eagerly shared their knowledge with my young students (see Figures 9.10, 9.11, and 9.12).

Figure 9.9. Jyree and Semaj observed a film strip closely. They noted that the pictures repeated and that the film was a new movie coming to theaters soon.

Figure 9.10. Araceli asked a concessionaire about the popcorn machine. She used letterlike shapes, letters, and drawings to record information. The concessionaire noted Araceli's focus and began to spell words for her (i.e., "large," "medium") as Araceli wrote them down on her worksheet.

Data Collections

Products (Individual or Group)

Figure 9.11. This is part of Araceli's documentation worksheet. She drew a rectangle to represent each size of popcorn. Araceli wrote the word "large" as the concessionaire spelled it. When the word "medium" did not fit in the rectangle she drew to represent it, she continued her writing of the word beside and above the rectangle with "i-u-m" above the question.

Figure 9.12. Araceli observed the popcorn machine closely while drawing it. She included many details in her drawing such as the kettle, cable, scoop, oil container, popcorn seed drawer, and popcorn cascading out of the top of the kettle.

Child Self-Reflections

Lists

Using Documentation to Revisit the Field Experience

The children encountered and documented a significant amount of information during the field experience. We needed to begin capturing and processing what the children had learned before it was lost. Therefore, we held a class meeting immediately following our field experience. I had the children state what they had learned, while Mrs. Noar wrote their comments onto a large piece of paper. The tired children eagerly shouted out answers, repeated one another's words at times, and stumbled over new vocabulary words such as *projector* or *popcorn seed*. The children used the information garnered and documented during this class meeting to plan and carry out constructions, operate equipment, and perform tasks common to a movie theater.

Child Self-Reflections

Records of Conversations

During the two days following the field experience, Mrs. Noar or I met with each team individually to review their field research and documentation. Each team reported on what they had discovered. The children referred to their documentation worksheets, touched their pretend writings as they commented, and labeled details in their drawings. We wrote down their comments and added word labels to their drawings with the children's permission. Each team demonstrated knowledge of how their specific item functioned during these team research reviews. Many teams' field drawings included details and were realistic renditions of specific pieces of equipment.

While meeting with individual teams, I had many "goose bump" moments. Our preparation and facilitation of the field experience had paid big dividends. I could tell from my documentation that all of my young students, including those with severe language delays, had gathered, documented, retained, and verbalized a considerable amount of information. The children's interest and passion for movie theaters helped them focus intently during the field experience, use their senses to gather information, and represent visually what they had experienced. The children were field researchers and documenters.

Assembling Documentation and Planning Boards

Children process and assimilate new information when revisiting an experience by reviewing and discussing documentation. I used the large-group review and individual team meetings to revisit the experience. In addition, I stimulated conversations by introducing photographs that I took during my preparation visit to the movie theater. We talked about the photographs' content as the children cut the photos apart and sorted them by topic. I told the children that we needed to start planning for the movie theater constructions. I showed the children how to organize information about specific subtopics or equipment. The children worked together to arrange and tape field drawings, photographs, writings, and dictations onto a large piece of poster board. For example, Evin, a 3-year-old, prepared a photograph of the movie projector's turntables for placement on a documentation board. I asked him to do this job to help him revisit the field experience and deepen his interest in the project (see Figure 9.13). Children also added titles and word labels to each documentation or planning board (see Figure 9.14). As documentation boards were completed, the children displayed each in the room and noted how much they had learned. This documentation process took several weeks with planning boards being completed, taken down and used as references for specific constructions, and returned to the room's planning board display area. In many ways, the children's documentation boards, such as the popcorn machine planning board featured in Figure 9.15, resemble documentation boards

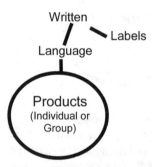

Figure 9.13. Evin arranged and taped photographs onto the movie projector's planning board. Evin's participation in the movie theater project became more focused after assembling this documentation board. Revisiting the field experience by reviewing the photos and accompanying documentation during the cutting and taping process sparked an interest in Evin, who later volunteered to help plan and construct the soda machine.

Figure 9.14. Faith, a 4-year-old, added labels to her signage planning board. She told Mr. Shernak what words she needed and asked him to show her how to write each word. Faith's awareness of print, letter formation, and confidence in writing grew as a result of this experience.

made by adults of children's learning, such as those seen in Chapter 12.

LEARNING FROM PRODUCT DOCUMENTATION

The Movie Theater Project provided rich opportunities for the children to produce several complex products, including all of the equipment needed to run a movie theater's amphitheater, projection room, ticket booth, and concession stand. Documenting the children's construction processes opened windows into the children's learning that otherwise would have been closed to me. Observing, documenting, assessing, and reflecting on the children's construction processes and accompanying documentation provided opportunities for me to strengthen both their tangible academic skills and less tangible learning qualities, such as creativity, planning skills, persistency, dispositions for learning, teamwork, and problem-solving skills. In addition, documenting the construction processes helped me understand and share the power of the children's learning as evidenced by their work.

Figure 9.15. This documentation board includes photographs taken in my preparation field visit; field drawings; field notes, including pretend writing, letters, and letterlike shapes created by Araceli and Ben, a 4-year-old; and a record of their comments from their team meeting. Many children referred to this documentation board as they constructed the popcorn machine, assembled items necessary to make popcorn, and operated the concession stand. The board was displayed in the room throughout the project and at the movie's premiere.

Ice Machine

The children selected the ice machine as their first piece of equipment to construct. The children struggled with selecting appropriate materials and assembling them during this construction's beginning. For example, Jyree selected a round container to represent the rectangular ice machine. Because of this difficulty, I referred the team back to the ice machine's photograph and discussed its shape. In addition, I sent the team to observe and draw the ice machine in our school's cafeteria. After these experiences, Jyree went back and selected a rectangular box for the ice machine's body and four cylinders for the machine's legs. Mr. Shernak and I guided the children in their selection of materials and construction techniques such as taping, stapling, and gluing during the beginning of this construction. I then stepped back and watched the construction process through the lens of my camera, which helped me focus on the process rather than the end product. I observed Trea Vion select a milk bottle for the ice scoop, draw a cutting line, and instruct Mr. Shernak to cut on his line. His actions, which represented his thought processes, told me that the children were now ready to take the lead in constructing equipment (see Figures 9.16 and 9.17).

Popcorn Machine

Before the field experience, the children knew that the movie theater sold popcorn, but could not describe how the popcorn was prepared. The children used documentation, including a videotaped demonstration of popcorn preparation, photographs, and their field drawings and notes, to conceptualize how to construct and operate a popcorn machine.

Jerriya took the lead in this construction. She started by constructing the top half of the popcorn machine. Jerriya selected a box for the popcorn warmer, drew the door, and told me to cut it out. She drew a rectangle for the window and selected clear plastic for the pane (see Figure 9.18). When the warmer door was completed, Jerriya referred back to the popcorn machine's planning board, selected materials for the popcorn kettle, and persisted when faced with the challenge of attaching the kettle to the warmer. I documented Jerriya's ability to approach these tasks with flexibility and inventiveness by photographing her construction process and marking Jerriya as "proficient" for this indicator on her Work Sampling Illinois Developmental Checklist.

While Jerriya worked on the popcorn machine, Semaj expressed his desire to join the construction

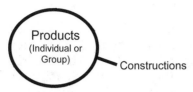

Products (Individual or Group) — Constructions

Figure 9.16. Trea Vion and Jyree carefully painted the ice machine. I encouraged them to check their work and touch up any missed spots. Learning to self-check their work is a life skill that will benefit my children throughout their school and work experiences.

Figure 9.17. Jyree and Trea Vion grew significantly in their abilities to select and use materials during this initial construction process. They strove for independence and included many details, including a scoop made out of a milk jug, a door made from a shoe box lid, legs made out of cardboard cylinders, and a sign that labels what is inside the machine, "ice."

Developmental Checklists

Observations of Progress and Performance

Figure 9.18. Jerriya worked intently on the popcorn machine's door construction for 45 minutes. She persisted when encountering several problems, including cellophane that easily tore, tape lengths that stuck together rather than to her work, and several mismeasurements and cuttings that left her with a window pane either too small or too big.

Captions & Signs
|
Written
|
Language

Products (Individual or Group)

Figure 9.19. After noting in a photograph that the popcorn machine had a sign, Jerriya asked Mr. Shernak to show her how to write the word "popcorn." Then, Jerriya carefully copied the word, drew popcorn kernels on each side of it, cut the extra paper off, and asked Semaj to help her attach it to the completed popcorn machine. I documented Jerriya's growth in her ability to seek help when encountering a problem on her Work Sampling Illinois Developmental Checklist.

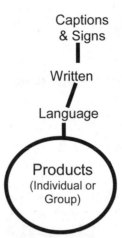

Figure 9.20. The completed popcorn machine includes a kettle with popped kernels flowing from it, kernel drawer, salt box, measuring scoop, and unpopped kernels. Semaj and Jerriya evaluated the popcorn machine's performance during a trial run with friends and stated that it worked excellently.

Figure 9.21. The children learned from their field research that soda was composed of two parts CO_2 (bubbles) packaged in tanks and syrup packaged in boxes, which were mixed together and dispensed through specific nozzles depending on the kind. Many children explained how the completed soda machine worked to classroom visitors and families.

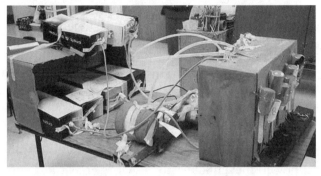

Figure 9.22. After observing a photograph of the soda dispenser and counting the number of nozzles, Semaj gathered enough pill bottles and tongue depressors to create them. Others joined him in labeling the nozzles by copying words from soda cans and water bottles gathered from the school's soda machines.

Figure 9.23. Evin taped a hose into its fitting (milk cap with a hole cut in it), while Mr. Shernak steadied it for him. The hose promptly detached itself and had to be retaped several times. Evin's persistence in completing a task grew as a result of participating in the soda machine's construction.

process by bringing found items to Jerriya, who promptly rejected them. Semaj then took his found items back and taped them together. I pointed out to Jerriya that Semaj was interested in working on the popcorn machine. After completing the major portion of the popcorn machine's construction, Jerriya allowed Semaj to help her paint it gray. This newly formed team reviewed the planning board and noted items that needed to be created. Semaj headed to the found item center, gathered materials and tape, and constructed a scoop for the popcorn seeds. Jerriya found a metal pan to store the seed in and a box for the popcorn salt, and created a sign that said "Popcorn" (see Figure 9.19). Semaj and Jerriya worked together to attach the sign to the newly finished popcorn machine pictured in Figure 9.20.

Soda Machine

The children also constructed a complex soda machine with CO_2 tanks, syrup boxes, and fountain controls, as shown in Figures 9.21 and 9.22. The children worked to solve several construction problems while replicating the machine over a 6-week period. Faith and Evin found it difficult to connect and keep connected the three parts of the machine with hoses and fixtures (see Figure 9.23). In addition, Trea Vion, Semaj, and Jerriya reviewed the soda machine's photographs and field drawings and noted many of the soda dispensing system's details, including the labeling. Individual children created each label by pretend writing and/or copying print from the photographs or real objects (see Figure 9.24). Observing and duplicating environmental print, signs, and labels, while engaged in activities meaningful to them, provided opportunities for the children to strengthen their writing as they learned letter formations, letter sounds, word formations and meanings, and that print provides useful information, such as the kinds of soda sold at a movie theater (see Figure 9.25).

Nacho Cheese Machine, Chip Warmer, and Chips

Jyree, Trea Vion, and Semaj volunteered to construct the nacho cheese machine. The children persisted and solved many construction problems through trial and error during this construction. They measured, cut, and adjusted the silver foam that they used to line the machine. They learned a lesson on gravity, since the wooden box that they selected to dispense the cheese was heavy and fell off the machine each time it was placed into working position. It had to be reinforced with much tape. Jyree was concerned that the cheese machine give out just the right amount of cheese, so he selected a gumball machine's base complete with lever to represent the "cheese switch." Finally, after the children taped the cheese dispenser box shut and in place, Jyree hypothesized that they needed to add some bottles to "keep the cheese from going everywhere." Figure 9.26 shows the interior of the nacho cheese machine.

Ciera and Earriana, both 3-year-olds, and Jerriya selected a box and stated that they were going to make the chip warmer. Over the course of a week, the girls drew and cut out windows, painted the box, and measured, cut, and installed display windows and shelving. Several children, including Ben, volunteered to draw and cut out nacho chips. Ben's excitement over making nacho chips served as a motivator for him to engage in two fine motor tasks that were difficult for him and a part of his IEP goals, drawing and cutting. He spent 30 minutes carefully grasping a marker, drawing circles, and cutting around each one. Ben's scissor grasp fluctuated, and he often resorted to short snips throughout this experience, according to an anecdotal note that accompanied a photo of cutting chips. When chips were collecting on a table, Semaj went to the found item center and selected used plastic plant containers to hold the nacho chips. The children enjoyed filling their new chip containers and placing them into the completed nacho warmer, which featured transparent doors complete with knobs, steady shelving, and a sign for advertising.

Candy Display Case With Candy

Replicating candy wrappers was a popular task. My documentation revealed that more than three-quarters of the class worked on creating candy wrappers. Many children suggested that their favorite candies be included in the candy display. Some even suggested what *not* to include in the display. A large candy-making team borrowed candy from the school office and used it as references. They busied themselves copying the illustrations and writing found on each wrapper (see Figure 9.27). The children produced more than enough candy to fill the yet-to-be-designed display case.

The display case team found its construction to be complicated. Earriana, Araceli, and Teiara (age 4) discovered how hard it was to get shelves to remain slanted, so that the candy could be displayed properly (see Figure 9.28). The solution was to have two girls hold each shelf while the third taped the shelf in place. After filling the finished display case with candy, the display team stood back and admired their work. The girls smiled proudly as they admired their completed construction.

Film Projector

The children had little experience with film projectors, and the field experience was the first time that the children had observed this complicated piece of equipment. Therefore, we needed to revisit the film projector several times before and during its construction. We used the film projector's documentation to help the children understand how to construct and operate a film projector. I helped the children review and reflect on several forms of documentation, including photographs, field drawings, observation drawings created while referencing photographs (see Figure 9.29), team notes (see Figure 9.30), and a video demonstration of how to operate the film projector. I hoped that our documentation reviews would empower the children to visualize, replicate, and conceptualize how the film projector worked, even though they had limited experience with it.

I soon realized how important details are to young children, as a team worked steadily for 2 weeks to complete the film projector's control panel. Jyree laid out the control panel's background areas using black paper on a blue background, while consistently referring to the panel's photograph. Next, Trea Vion and Jyree selected materials suitable for buttons and affixed them to the panel in rows (see Figure 9.31). They carefully counted the number of buttons in each row and matched their button layout with the original panel. Trea Vion observed the panel's photograph and noted the difference in the panel's switches compared to its buttons. He selected spongy black foam to give the panel's switches more depth than the flat buttons. Faith and Ciera added a letter, number, or symbol to each button, just like in the panel's photograph. When I compared the children's completed panel to the original panel's photograph as in Figure 9.32, I was awestruck by the sophistication and details included in their reproduction.

Ben, Trea Vion, Jyree, Jerriya, and T'Nahleg, a 4-year-old, tackled the construction of the projection unit. The team replicated the projector's powerful light bulb, cogs, exhaust pipe, and signage that noted the projectionist's number, film title, and run times. They secured everything with tape and prepared to move it into the hallway, our project storage area. As the team and Mr. Shernak struggled with pushing the huge machine along the floor, Trea Vion stated, "Alls this thing needs is wheels." The team pushed the projector back into the room and helped Trea Vion attach castor wheels that he retrieved from the construction materials area. When all was complete, Trea Vion pushed the projector by himself (see Figure 9.33), and stated "There, that's better."

Figure 9.24. Trea Vion used a soda can as a model for his printing. He was very proud of his word label and volunteered to write several more labels. His awareness of print and disposition for writing increased as a result of this experience.

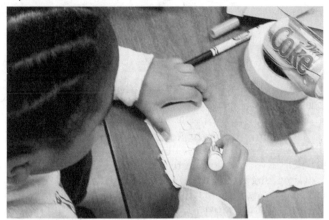

Figure 9.26. The selection of materials was key to the cheese machine's construction. Jyree, Trea Vion, and Semaj visualized what the interior of the machine should contain; even though they had never seen the interior or documentation about what it contains.

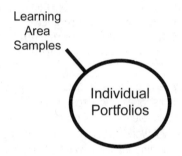

Figure 9.25. The work sample on the left is Evin's first attempt at copying a word ("Coke") while making labels for the soda syrup box labels. The work sample and accompanying anecdotal notes revealed that he struggled with his marker grip and letter formation. The work sample on the right was Evin's fifth attempt at copying a word ("Sprite") for the soda syrup box labels. Evin's growth in his ability to form letters and copy letters in left to right order is evident when comparing the first work sample with the second. I used these two samples to illustrate his growth in writing and difficulty with marker grasp to his mother during a family/teacher conference.

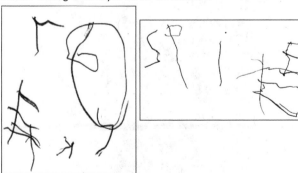

Figure 9.27. Jerriya chose to replicate a KitKat bar's wrapper. She observed the wrapper closely, chose paper and markers that matched the colors on the wrapper, carefully copied the wrapper's design and print while working from the left to right, and cut out her completed wrapper. I captured this experience for Jerriya's portfolio by photographing her while she worked and then photographing the completed replication.

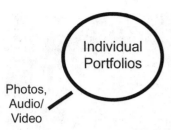

Photos,
Audio/
Video

Figure 9.28. Earriana worked to find the end of a tape roll while Araceli cut a piece of tape and Teiara tried to tape a shelf into place. Each was working on the candy display independently until they realized that the shelves would not stay in place while being taped unless someone held them. Their dilemma created a need to work together in order to be successful.

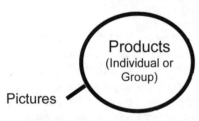

Pictures

Figure 9.29. While observing a photo of the film projector's stringing box, Avierre, a 4-year-old, drew it, complete with dials, cogs, and film strip stringing out of the top. The process of revisiting a piece of equipment by completing an observation drawing of its photograph helped Avierre note details that he had previously overlooked. Also, the children who constructed the film projector's stringing box referred to Avierre's drawing and included several details, such as the cogs, in their construction (see Figure 9.34).

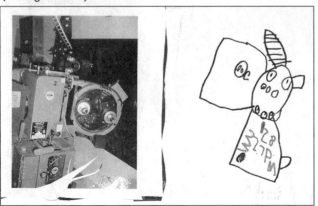

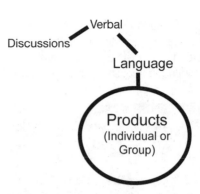

Figure 9.30. Avierre and Evin's documentation notes revealed their understanding of how the film projector worked. They were able to form a basic conceptualization of how the projector worked even though they were only able to observe it briefly during our group tour, due to the theater's safety policy.

Film Projector Research Team Notes
by
Avierre and Evin

Avierre: Plug it (projector) up. Plug it with a cord.
Evin: Through the machine. (Pointed to film strip)
Avierre: Put the movie (film strip) on circles to the machine. Buttons light up. To turn on the movie. A Projector. Buttons. A light—took pictures. (Pointed to parts of the film projector while labeling them.)
Evin: Machine (Pointed to film projector.)
Avierre: The light. 1 + 6 stands for machine. (Pointed to number label on projector.) It (film) plays 3 (times).

Figure 9.31. Jyree and Trea Vion selected materials, cut them into representative shapes and sizes, and affixed them to the control panel, while referring to its photograph. Mr. Shernak supported the boys' work by being present; asking open ended questions; encouraging the team to refer to the documentation board; verbally describing the boys' work; encouraging the team to persist when faced with a difficult task or problem; noting the team's progress; and being ready to assist, if asked, and if the task was something the boys could not do alone (i.e., retrieve adult scissors from teacher shelf).

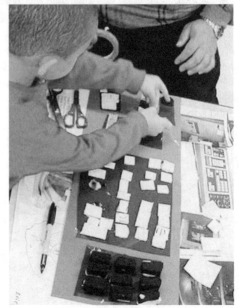

Figure 9.32. The children's control panel (top) closely resembles the real control panel (bottom), including color, texture, layout, symbols, and print.

Figure 9.33. Trea Vion recognized a problem, offered a solution, worked with others to employ his solution, and evaluated its results. The pride in his accomplishment was revealed in his facial expressions, as he quickly moved the film projector to the hallway and deemed the problem solved.

Figure 9.34. T'Nahleg retrieved the film strip from the documentation wall and carefully attached its end to the stringing box's cogs, passed it in front of the light bulb, wrapped it around a film disk axle, and spun it forward and backward. As the film unwound onto the floor and detached from the disk tray, he noted that he had to tape the end to the tray.

Drew, T'Nahleg, and Ciera selected materials for the film disk trays, which hold the projector's film reels. The children observed the film projector's planning board and stated that the film trays needed to go in circles (rotate). The team selected three large flat disks for the film tray, placed them on top of each other, and tested the film disk tray by spinning the top tray. Drew and Ciera discovered that spinning their construction was fun and noted that the top tray fell away as they spun it. They had a hands-on experience with centrifugal force (physics concept) and were able to identify the problem: lack of a stabilizing axle. The team had difficulty finding just the right item to serve as the disks' central axle. Each item that they tried was either too thin or too wide to fit in the two trays' center holes. When the team was about to give up, I suggested that they try a thick pencil. It worked, but fell out each time T'Nahleg spun the trays. Drew fixed this problem by placing a plastic spring over the top of the pencil and securing the axle with an abundant supply of masking tape.

When the projector's three components were all complete, T'Nahleg strung the film onto the projector's cogs (see Figure 9.34). He referred to the projector's documentation board and noted that the film must be in front of the light bulb in order for the movie to show up on the screen. After 6 weeks of intense work, the children declared the complicated film projector ready for operation.

Chairs With Cup Holders

Drew and Corey, 3-year-olds, tackled constructing the theater seats with cup holders. They used critical thinking and problem-solving skills to plan, select materials, and complete their constructions. Until this construction, Corey had not engaged in any constructions and rarely observed teams working on constructions. He could usually be found working in the block or living area during our work times. I was pleasantly surprised when I observed and documented him volunteering, gathering materials, persisting when the construction process became difficult, and smiling ecstatically when he realized his success in completing the construction (see Figures 9.35, 9.36, and 9.37). Drew observed Corey working on his chair, left the construction area, and quickly returned with all his needed materials. He completed his construction and tried it out (see Figure 9.38). Drew sat in his theater seat often; placed it in the front row at the movie's sneak preview in our classroom; and sat in it during the movie premiere, even though it was part of a documentation display located away from the

Figure 9.35. Corey selected a hard plastic cylinder with a hole in it for his cup holder. He persisted when faced with the difficult task of cutting the hole bigger, so that his cup would fit correctly. He was empowered by Mr. Shernak, who held the cylinder for him and encouraged him to continue on when the cutting became difficult and tiresome.

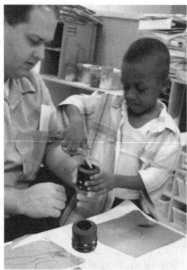

Figure 9.36. Corey referenced the theater chair planning board, selected two commercial egg cartons from the construction materials area, and asked Mr. Shernak to hold the cartons while he tested them with his arms. He then took the egg cartons and carefully taped them to the back and seat of a classroom chair.

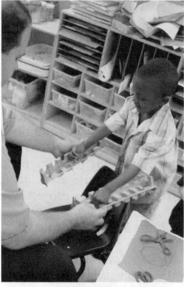

Figure 9.37. Corey's pride in his work was evident as he sat in his completed theater seat.

Indicators of Dispositions

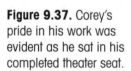

Observations of Progress and Performance

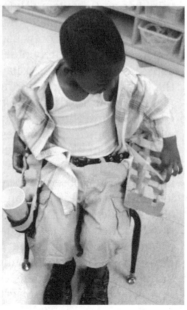

Figure 9.38. Drew used a bucket, hard plastic packaging, and cardboard to construct his theater seat.

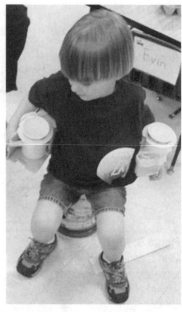

Figure 9.39. The completed computer screen includes a list of buttons with the titles of movies showing, a number key pad, and some additional unlabeled buttons.

Figure 9.40. This sign team worked out a system for taping the box letters (RAVE) to the sign's background. Kyler unrolled long lengths of tape from its dispenser and handed the end to either Avierre or Trea Vion, who placed the strips across each box, while Kyler worked to cut the other end off the roll.

premiere's movie screen. While observing and documenting Drew's actions, I realized that his theater seat had become real to him.

Ticket Booth Computer and Ticket Printer

Araceli and Avierre (age 4) replicated the ticket booth computer and printer. Araceli used a ruler to draw buttons, copied the numerals found on the computer's key pad, and wrote the list of films showing at the Yellow 2 movie theater (see Figure 9.39). She referenced a photograph of the computer screen as she copied the numeral key pad and recalled that the buttons were used to punch in the number of tickets. Avierre constructed the ticket printer. He used a roll of adding machine paper to represent tickets coming out of the printer. He adjusted the size of the ticket slot several times. Avierre struggled with how to keep the ticket roll from unrolling onto the floor. He solved the problem by taping the roll onto the inside of the box. After several trials, Avierre determined that the tickets could be printed and retrieved from the ticket slot. Araceli and Avierre affixed the computer screen onto the ticket booth, tested their construction, and stated that it worked.

Marquee

Several teams completed the multiple steps needed to build the marquee. The marquee's construction, as with many other constructions, provided opportunities for the children to develop social skills, including sharing, taking turns, voicing ideas, using words to resolve conflicts, and compromising. Ben and Faith worked side by side while painting the background red. Then, Ben and Araceli sprinkled glitter from a common bowl onto the marquee's background. In addition, Teiara and Michaela worked together to paint the marquee's sidebar and copied the words *Motion Picture* using the marquee's planning board as a reference. Kyler, 4 years old and new to the project; Trea Vion; and Avierre worked together to attach the letters for the name of the theater, RAVE, onto the background. The boys had difficulty dispensing tape at a workable length and used teamwork to propose, evaluate, and implement a solution to this problem (see Figure 9.40).

While reviewing the marquee's documentation board, Avierre noted the blue rectangular border that surrounded each letter on the original sign, gathered materials, and created a blue border for a letter. Then, he demonstrated and told Trea Vion how to cut the borders. However, Trea Vion continued to work on his own, drawing rectangular shapes and cutting them into narrow strips (see Figure 9.41). After many unsuccessful attempts at cutting a rectangular boarder and faced with a pile of blue scraps, Trea Vion asked Avierre to show him again how to draw and cut the borders. Trea Vion used Avierre's method and was successful in completing the task. The boys then worked together to frame each letter (see Figure 9.42). I documented Trea Vion's growth in Social and Emotional Development, particularly his growth in handling frustration and asking for help, on his Illinois Work Sampling Developmental Checklist and added this Individualized Item to his portfolio. The children displayed the completed marquee outside our room. Many visitors commented on the marquee's details and how it realistically represented the one found at the RAVE movie theater (see Figure 9.43).

Movie Screen

Jyree, who worked on the project almost every day, heard me mention to Mr. Shernak that we did not have a movie screen yet. Jyree perceived the need for a movie screen, took initiative, and followed through on fulfilling that need. He went directly to the art area and independently planned and constructed a frame using mat board scraps and tape. After completing his construction, he declared, "Here is our movie screen." He held it up for me to document with my camera. Jyree asked for help in attaching the frame to a door. Later on, he and Earriana added a white paper screen and poles to his frame. The movie theater project helped Jyree and others learn to plan and complete tasks independently. I was able to document (anecdotal notes, photographs, work samples, checklist) several of Jyree's less tangible qualities during this project, including his abilities to define problems and suggest solutions, work creatively, use language to resolve conflicts, and persist when faced with a difficult task.

CREATING AND USING DOCUMENTATION DURING MOVIE CREATION AND PRODUCTION

Our Movie Theme Decision-Making Process

The children began to talk about making a movie midway through the project. Faith, Michaela, Earriana, and several others formed a team and began to draw pictures related to their favorite movies. I had the team organize and document each story by placing their drawings onto storyboards that we displayed in the room.

Figure 9.41. Trea Vion used a marker to draw narrow rectangles onto his paper and then attempted to cut them out.

Individual Work Samples

Individual Portfolios

Figure 9.42. After allowing Avierre to show him how to cut the blue rectangular borders and experiencing some success at the task, Trea Vion's demeanor changed from frustration to confidence, as seen in his facial expressions and body language.

Figure 9.43. The completed marquee (left) is a close match for the actual RAVE marquee (right).

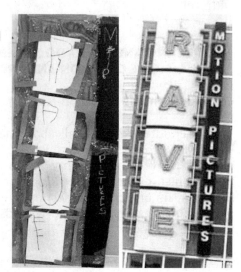

After several days of storyboard making, I held a class meeting to discuss the type of movie we wanted to produce. Most of the children wanted to create a movie based on their favorite cartoon shows or movies. I reflected on the children's discussion, the opportunities these movie topics would bring for meeting our curriculum goals, and my own lack of knowledge regarding children's cartoons. I also reflected on my class's favorite books and the benefits of producing a movie based on a book. I decided that a plethora of curriculum goals could be met with the children writing a script, creating props, acting out roles, and producing a movie based on a book rather than a cartoon. I shared my decision with the class, who received it enthusiastically. The children selected two books and voted on which one they wanted as their movie theme.

The class selected *Alphabet Adventure* (2001) written by Audrey Wood and illustrated by Bruce Robert Wood. The children had read this book many times, and most could retell it in their own words. In *Alphabet Adventure*, a group of lowercase letters travels on a field trip with their teacher. During the field trip, the lowercase "i" loses her dot. The dot is actually hiding and can be found in every illustration. A wise uppercase letter informs the class that if they bring items for the "i" to use in place of her dot, the dot will eventually come out of hiding. Each item that the "i" tries to use as a replacement does not work until she tries "c"'s cherry, which is red and round like the dot. Precisely when the "i" places the cherry on her head, the dot reappears and returns to its proper place.

Prop Planning and Script Writing

We created a prop and letter chart by having the children name nouns that began with each letter and were suitable for dotting the "i." Each child used the prop chart to select a letter role to play in the movie and a prop to create. The children referred to the chart often, including when they needed to make their letters and props, write the script, rehearse lines, and perform letter roles. I observed and documented individual children reviewing the chart alone or in small groups. The children enjoyed identifying and labeling letters, pretend reading words, suggesting nouns to add to the chart, adding marks to the chart, and re-creating the charting experience in their own way on the easel. The charting experience provided opportunities for the children to explore letter identification, formation, and sounds; learn new vocabulary; participate in a meaningful group writing experience; and use their documentation as a reference.

After the chart was complete, the children wrote the "Alphabet Adventure" movie script. Each actor selected a letter character and prop to dot the "i," considered the "i"'s possible reaction to the prop, and dictated the "i"'s verbal response. In addition, the children created a short introduction and conclusion to the movie at the end of the movie's production.

Letter Constructions

The children explored spatial relationships, cause and effect, and shadows during letter construction. My young students used a paper die-cut press to create each letter's pattern (see Figure 9.44). Then they placed each letter onto an overhead and traced its outline onto poster board (see Figure 9.45). Tracing letters using an overhead was a new technique for the children. Each child learned how to move his body out of the way, so that he did not block his view of the letter with shadows. Lastly, the children selected colors for each letter and painted them.

Prop Constructions

The children selected props from the prop/role chart to create. They used books, pictures from the Internet, and real objects to research the props' shapes, colors, and textures. In Figure 9.46, for example, Michaela and Jerriya observed a vase of flowers while drawing it with pens. After drawing a prop onto poster board, each child painted a black outline and filled the painting in with color (see Figure 9.47). The class displayed the letters and props in the room as they were completed (see Figure 9.48). After the completion of the Movie Theater Project, I used the letters and props as artifacts representing our class history and displayed them as an alphabet set along the top of the walls in our room. The following year, many of the 4-year-olds, who had been 3-years-old during the project, recalled events from the project, as they often reflected on the alphabet and reviewed its history.

Movie Production

We started filming scenes for the "Alphabet Adventure" movie with a video camera as soon as the first props were completed. A child assistant cinematographer, a child director, and I instructed the actors during a short rehearsal before each filming. The children referred to their written script and used the prop/role list as a scene schedule during filming. Each scene consisted of a letter character offering his prop to Araceli, the "i," who stated the reason why it would not work. The actors and film crews took the filming seriously. All wanted to see the performances on film. The children gave specific feedback on each scene's quality and decided to retake many scenes. In the final scene of

Figure 9.44. Ciera slowly turned the crank of the paper die-cut press, while she and Avierre observed the letter "w" being formed by the die cut. Ciera was fascinated by the cutting process and volunteered to cut letters for several others.

Figure 9.45. Christian, a 3-year-old, used a black marker to trace his letter, "c," onto poster board. He made several mistakes at first, as he learned to manipulate the marker and adjust his body in order to avoid having his shadow cover up the letter's outline. When Christian was finished outlining his letter, he stepped back and observed his work.

Figure 9.46. Michaela and Jerriya were commissioned to paint a prop, a vase, for Dr. Bussan, our principal, who played the letter "v" in the movie. The team incorporated many details in their observation drawing, including the flowers' blooms, stems, leaves, and buds. They worked well together and were able to resolve several conflicts about who was going to draw or paint particular areas.

Written ━━ Letters

Language

Products
(Individual or
Group)

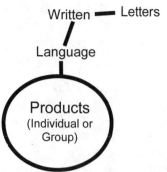

Figure 9.47. To prepare the prop for the letter "t," Teiara carefully outlined her drawing with black paint, and then filled in open areas with color, while referencing a picture of a tiger that she found in a book.

Figure 9.48. Ciera proudly displayed her letter "w" and wagon prop. Ciera, as with all of our 3-year-olds, was empowered by this experience, and completed a prop that was realistic and detailed. I was amazed by the quality of all the children's props.

Figure 9.49. Christian volunteered to paint several letters for the poster. For each letter, he referred to the book, called out a letter name, selected a color for it, and painted it onto a small sheet of poster board. I documented the lowercase letters that Christian recognized and labeled during this process. I also documented those letters he was able to form without assistance and those he formed after a demonstration.

Figure 9.50. Drew assembled the poster while referring to the book's cover. He took the job seriously and carefully placed each letter into the boat, while making sure it was visible.

Figure 9.51. Jerriya operated the soda machine. She carefully placed the cup under the spigot and against the flow lever, watched to make sure the soda did not overflow, and handed the cup to her waiting customer, Semaj.

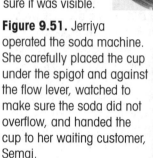

Figure 9.52. Drew (left) prepared nachos. He carefully turned the nacho cheese control button and observed the pretend cheese dripping onto the nacho chips. He said, "This machine gives just the right amount of cheese." Faith (right) prepared bags of popcorn for customers, using the scoop to fill each bag.

Figure 9.53. Teiara performed the role of cashier. She entered customers' purchases on the computer, told them the amount due, collected money, returned change, and thanked them for their business.

the movie, the dot, which can be seen in the background in every scene, comes forward and returns to his proper place above the "i." Filming scenes and editing film footage took 3 weeks. The final film lasted less than 5 minutes and was in great demand by families and friends after its premiere.

Movie Poster

The children had observed several movie posters at the theater and decided to create one of their own for the "Alphabet Adventure" movie. Several children volunteered to make the poster. They decided to use the *Alphabet Adventure* book's cover as a reference for their drawing, painting, and writing. I observed and documented children drawing and painting the ship's hull, writing and painting letters, and assembling the final three-dimensional poster (see Figures 9.49 and 9.50). The completed poster included a title and a ship full of lowercase letters traveling on a body of water and was displayed outside our room by the marquee.

LEARNING FROM DOCUMENTATION OF CHILDREN'S DRAMATIC PLAY: THE OPERATION OF THE MOVIE THEATER

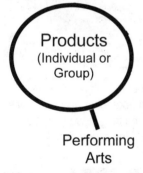

After 4 months of work, the theater was complete and ready to open. The children determined where to locate the auditorium, projection room, concessions, and ticket booth. They selected jobs (i.e., concessionaire, concierge, ticket seller) and viewed a training video (i.e., field experience video). Then all employees eagerly took their positions and performed assigned tasks. The theater became real to the children, as they reenacted roles and performed specific tasks that they had researched and prepared for over the last few months. I observed the action, focused on documenting the depth and intensity of the children's dramatic play, and kept my camera shutter clicking, capturing their actions, facial expressions, and body language (see Figures 9.51–9.53). After the movie theater employees and patrons sold and purchased their concessions and were seated in the auditorium, the projectionist started the featured film, "Alphabet Adventure." The audience—my class—laughed throughout the first showing and insisted that the film be shown several times, so that they could catch dialogue previously missed. The depth of the children's pretend play and

excitement about their movie performances gave me goose bumps, as I reflected on how far they had come, how much they had learned, including increasing their vocabulary, both as a class and individually while engaged in this project (see Figure 9.54).

SHARING DOCUMENTATION THROUGH A CULMINATING EVENT: OUR MOVIE PREMIERE

After 4 months of intense project work, the class began to prepare for the culminating event, a movie premiere. A team created and distributed invitations to the event. We invited family members, teachers, administrators, and community members. Mrs. Noar told the children about the red carpet that is rolled out for the actors at movie premieres. Several children constructed a red carpet complete with stars inscribed with actors' names. Another team constructed standards and ropes to protect the carpet from enthusiastic fans. A group moved all the equipment into the school's large activity room. We created a program for the evening, complete with children's artwork and writing. After Earriana mentioned that we needed tickets, several children created tickets, reproduced them using a copying machine, and cut the tickets apart. We worked steadily for 3 days preparing for the premiere.

Meanwhile, I spent each evening downloading and printing pictures of the children working on the project. I carefully selected photographs that captured key moments in the project and wrote display text to accompany each one. I wanted to express to the project's viewers the life of the project. Therefore, I kept my display text short, moving, and action focused. I wanted the documentation viewers to step inside the project, as they made their way through the displays. I placed my documentation next to the children's documentation (i.e., planning boards, webs, and lists), beside the appropriate pieces of equipment. After all of the documentation, equipment, and refreshments were in place, I checked to make sure that the real movie projector was working. We were ready for the final event.

The premiere was held during the evening, so that most families could attend. As family members and friends came into the school, the children immediately took ownership of the event. Earriana and others became ticket sellers in the box office located in the hallway. T'Nahleg and friends became concierges taking tickets, tearing them in half, and directing family members to the activity room. As patrons reached the activity room, they received the program and a few tips on how to view the children's work and documentation. The activity room became

Figure 9.54. Observing, touching, documenting, replicating, using, and conversing about objects while researching, processing, and reenacting concepts related to the movie theater during dramatic play experiences helped my children "own and use" many new words, including those found on this list.

Cinema	Advertisement	Edit
Concession stand	Uniform	Action
Auditorium	Ticket	Cut
Lobby	Ticket stub	Video Camera
Ticket booth	Signage	Tripod
Projection room	Coin	Popcorn kernel
Storage room	Bill	Popcorn seed
Stock	Change	Oil
Employee	Receipt	Seasoning salt
Boss	Movie schedule	Soda syrup
Supervisor	Computer screen	CO2
Concessionaire	Medium	Tank
Usher	Script	Hoses
Concierge	Poster	Spigot
Projectionist	Production	Nozzle
Ticket seller	Film	Lever
Concessions	Trailer	Switch
Counter	Credits	Projector
Price	Scene	Control Panel
Cash register	Prop	Disc tray
Display	Role	Film strip
Customer	Lines	Cup holder
Patron	Actor	Theater seat
Buy	Director	Safe
Sell	Writer	Elevator
Service	Shoot	Screen

Reports/
Presentations

Language

Products
(Individual or
Group)

Figure 9.55. Trea Vion helped his mom find his star and told her how he had traced around a star stencil with a marker, cut on the resulting lines with scissors, and wrote his name all by himself.

Figure 9.56. Semaj excitedly described for Jaylin, his brother, how the movie projector worked. He enjoyed showing how to push buttons and turn the film discs. Jaylin was impressed by Semaj's presentation and the film projector.

Figure 9.57. Ben and his grandmother observed the candy display and accompanying documentation. Ben named for his grandmother several kinds of candy made by the class. They then purchased a few of his favorite candy bars from the concession stand and took their seats.

Figure 9.58. Earriana and her mother moved around the room carefully viewing products, photographs, and narratives. Earriana enthusiastically described the project work, while her mother viewed the work and read the accompanying narratives either out loud or silently.

a living museum and theater. Children pointed out to family members what they had made, their pictures in photographs, and described their work as in Figures 9.55–9.57. Adults focused on viewing the work, photographs, and accompanying documentation (see Figure 9.58). Many adults stated that they did not know that young children could do so much.

As patrons snacked on food from the concession stand and finished viewing the exhibit, I announced the entrance of the actors, who lined up at the door and entered via the red carpet. The audience applauded. I thanked our families and friends for their support and introduced and started our 5-minute movie, "Alphabet Adventure." There was laughter and applause throughout the movie. We showed it again . . . just in case someone missed something. After the final showing, the children stood proudly as they received several rounds of applause.

The evening was a celebration and sharing of learning with our families and friends. It was a culminating event that brought joy to my heart, as I watched my empowered young students share what they had accomplished . . . some of which many people did not know that they were capable of doing. Thus, project viewers were amazed by my students and their work on an in-depth study about a movie theater. My students became experts on a topic, sharers of knowledge with adults and other children. They became children who know the power of learning and are able to be colearners with anyone. . . . This is what I celebrated deep within my heart late that evening, as I reflected on what I had just experienced.

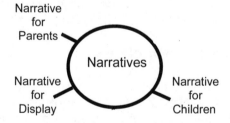

REFLECTIONS ON THE MOVIE THEATER PROJECT'S DOCUMENTATION

What people see through an open window, such as a window on a learning experience, can be as diverse as the people looking through the window, just like the different points of view seen in the doll-drawing experience in Chapter 3. People's experiences, expectations, and roles, among other things, influence their perspectives on learning and learning experiences, such as the Movie Theater Project. In order to sample these different points of view, I asked a colleague, my principal, a coteacher, two parents, and a Yellow 2 student to reflect on our project and its accompany-

ing documentation. All of these project viewers observed the children's work in progress, heard the children talk about their work, and attended the movie's premiere. Everyone, except for Mr. Shernak, reviewed photographs of the project, right before writing (or dictating by Corey) their comments.

I invite you to reflect on each viewer's perspective and consider what each person saw through an open window on learning via the Movie Theater Project's documentation. In order to guide your reflections, I have provided a few questions to consider when reading an individual's reflection. These questions are not inclusive, just starters to help you reflect from your own perspective, as you look into a window on learning.

A Colleague's Point of View

Tammy Shinkey teaches preprimary students in Yellow 1, a classroom adjacent to mine at Valeska Hinton Early Childhood Education Center. She uses project work within her classroom. I often dialogued with Miss Shinkey about my students and my teaching, including our work on the Movie Theater Project.

> Premiere night was truly inspiring. . . . What sticks most in my mind was the ownership the children took in their work. They were the experts . . . the ones doing the teaching in the room, describing and demonstrating how everything worked. The learning was evident in the documentation and dispositions of the students. There was pride, excitement, and awe on the faces of the adult family members, as they saw laid out before them the empowerment of young children through project work.
> —Tammy Shinkey, Early Childhood Teacher, Yellow 1, Valeska Hinton Early Childhood Education Center

Reader Reflection

- In what ways do projects empower young children, according to Miss Shinkey's reflection?
- What is the value of teachers sharing documentation with others, including colleagues, families, and community members?

A Principal's Point of View

Dr. Beth Bussan is the principal at Valeska Hinton Early Childhood Education Center. The Movie Theater Project occurred during her first year at our school. She is responsible for evaluating my performance, guiding curriculum, and providing resources for instruction, among other things.

To witness the power of planning . . . observing the topic emerging . . . notice the development of child engagement . . . see, hear, feel the empowered, enthusiastic, energized, passionate children . . . observe the webbing . . . the emergent awareness, growing knowledge . . . shared experimentation . . . note individual's growth and development as common interests appear . . . as teachers examine the phases of project work . . . skillfully navigating through the webs . . . questioning, examining, facilitating, reexamining . . . linking skills and concepts . . . the exciting field work . . . site visit . . . WOW . . . documenting observations . . . models . . . collecting data . . . growth and development of teamwork . . . flexible parameters . . . a variety of learning styles with adaptations and modifications for individual children . . . miniprojects within the big project . . . Phenomenal Constructions!! resources from a variety of sources constantly at the children's fingertips . . . children in charge of their learning . . . actual movie cinema . . . WOW! [The ellipses are part of the original quote.]

—Dr. Beth Bussan, Principal, Valeska Hinton Early Childhood Education Center

Reader Reflection

- What evidence of learning did Dr. Bussan see exhibited by the children, their work, and accompanying documentation?
- What are the benefits of including project work in the curriculum, according to Dr. Bussan's reflection?
- What is the teacher's role in an early childhood classroom, according to Dr. Bussan's reflection?
- What are the benefits of sharing documentation with decision makers, such as administrators?

A Coteacher's Point of View

Mike Shernak and I had been coteachers for 3 years when the Movie Theater Project occurred. He taught 60–75 minutes a day with us in Yellow 2, helped facilitate project work, engaged all of our students (especially those with IEPs) in classroom learning experiences, and dialogued with me often about our teaching strategies. He was a part of the Yellow 2 team and a fellow colearner.

As the special education teacher, I found my children reaching new heights through the process of being an integral part of a project that meant so much to them. The work of the children was such that I would have never imagined their being able

to create. The process the kids went through to make connections to their prior knowledge and consequently connecting their knowledge to the work on the project was great!

I saw readiness skills being put into real life action by my kids as they counted, matched, and named colors, and described, identified, and formed letters and shapes. Such concepts as understanding spatial concepts, following directions, and completing a task without prompts increased with my children's love and interest in the Movie Theater Project. I know there were many times we as teachers tried to align or encourage my children to join specific project activities in order to develop specific IEP goals, such as cutting with scissors. It was amazing when I saw progress made in many areas by my children. Their individual enthusiasm for learning increased, and they continually wanted to do more work related to the movie project.

—Mike Shernak, Early Childhood Special Education Resource Teacher, Valeska Hinton Early Childhood Education Center

Reader Reflection

- How does project work benefit young children, including those with special needs, according to Mr. Shernak's perspective?
- What expectations can teachers, like Mr. Shernak, have for children with special needs engaged in project work?
- How can project work be used to meet IEP goals?
- How can IEP goal performance be documented when children are engaged in project work?

Two Parents' Points of View

Cherita Freeman, Ciera's mother, and Theresa Miller, Michaela's mother, were mothers of 4-year-olds who had started in my room and who actively participated in the life of our school, attended family/teacher conferences regularly, and volunteered in Yellow 2 periodically.

I was lucky enough to go to the theater with the kids, when they started the project. I would have to say that they did a remarkable job! They created a very worthy "opponent" for "RAVE" [movie theater]. I am amazed at the skills and abilities of these 3- and 4-year-olds. I not only enjoyed the movie they made, but I was impressed with the props they created and with the way they had the "theater" set up. Everything from the ticket booths to the "Walk of Fame" red carpet at the entrance was done by the children. This was the most enjoyable experience that I have seen from children this age.

—Cherita Freeman, Ciera's mother

I thoroughly enjoyed seeing the children so proudly present their project to their parents and everyone else. They all seemed to have been so motivated and engaged in the making of this project. I can tell by the final presentation and by viewing the pictures that the children worked extremely hard and were very proud of what they had created.

This was a very creative experience for the children to have had. I feel that through direct observation and research, this learning experience was more meaningful to them. They were able to find answers to new questions, so they could build upon the knowledge they already had about a movie theater. I am impressed by the great attention to detail that these preschool children used. I was, and am still, amazed by the determination and effort put forth by each and every student in the construction of this project. Not only did they make everything themselves. . . . They were even the stars of the show!! And they didn't forget the credits!

I believe the students had an enormous amount of fun while also learning about responsibility, decision making, and problem solving through the creation of this Movie Theater Project. It is a remarkable accomplishment of such incredible kids!!

—Theresa Miller, Michaela's mother

Reader Reflection

- According to these parents' reflections, what are children learning in Yellow 2 through project work?
- What insights into the capabilities and development of young children did the movie theater's documentation provide for these parents?
- What action words or verbs did these two parents use in their reflections? How are these verbs related to the power of documentation?

A Yellow 2 Student's Point of View

Statements on Dispositions

Child Self-Reflections

Corey, 3 years old, was a Yellow 2 student and participant in the Movie Theater Project. In particular, he participated in field research, built two seats with cup holders for the theater's auditorium, created a letter and prop, and played the role of the "r" in the "Alphabet Adventure" movie.

I made that! That was me? . . . I made all that? Dang! That is me!

—Corey, Yellow 2 Student
(3-year-old), Valeska Hinton
Early Childhood Center

Reader Reflection

- What dispositions did Corey express in his self-reflection?
- What are the benefits of a teacher sharing documentation, such as photographs of a child's participation in a learning experience, with individual children like Corey?
- What kinds of questions can a teacher ask to help a child, like Corey, evaluate and reflect on his own work?

My Own Reflection

Documentation sometimes keeps me up at night. During the Movie Theater Project, I found myself reflecting on an "aha" moment and what it meant, crafting teaching strategies to move an individual child or my class onto next steps based on evidence provided by my documentation, thinking about how to best open a window onto my students' learning, or just enjoying the proof of the children's growth and learning. The process of documentation along with the documentation itself opened windows for me. Documenting the Movie Project empowered my teaching and enhanced my perspectives on children, families, learning, teaching, and life.

CHAPTER 10

Documentation for Teacher Growth

The Movie Theater Project discussed in Chapter 9 documents the knowledge, skills, and dispositions not only of the children but also of their teacher, Kathy Steinheimer, and the other adults who interacted with the children in this project. Showing (or teaching) others about their children and what is happening in their classroom is a task familiar to most teachers. Teachers do this every day, and this task alone is sufficient in impact to justify the time and energy needed for documentation. This is a valid, worthwhile reason to document. The focus of documentation in this instance is outside the teacher; it is another way to communicate with others. However, the greatest value of documentation may be the opportunity that it provides for the teacher to focus inward, on her own skills and knowledge, and in this way it assists the teacher in improving as a professional. Reflection on their own teaching is a recognized and encouraged method for teachers to develop their skills as professionals (Jalongo, 1991; Jones, 1993). Reflection on a regular basis is a valid way to grow professionally. Loris Malaguzzi (1998) also affirms the value of self-reflection:

> Teachers must possess a habit of questioning their certainties, a growth of sensitivity, awareness, and availability, the assuming of a critical style of research and continually updated knowledge of children. (p. 69)

Teacher reflection has become the centerpiece of a number of educational reform approaches. Teachers of young children will find that there are many models of reflective practice that are applicable to their work. These models are based on the idea that members of a learning community can subject their personal views and practices for critical analysis and that this will result in improved outcomes for children (York-Barr, Sommers, Ghere, & Montie, 2001).

DECISION MAKING

Teaching is a personal process that is often described as a process of continuous decision making. Examples of decisions that a teacher must make include deciding what kind of environment to provide, how lessons and experiences should be structured, when to move on to a new activity, or how an activity should be modified to meet individual needs. As teachers mature and gain experience, they improve that decision-making process. Documentation supports the teacher in making these decisions by focusing on children's knowledge, skills, and attitudes as she collects and provides evidence for reflecting on the effectiveness of that decision making.

Making a good decision depends on the accuracy, relevance, and reliability of the evidence on which the decision is based. Typically in the past, many decisions, such as when to introduce a concept, were made without analysis or consideration of what the children already knew, what they didn't know, what their disposition was to learn the task, or what else was occurring in the classroom. Timing of the introduction of a topic was often determined by a grade-level guideline that may or may not have been appropriate for a specific child or group of children or by a teacher's arbitrary calendar schedule. If a teacher regularly documents children's work, he knows what skills and knowledge the children have, and he can use that to assist in making a decision about what skill is appropriate to be introduced.

When Beth Crider-Olcott first began to document learning in her classroom for 3- and 4-year-olds, she was teaching sorting as a mathematical thinking skill. She had selected materials that enabled children to sort, she organized circle-time activities in which children sorted together, and she interacted with children in play, such as block play, by calling attention to likenesses and differences and the sorting process. When she began to collect evidence of their sorting skills for their portfolios, she discovered that all the examples she had collected were examples of sorting by one attribute, color. In examining the portfolio items that she had collected, she was also surprised to discover that all of her children already knew how to sort by color. This evidence had a powerful influence on her decisions for the rest of the year. She made changes in the toys available for children's play by adding toys that involved sorting by shape, size, or use, and adding more advanced classifying schema, such as farm animals and pets. Activities in circle time focused on sorting items with several attributes instead of only one.

As the variety of opportunities increased for children to do mathematical thinking regarding sorting and classifying, Ms. Crider-Olcott documented how the children responded to the increasing complexity of the tasks. She was able to see the variations in the skill levels of the children. With this information, she then focused on her interaction patterns with individual children. She assisted children who had difficulty sorting according to two attributes by modeling and by talking with them as they thought through the sorting process. She was able to challenge the thinking of children who had mastered sorting according to two attributes by adding additional attributes or adding more complex sorting criteria.

The example of Beth Crider-Olcott and her class's experiences with sorting illustrates how the investment of time and effort in documentation can result in fundamental changes in how the teacher makes decisions. It also shows how these changes are integrated into the classroom and how they result in more effective teaching.

To examine more closely how documentation supports teacher decision making, it is helpful to return to the three windows introduced in Chapter 2—the window on a child's development, the window on a learning experience, and the window for teacher self-reflection.

THE WINDOW ON A CHILD'S DEVELOPMENT

To create a window on a child's development, the teacher uses documentation to examine the individual child's growth and development. This documentation provides insight into the child's knowledge, skills, and dispositions, and serves as a basis for the many important decisions made on a daily and weekly basis. In addition, the teacher often needs to make recommendations regarding placement, referral, or allocation of special resources. The types of documentation that are most helpful for a teacher in this decision-making process may be those that are individually produced or that focus on individual children. These include portfolio items such as samples of the child's drawing, writing, constructions, or songs. Anecdotal notes of teacher observations capture skills and knowledge that were demonstrated in the classroom. Developmental

checklists on each child are, obviously, extremely valuable in decision making in this window.

Decision Making in Action

Of the various types of documentation, children's products provide an especially rich source of information about their development, especially when accompanied by anecdotal notes that describe the process of making that product. Products enable the teacher to make judgments about the quality of the child's work by comparison with products of other children the same age. This is useful for planning lessons and selecting materials and resources. In addition, the teacher develops an understanding of the unique ways in which children approach problems and learn concepts.

In the following example from the Bicycle Project, teacher Jolyn Blank collected the work of Patience and Samuel for their portfolios and recorded her observations of how they approached the new task by working through it on their own and how they sorted out their knowledge.

Today I introduced the bike parts I collected from a local bicycle repair shop. The children got their hands on the parts and studied them carefully. They eagerly began drawing them. Samuel and Patience told Mrs. Boos, "We don't need any help." They then became immersed in their drawing. Patience put extreme care into her drawing of the chain and the chain wheel and then decided to create a second draft. In her second draft, the chain was connected to the chain wheel. Although this was not the case on the parts displayed on the table, she represented that she knew how they were assembled on the bike.

This documentation provided an insight into how Patience liked to work. Ms. Blank realized that Patience liked to figure things out on her own and would carefully work and rework an idea. The next time Ms. Blank made a decision about how to plan a learning experience in which Patience was involved, she added opportunities for Patience to approach learning in this way. The combination of the teacher's anecdotal notes and the product, her drawing, provided this insight.

Many teachers in this book have reported that increasing their documentation enabled them to do a better job of making decisions about whether to introduce new content and skills or reinforce concepts with additional practice. This "teaching to Vygotsky's zone of development," as described in Chapter 1 (refer to Figure 1.3) has enabled them to be more efficient. An example of this is Michelle Didesch's experience with a 4-year-old who was interested in learning to write. Ms. Didesch had been carefully documenting this child's progress in understanding the writing process. She knew that the child understood that writing had a purpose, that writing was done by using letters in a specific order. Ms. Didesch also realized that the child was beginning to understand that there was a relationship between letters and sounds. One day, the child was playing in the housekeeping area, pretending to be a new mother. She came to Ms. Didesch and asked her to make a sign. She wanted it to say, "I just had a baby!" Ms. Didesch had a decision to make. She could write the sign for the child, she could write the words for the child to copy, or she could encourage the child to try invented spelling. Her documentation assisted her decision making. Ms. Didesch told the child that she could figure out the letters by listening to the sounds. By slowly saying the words with her teacher, the child wrote, "I jst hd a babe." From that point on, the child tried to write with invented spelling.

Had Ms. Didesch not documented this child's progress toward writing, she might have responded by relying on her knowledge of the typical development of 4-year-olds and responded by making a sign for the child. Challenging a child to painstakingly sound out each letter at this age could have been developmentally inappropriate and damaged the disposition to want to write. For many 4-year-olds, who are just learning that there are such things as letters, a model to copy would also have been an age-appropriate response. Because of her documentation, Ms.Didesch was able to make the right decision for that child at that time and encouraged her skill development.

Decisions that inform the teacher about one child's development do not always have to be based on observations or products created by the child alone. A child's participation in a group can also reveal individual knowledge, skills, and dispositions and provide information on the ability of the child to work with others. Parents often provide documentation of what the child does at home, which can also assist the teacher in making decisions about an individual child.

Documentation can lead to much more informed decisions about educating individual children than can individualized information that comes from standardized tests. Information from group-administered standardized achievement tests usually provides a profile of a child's knowledge and skills at a particular point in time. However, because results are not known for some time, the profile is often not up-to-date or specific enough to inform day-to-day decisions.

THE WINDOW ON A LEARNING EXPERIENCE

As described in Chapter 2 in the discussion of the window on a learning experience, the teacher uses documentation to examine and give others a view of learning processes, such as a project, which involve a group of children. Documentation can show how children's thinking changed and what concepts, skills, and dispositions were applied and/or developed through the course of the experience. The teacher can share the impact of the experience with others, such as other children, parents, school administrators, and members of the community. This enables all constituencies to examine the effectiveness of a learning experience. The teacher makes many important decisions before, during, and after each learning experience in which the children are engaged. Here are some questions frequently asked by teachers and others when making decisions about project work:

- Are children engaged in meaningful learning?
- Are there opportunities to develop language, literacy, and numeracy?
- Are there opportunities to practice thinking skills such as problem solving?
- Are children learning to work together?
- Are children learning to use traditional library references?
- Are children learning to interview experts, survey, experiment, and observe on site?
- Are children representing what they know by drawing, writing, building, or discussing?
- Are children developing dispositions to question and seek answers and school skills?

Some types of documentation that come directly from the learning experience are especially helpful. These enable the teacher to direct the experience to maximize the knowledge acquired and the skills developed. Webs completed throughout a project or unit of study assist the teacher in identifying what knowledge children are gaining. The written and verbal language of songs provides insight into growth in both knowledge and skills as well as in vocabulary and the ability to use language to represent learning. An observant teacher can assess children's knowledge when they make and use materials and equipment to construct play environments representing a real place, and when they represent their ideas with blocks, Legos, or sculpture. Additional experiences can then be provided to extend learning. Observation of details and words to describe these details in children's drawings and paintings reveals their growth in knowledge about topics and provides an opportunity for the teacher to see if children are incorporating new vocabulary. Displaying Time 1 and Time 2 versions of the same drawing together provides especially strong evidence of children's learning while it demonstrates the effectiveness of the experience to stimulate that learning. As these are collected during the process of the experience, they also guide the experience.

The best type of documentation for answering questions about the process of a learning experience, however, may be narratives, those various ways in which children and teachers tell the story of the experience. History boards with photos, books for parents, videos, notes to accompany displays, teacher journals, and project journals are often interesting, thought-provoking, and persuasive. They enable the teacher and children to trace the trail of their learning and see how decisions affect outcomes at various points in the process. Group learning experiences provide unique opportunities for children to learn how to work together. Group interaction skills include how to listen to each other, how to give and receive feedback, and how to cooperate to achieve a common goal. Narratives can provide information about the effectiveness of an experience in developing these skills.

Decision Making in Action

An example of how narrative documentation assists the teacher in monitoring the development of group interaction skills is present in this passage, also from the Bicycle Project. It is an excerpt from a narrative written by Suzi Boos and Jolyn Blank describing the progress of their project.

> We have been working on a wall story about bikes. During a small-group discussion, Raymond developed the writing structure for a story: "_____ likes to ride _____ (descriptive phrase)." We began to use our end of the day whole-group meeting as an opportunity to critique the work they had done. We worked on the book over a period of time. A sample of the children's suggestions for improvement is documented here in reference to certain children's work.

Work: Brittney Likes to Ride in the Spring

Justin M: It's pretty.
Justin D: Good drawing.
Teacher: What do you suggest Brittney could change if she did her page again?
Justin D: Change this to brown. (Justin pointed to a drawing of a puddle colored blue)
Ariane: Yeah, it's a mud puddle.

Work: Sarah Likes to Ride and Do Wheelies

Lakeshia: Sarah is the best drawer. She did a good job on the street and took her time.
Justin D: That's what a street looks like!
Ariane: She needs to put the clouds and the sun in.

This was the children's first experience with doing this. It was a powerful way to involve children in reexamining and reflecting on their work and motivated some of them to revise and increase their own expectations for the quality of their work. This was also the teachers' first experiences with this. We found it very beneficial and will continue to use this technique.

This teachers' narrative provides a window on the learning experience and how it enabled the teachers to see how one strategy, making a wall story, provided an opportunity for children to develop the skills of giving and receiving feedback. The teachers were able to review how the strategy contributed to promoting the group interaction skills they desired. The same piece of documentation also enabled the teachers to reflect on their own decision to incorporate the strategy into the project. This is teacher self-reflection, which is the focus of the next window.

THE WINDOW ON TEACHER SELF-REFLECTION

In the window on teacher self-reflection, the teacher focuses on his own knowledge and skills and on his role. The teacher uses the documentation to reflect on how his teaching might be strengthened, improved, or modified. Decisions in this area can have a profound effect on children's learning. As the teacher documents and reflects on the documentation, he becomes a better teacher as the results or lack of results of his teaching become visible. If the teacher improves his knowledge and skills while working with one child or one experience, these can carry over from child to child and class to class, affecting many children. Thus documentation, as shown in the web in Chapter 3 (refer to Figure 3.1) and in Chapters 4 through 8, has enormous potential for having an impact on education. Decisions in this window are important decisions.

Most types of documentation can be used by the teacher in some way to examine her teaching and improve its quality and effectiveness. An obvious place for a teacher to start would be to look at children's products. The teacher might ask herself, "What are the children producing or not producing?"

Here are some questions teachers can ask themselves about their own development as teachers:

- Do I understand child development and plan to meet unique needs and potentials?
- Do I create a safe, secure learning environment for all children by showing appreciation of and respect for the individual differences and unique needs of each member of the learning community?
- Do I employ a variety of methods to systematically observe, monitor, and document children's activities and behavior, analyzing, communicating, and using the information to improve my work with children, parents, and others?
- Do I promote all domains and organize the environment to best facilitate learning?
- Do I use multiple teaching strategies for meaningful learning and social cooperation?
- Do I design and implement developmentally appropriate learning experiences that integrate within and across the disciplines?
- Do I use multiple teaching strategies, using a variety of practices and resources to promote individual development, meaningful learning, and social cooperation?
- Do I work with and through parents to support children's learning?
- Do I regularly analyze, evaluate, and strengthen the quality and effectiveness of my work?
- Do I work work as a leader and collaborator in the professional community to improve programs and practices for young children and their families?

These questions come from a summary of the nine, standards for National Board Certification as an early childhood/generalist (National Board for Professional Teaching Standards, 2002, pp. 5–6). These questions can also be used to select and organize documentation for the purpose of providing evidence of professional knowledge, skills, or competencies as delineated by an agency, organization, or supervisor. In this way, documentation can not only assist the teacher in reflecting upon her own professional development but enable her to demonstrate her expertise to others.

Decision Making in Action

In the following two excerpts from Dot Shuler's journal of the project they did on rocks in her second-grade class, you can see how Ms. Shuler followed the progress of her class toward the goal of "using references to gain information" and then "using information in representations."

> While silent reading this morning, Troy also found a hardness scale of sorts. It showed talc on one end and a diamond on the other. They're beginning to discover the information without my telling them a thing. I am so proud of them!
>
> From the journals that were read aloud today, we had a story about the softness of talc, one about the three kinds of rocks, and one about the layers of the earth—all of them were the result of silent reading. They are discovering on their own!

In the next passage, her journal shows how she had been evaluating the quality of the work they were producing and had concerns about it. She felt that they did not understand the importance of quality, so in response she opened a discussion of the problem.

> One day this week, we stopped for a class discussion on the quality of work and its importance in representations like graphs. I just discussed it, with concern and interest. They said they understood, and upon going back to centers, two asked me if they could do their graph over.

The result of her calling attention to her goals resulted in children's redoing their work voluntarily. When deciding what to do in future experiences, Ms. Shuler will most likely alter her instructions to address this issue before work begins.

Mary Jane Elliott shares the following reflection on her teaching. It is a narrative of a conversation that she had with her students after she showed them a documentation board on the Apple Project that they did in her kindergarten. She had prepared the display for presentation to a professional audience.

> Erica raised her hand and said, "You know, Mrs. Elliott, that all of those ideas on the board were the children's. We did the investigations, and those were our words you typed and put on the board. The only thing you did was go around and take pictures!" This was the best compliment I have ever received about my teaching. Indeed, the work on the board was the project work designed and directed by the children themselves. I was a colearner and a facilitator. That one of my children actually recognized my role for what it was still astounds me!

After this reflection, it is very likely that Ms. Elliott will again decide to put her children in charge of their own learning.

Both of the previous examples of documentation supporting teacher self-reflection resulted in insight into the effectiveness of teaching strategies and benefited these teachers and the children in their care. Other teachers also gained from these insights through discussions in which they vicariously experienced the decisions made. Another way that teacher reflections can be shared with other teachers and administrators is through history books and displays. All of these methods of sharing documentation help others see the teacher as a learner who is growing professionally and encourage colleagues to reflect on their own teaching.

PUTTING TOGETHER A TEACHER PORTFOLIO

How documentation supports teacher growth is demonstrated in the portfolio process for National Board Certification. Teachers applying for certification with the National Board for Professional Teaching Standards (NBPTS) commit to documenting and analyzing their teaching for a specific purpose, NBPTS certification. Applicants, commonly known as candidates, use a clearly defined and detailed portfolio format that includes work samples, videotapes of classroom practices, documentation of accomplishments outside the classroom, and accompanying narratives answering specific questions. The candidates' completed portfolios are scored using set criteria. Studying and analyzing is inherent to the National Board for Professional Teaching Standards portfolio preparation process. The purpose of the portfolio is to provide evidence as to how the teacher embodies their teaching standards (NBPTS, 2002). The portfolio documents the candidate's practice of and commitment to the National Board's five core propositions:

Teachers are committed to students and their
    learning.
Teachers know the subjects they teach and how to
    teach those subjects to students.
Teachers are responsible for managing and monitoring student learning.
Teachers think systematically about their practice
    and learn from experience.
Teachers are members of learning communities. (p. 3)

In addition to developing portfolios, candidates complete five exercises, essay tests based on applying knowledge within specific content areas. The NBPTS certification process requires a commitment of 1 to 3 years, depending on when certification is achieved. Many candidates utilize mentors, who are National Board certified in their certificate areas, to critique their portfolio entries and encourage them to continue on when the process becomes tedious or overwhelming. These mentors and fellow candidates often form a core group and serve as candidates' professional learning communities during and after the completion of the certification process.

Collecting and analyzing documentation of children's learning is essential to the National Board Certification process. Candidates collect children's work samples and use anecdotal notes to record details concerning the learning experiences that produced the work samples the child's specific actions, accompanying child comments, and signs of dispositions for learning. In addition, the candidate may record her own thoughts on the work samples and related learning experiences in a teacher journal. The candidate uses this raw documentation to analyze her teaching as she answers questions that require her to, among other things, assess the child's strengths, interests, and needs; identify effective and ineffective teaching strategies related to the work samples; and consider next steps in the child's development and/or acquisition of knowledge, concepts, or skills, along with accompanying teaching strategies. The process of revisiting and thoroughly analyzing the raw documentation multiple times helps the candidate to become aware of her own teaching practices and how they relate to the NBPTS.

In addition to collecting documentation related to specific children's learning, the candidate documents specific learning experiences and his role in those experiences by videotaping his teaching and the children's participation in the learning experiences. The candidate benefits from carefully reviewing the videotaped learning experiences and documenting them with a transcript of verbal comments and accompanying descriptions of the children's and candidate's actions. Placing comments and behavioral descriptions on sticky notes that can be rearranged into specific categories (i.e., child self-reflections, evidence of a particular learning goal) helps the candidate begin to assimilate the raw data and use it as documentation when answering specific portfolio questions. In addition, he may jot down key reflections in his teacher journal and/or review his videotape with his professional learning community. The candidate uses the videotape and accompanying raw documentation for many purposes, including assessing the children's understanding of knowledge, concepts, and skills presented or practiced during the learning experience; identifying challenges and opportunities inherent to the learning experience; and assessing teacher strategies used during the learning experience. This intense analysis and reflection on a single learning experience helps the candidate assess his teaching practices and prepare to write the necessary documentation narratives that will accompany his videotape and serve as evidence for his ability to meet NBPTS.

Teacher growth is inherent to collecting and analyzing documentation during the NBPTS portfolio creation process. Collecting documentation and utilizing it to systematically assess children's learning, guide instruction, identify teaching strengths and needs, and share with mentors, fellow candidates, and NBPTS assessors increases the candidate's knowledge of pedagogy, content, and teaching strategies. This analysis improves teaching practices, increases abilities to reflect on one's teaching, and enhances dispositions for teaching and learning. Teachers are encouraged to partake in the process and begin a journey of awareness, reflection, and growth as professionals.

LOOKING AT DOCUMENTATION COLLABORATIVELY

Sharing documentation with other teachers is a productive way to support teacher growth. Documentation has become an integral part of group reflection and teacher portfolios for professional learning communities. A professional learning community asks each teacher to share her professional expertise, insight, and creativity with her colleagues as they describe individual children's work and play. The community learns continuously as insights and experiences are shared, and the school becomes a "learning organization." Within this general format, a number of variations of professional learning communities have been developed. Most of them use some structured way to gather professionals together to share observations, reflect upon the meaning of children's work, and enhance their practice (Roberts & Pruitt, 2003). In this section we will highlight two programs specifically related to early childhood teachers: those of Project Zero and the Chicago Metro Association for the Education of Young Children.

Project Zero and Making Learning Visible

Project Zero, an educational research group at Harvard University, has been involved in a collaborative project, called Making Learning Visible, with the preschools of Reggio Emilia and local schools in Massachusetts. The researchers have studied the effect of the use of documentation on both children and teachers. In *Making Teaching Visible: Documenting Individual and Group Learning as Professional Development* (Project Zero, 2003), they describe the practice of documentation to include the following features:

1. Documentation involves a specific question that guides the process, often with an epistemological focus (focus on questions of learning).
2. Documentation involves collectively analyzing, interpreting, and evaluating individual and group observations; it is strengthened by multiple perspectives.
3. Documentation uses multiple languages (different ways of representing and expressing thinking in various media and symbol systems).
4. Documentation makes learning visible; it is not private. Documentation becomes public when it is shared with learners, whether children, parents, or teachers.
5. Documentation is not only retrospective, it is also prospective. It shapes the design of future contexts for learning.

Their research has shown the rich opportunity for adult and child growth through reflection on child work.

Chicago Professional Learning Communities

The Chicago Metro Association for the Education of Young Children (AEYC), under the leadership of Tom Layman and funded by the McCormick Tribune Foundation, has developed a program for professional learning communities in 10 early childhood centers in Chicago. Tom Layman contrasts their professional learning communities approach with a more "traditional approach," in which administrators decide where teachers are weak and bring in outside experts or trainers. He says,

> The traditional approach looks for teachers' weaknesses, while the professional learning community approach builds on their strengths and encourages teachers to define areas where expertise is needed. A professional learning community approach challenges teachers to be insightful and creative, and its teachers generally meet the challenge.
>
> Another difference is that the traditional approach, depending on outside trainers, often recommends standardized or generalized teaching practices, that may or may not work in particular situations, while the professional learning community approach creates unique teaching strategies based on children's unique strengths and needs. (Chicago Metro AEYC, 2004, np)

Teachers in professional learning communities find that listing desired and highly valued child outcomes is an important first step toward achieving them. But it can only work if they take two additional steps:

1. They must find ways to engage the mind and imagination of each child in their program.
2. They must find time for teachers to meet regularly to examine children's work and play.

Octavia Durham and Dexter Smith, who worked with early childhood programs in developing communities of practice, describe their process in this way:

> A Professional Learning Community is a group of teachers and other staff at a school or center who meet regularly to examine individual children's work and play, and brainstorm possible next steps. They share guesses and insights about individual children's knowledge and interests, and plan (or experiment with) new activities designed to take children to the next level. Over time, they develop a shared set of teaching strategies that have worked before and might work again—depending on the children and circumstances encountered on each new day. They become seasoned professionals. (Chicago Metro AEYC, 2004, np)

Chicago Metro AEYC has identified three key elements to effective professional learning communities in early childhood programs:

- Emergent Curriculum—Building on children's interests
- Child Outcomes Orientation—Extending activities to achieve learning goals
- Shared Documentation—Meeting to examine a child's work and play

Each of these works to support the others, as shown in the diagram in Figure 10.1.

Figure 10.1. Three keys of a professional learning community.

Key 1: Emergent Curriculum. This is an approach to curriculum that takes advantage of children's interests and curiosity and is flexible enough to change based on children's interests and knowledge. Teachers observe children to learn what they are interested in and what they know about it. Then they find ways to help children pursue their interests and learn more about them. Using an emergent curriculum does not exclude the use of teacher-directed activities, whole-class learning experiences, or the introduction of topics that the teacher feels are worthwhile for children to learn, but ideally such activities should be related to children's interests or current projects.

Documentation is an essential part of emergent curriculum. It is critically important for teachers to document what children do as they pursue their interests. This documentation is then shared with other teachers and parents as evidence of learning and as the starting point for planning new activities.

Key 2: Child Outcomes Orientation. Reaching consensus on learning goals for children—and making those goals explicit—is one of the keys to an effective professional learning community. However, while programs often embrace all of the outcomes listed in published frameworks or "early learning standards" (usually more than 100 items), no teacher can focus on all of those outcomes at once.

It is important for the entire staff of a center or school to meet periodically (perhaps quarterly) to choose a few learning outcomes for special attention over the next several weeks. This discussion helps teachers become more aware of their own values for children's learning, and it helps them think about differing values that colleagues or parents might have. The child outcomes chosen at these quarterly meetings will provide focus for teacher observations and discussions in the coming weeks.

Key 3: Shared Documentation Meetings. The heart of a professional learning community is its regularly scheduled teacher meetings to share documentation. These structured meetings last from 30 to 45 minutes. The entire staff does not need to be present, but each meeting should include the entire teaching teams from two to four classrooms, in order to have enough people for brainstorming. A facilitator is chosen to guide the meeting, using the format of a "tuning protocol" (Allen & McDonald, 2003). A form for the tuning protocol, which serves as an agenda for a documentation meeting, is provided in Chapter 13. All teaching team members are treated as equals in these meetings. Aides and volunteers are able to collect documentation and present it to the group.

Figure 10.2 shows a group of teachers in a professional learning community meeting using the tuning protocol.

At each meeting, one teacher presents documentation she has collected on one child, and poses a question for brainstorming by her colleagues. She usually asks for ideas on (a) *next steps to build on the child's interests* as reflected in the documentation, so the child achieves deeper knowledge or more complex skills in that area; or (b) *next steps to pursue a particular learning outcome* with the child, in light of what the documentation reveals.

After describing the child's work and play and posing her question, the teacher listens quietly, perhaps making notes, while her colleagues brainstorm possible answers to her question. This is not planning; the teachers are simply imagining some possibilities for future curriculum or new teaching strategies. At the end, the teacher who posed the question makes a brief response and thanks her colleagues. She might not try any of their suggestions, but the entire group leaves with a deeper understanding of one child, and a number of ideas for the future.

MAKING REFLECTION A PRIORITY

A critical element in the use of documentation for decision making is time to reflect. In Chapter 12, there are ideas for teachers of how this can be ac-

Figure 10.2. Professional learning community meeting.

complished in the section "Setting Aside Time for Reflecting About Documentation." Time is needed to reflect on the documentation and to organize displays; teachers also need time to discuss with and provide input to one another through professional learning communities.

Administrators who schedule planning and preparation periods so that teachers can meet together and who provide materials and space for documentation encourage teachers to document. These administrators are likely to be rewarded by improved quality of decision making in their programs and greater progress toward meeting their goals for children and families.

CHAPTER 11

Documentation as Assessment: Building Credibility

credibility: —1. The quality, capability, or power to elicit belief.
—*American Heritage Dictionary*, (2000)

In the previous chapters we have seen how documentation provides three windows for viewing the educational process, how the teacher can create those views, and how they can be used to inform instruction. However, documentation can also have a far-reaching impact outside of the classroom. Therefore, if we are to retain the opportunity to teach in ways we know are best for young children, we must also make use of the potential of documentation to help those outside the classroom understand the effectiveness of active, child-sensitive, meaningful learning experiences. "What happened in school today?" is the question that Lilian Katz raises in the Foreword to this book. She reminds us that fostering a beneficial relationship between the school and the parent is only one of the reasons for documentation. Documentation is also a vehicle to increase the understanding by the outside world of the merits of high-quality early childhood education. How then can we, as educators, use documentation to inform those on the outside of the school about the how, why, and what children are learning, so that they can answer Professor Katz's question with some confidence?

It may be helpful for readers to create an image of a school with the three windows, and then imagine themselves backing away and looking at the school from afar. From this vantage point, the school is surrounded by other buildings, other institutions, and by a community with diverse people who have multiple needs and beliefs. We can see children, staff, and families with a variety of attitudes and points of view entering and exiting the school. We see those outside who do not enter the school, and we realize they also have expectations and philosophies about the school and education.

This image is a metaphor for the situation our schools are currently experiencing. The world outside the school is engaged in turmoil with discussion and debate about school reform, evidence-based assessment, national and state standards, and statewide testing. At the same time, leaders in many states are seeking support for innovative initiatives such as universal preschool. For this reason, it is important that the process of documentation have credibility; that is, that those outside of daily classroom activities have confidence that what they are viewing in the children's work is indicative of their growth and development; that information is being gathered in a systematic, reliable way; that children are receiving equal opportunities to demonstrate their knowledge and skills; and that valid interpretations are being made. Early childhood teachers must have a firm grasp of the complexity of assessment and evaluation, both to make sure that the documentation process informs their own teaching and also to be able to converse knowledgeably with others of divergent backgrounds and outlooks.

DEFINING ASSESSMENT

How does the term *assessment* relate to documentation, as described in this book? Assessment is defined by the National Association for the Education of Young Children (Bredekamp & Rosegrant, 1995) as

> the process of observing, recording and otherwise documenting the work children do and how they do it, as a basis for a variety of educational decisions that affect the child, including planning for groups and individual children and communication with parents. (p. 11)

Assessments typically take either a *quantitative* or a *qualitative* perspective (Losardo & Notari-Syverson, 2001).

> From a **quantitative perspective**, assessment is viewed primarily as an objective measurement process that results in a numerical representation of children's behaviors and abilities. The process begins with the identification of well-defined target behaviors, which are usually tested in pre-specified

and standardized conditions. From a **qualitative perspective**, assessment is viewed as the documentation of more complex and holistic behaviors as they occur in the natural environments. Methods such as observations, interviews, and questionnaires provide information on qualitative aspects of behaviors rather than mastery of skills. (p. 14; boldface in original)

Performance assessment, another frequently used term, refers to a type of qualitative educational assessment in which the judgments made are based on a child's performance, such as behavior or products (Stiggins, 1994). Yet another frequently used term is *authentic assessment*. "Assessment is authentic when we directly examine student performance on worthy intellectual tasks" (Wiggins, 1990, p. 1).

All of these terms and their definitions apply to the types of documentation explained in this book, although many early childhood teachers may not be accustomed to thinking of classroom documentation as a type of assessment. Tynette Hills (1992) points out that when early childhood teachers are asked what they associate with assessment, they typically list such things as testing, screening, observation, records, and report cards. They seem to take a view of assessment primarily in quantitative terms. "Distressingly often, they speak of assessment methods that are incongruent with the goals and objectives of their programs" (p. 44).

There are many reasons to assess, and it is important to remember to identify the purpose of assessment when discussing assessment issues. Hills (1992) describes assessment as *formal* or *informal,* with formal assessment including readiness, developmental screening tests, criterion-referenced achievement tests, and developmental assessment tests that have high reliability and validity. Formal assessments are typically based on a quantitative perspective. According to Losardo and Notari-Syverson (2001), they provide "information on a preset content and have specified guidelines for administration. Information is usually collected on a one-time basis and compared with normative data. Standardized tests belong in this category" (p. 15). On the other hand, informal types of assessment, according to Hills (1992), includes observation, parent reports, error analysis of children's work, structured observations, teacher-made tests, and analysis of work samples. She concludes:

> Informal types of assessment, done systematically and well, can serve all purposes except the purpose of identifying and diagnosing children with special needs. . . . In fact, informal methods should be the primary form of assessment in early childhood programs to assure that teaching and assessing are complementary and developmentally appropriate approaches are employed. (pp. 48–49)

One of the goals of this book is to open teachers' eyes to additional opportunities for assessing the learning of young children and to give teachers the confidence to use documentation of what children say, what they make, and what they do as evidence of their learning.

CURRENT PRESSURES FOR ACCOUNTABILITY AND PERFORMANCE ASSESSMENT

The enactment of the No Child Left Behind Act (NCLB) in 2001 has brought a great deal of pressure for accountability to bear on public schools. "It is widely believed that tangible rewards or punishments will provide strong incentives for schools, teachers, and children to improve their performance" (Bowman, Donovan, and Burns, 2001), and consequently, states are required to have grade-level standards and corresponding assessments to test whether these standards have been met. Schools are required to give children in grades 3 through 8 annual tests in reading and math. Schools that do not make annual yearly progress (AYP) on these tests are held accountable and are in danger of losing state or federal funding. In an effort to boost achievement on these tests, many school districts have begun to prepare children for formal academics at younger and younger ages. And in some cases, standardized tests are being given to young children in an effort to demonstrate efforts to be accountable.

Many early childhood educators are in the difficult position of trying to teach children in ways that are optimal for children's learning, while avoiding the pressure from grade levels above them to teach narrow, academic skills at an earlier age. As one teacher put it, "I feel like I'm being asked to put the roof on the house, before I've even laid the foundation!" They want to use assessment methods that will assist them in determining how to teach the individual children in their classrooms.

GUIDELINES FOR APPROPRIATE ASSESSMENT

In response to the trends for accountability and assessment, major organizations in the field of early childhood education have issued position statements on appropriate assessment for young children. For example, the Division for Early Childhood (DEC) of the Council for Exceptional

Children recently published a chapter on recommended practices in assessment in their new book, *DEC Recommended Practices: A Comprehensive Guide for Practical Application in Early Intervention/Early Childhood Special Education* (Sandall et al., 2005).

In a joint position statement issued in 2003, the National Association for the Education of Young Children (NAEYC) and the National Association of Early Childhood Specialists in State Departments of Education (NAECS/SDE) published a list of indicators of effective assessment practices:

- Ethical principles guide assessment practices.
- Assessment instruments are used for their intended purposes.
- Assessments are appropriate for ages and other characteristics of children being assessed.
- Assessment instruments are in compliance with professional criteria for quality.
- What is assessed is developmentally and educationally significant.
- Assessment evidence is used to understand and improve learning.
- Assessment evidence is gathered from realistic settings and situations that reflect children's actual performance.
- Assessments use multiple sources of evidence gathered over time.
- Screening is always linked to follow-up.
- Use of individually administered, norm-referenced tests is limited.
- Staff and families are knowledgeable about assessment. (p. 2)

With these indicators, NAEYC and NAECS/SDE assert that professionals have "a shared responsibility to make ethical, appropriate, valid, and reliable assessment a central part of all early childhood programs" (p. 1). These indicators provide a framework for examining documentation practices.

Ethical Principles Guide Assessment Practices

To assess children in an ethical manner, the styles, methods, and content of assessment must become compatible with, rather than at odds with, the behavior and interests of young children. By using authentic assessment to document the learning of children in the natural classroom environment, we avoid pulling them away from the natural setting and/or routine and putting them in artificial situations where they are uncomfortable and may not be able to perform to their potential. "Contrived tasks and materials as well as unfamiliar people and circumstances are not optimal for true appraisals of what children really know and do" (Neisworth & Bagnato, 2005, p. 48).

Ironically, some teachers may believe they are gathering more precise information when they administer a formal quantitative assessment, but they are more likely to get a true picture of what children know and can do by documenting their learning over time in the classroom setting. When the purpose of assessment is to improve learning, authentic assessment practices, such as documentation, are more likely to be useful—and considered ethical.

Assessment Evidence Is Used to Understand and Improve Learning

Documentation is meant to help teachers make decisions about how, when, and what to teach individual children in the class and the class as a whole. In contrast, more formal assessments are designed to compare children, either with a normative standard for a child's age or grade, or with one another. Formal assessments generate a number that can be used to compare the performance of a child to that of other children at one point in time. They compare and rate children, but they do not tell us important information about what children are beginning to know or understand.

When observations take place over time and in the natural classroom setting, teachers may discern patterns in children's learning and behavior, gather accurate evidence of children's performance, and guide them toward experiences that challenge them and lead to progress, rather than teaching skills they are not ready to attempt or those they have already mastered. Documentation practices can help teachers know the children in their classroom better, so they will be better able to plan curriculum and teach them.

Assessments Use Multiple Sources of Evidence Gathered Over Time

As discussed in Chapter 5, commercially produced systems are available to support ongoing observation of young children in the natural classroom environment, such as the *Work Sampling System* (Dichtelmiller, Jablon, Dorfman, Marsden, & Meisels, 2001) and the High/Scope *Preschool Child Observational Record* (COR) (High/Scope Educational Research Foundation, 2003). Curriculum-embedded assessments such as these assure teachers that the information they are gathering will help them make good decisions as they plan for children's group and individual learning experiences. They are meant to be used on an ongoing basis, and they provide teachers with suggested routines for periodically stopping to organize and reflect on the observations they have gathered. These systems are flexible, and teachers who use them are encouraged to incorporate other forms of documentation, such as anecdotal notes and portfolios, which were discussed in Chapter 6. The more ways a teacher finds to document children's learning, and the more points of view she can take into consideration in evaluating the documentation she has collected, the more likely she is to make useful decisions about children's learning.

Assessments Are Appropriate for Ages and Other Characteristics of Children Who Are Being Assessed

Understanding the developmental stages that apply to the children he teaches can help a teacher notice significant moments and products to document when he is with those children. Some commercially available assessment systems include developmental guidelines that are aligned with the items on a checklist, as discussed in Chapter 5. These developmental guidelines can help a teacher fairly determine how to rate a child on a particular checklist item.

In many of today's early childhood classrooms, a teacher may have students from several different cultural and ethnic backgrounds. Learning about these cultures and developing cross-cultural competence (Lynch & Hanson, 2004) will help the teacher better understand and document the learning of the child.

Children who are hearing-impaired, nonverbal, or second-language learners are particularly likely to have difficulty responding to on-demand verbal assessments. By watching these children at play, teachers can gather a great deal of useful information about their abilities, interests, and ways of handling various situations, as well as taking cultural differences into consideration in assessing progress and performance.

Assessment Evidence Is Gathered From Realistic Settings and Situations That Reflect Children's Actual Performance

One of the great strengths of documentation is that it takes place in the natural classroom environment and is applied directly to planning for individual children as well as for the class as a whole. Teachers who practice ongoing documentation are able to observe children's performance in many situations. They can assess whether a child has actually internalized what has been taught, and they can collect evidence of the child's interests and dispositions, as well as knowledge and skills. For example, Ruth Harkema documented the interest of 3-year-old Willie's growing interest in guinea pigs:

When the children voted to study guinea pigs, Willie, new to the class and from a family that speaks Mandarin Chinese, pushed his English word book into my hands and said, "Gilly pig, what is it?" Photographs of the guinea pig's first visit revealed him peeking between other children to satisfy this need to learn and do it quickly (see Figure 11.1). We made sure Willie had time to see, hear, touch, do, ask questions, respond to answers, and create. He was the first child to make a three-dimensional guinea pig (see Figure 11.2). Quick to observe that volunteers were helping children with the glue, he brought his mother to the next class session. She shyly smiled and asked if she could stay, saying that she would dedicate herself to helping Willie. He parked her at a table and proceeded to create a second stuffed guinea pig. During our guinea pig celebration, he hugged and paraded his two very different guinea pigs.

This is an example of how observing children in action can provide an accurate understanding of the child's dispositions, knowledge, and skills. We can see that Willie is a curious child and has a positive disposition for investigating and learning about new things. We see evidence in this anecdote that Willie has an understanding of the value of books and a positive disposition for reading because he turned to his book for information and used it to start a conversation. Even though he does not speak the dominant language of the classroom, he is comfortable with other children and asks for assistance and information from the teacher when he needs it.

We can also see from the photo documentation that Willie also has an accurate understanding of the parts of guinea pig and is able to represent his learning using classroom materials. All of these observations provide insight into Willie's development and information that the teacher can use for planning subsequent learning experiences and teaching strategies. These insights into Willie's development were possible because the assessment of Willie's performance occurred in the natural setting of the classroom environment.

To provide the most accurate assessment of children's performance, documentation should be ongoing and a regular part of the classroom routine. Opportunities to document children's knowledge, skills, and dispositions occur from the moment they arrive in school and until they leave at the end of the day.

In the 1995 guidelines for planning instruction and assessment, Bredekamp and Rosegrant recommend that assessment indicate both "what children can do independently and what they can demonstrate with assistance, because the latter shows the direction

Figure 11.1. Willie joins a group of children petting a guinea pig.

Figure 11.2. Willie holding a three-dimensional representation of a guinea pig.

of their growth" (p. 17). This guideline emphasizes the importance of collecting children's work even when the child is working with another child or is being assisted by the teacher. As shown in the examples provided in this book, it is equally important to indicate in an anecdotal note or narrative accompanying a product whether assistance did occur. One area of learning where this indication is particularly significant is in assessing writing. A child may create a sign

to label a construction that he built. To use the sign as evidence of the child's skills in writing, it is critical that the teacher note whether the sign was copied from a teacher model, whether the teacher helped the child by saying the words slowly as the child chose the appropriate letters, or whether the child wrote the sign independently. When such documentation is carefully dated and includes the context from which the sample emerged, it is valuable for assessment.

Assessment Instruments Are in Compliance With Professional Criteria for Quality

Reliability and Validity. Teachers who use informal assessments may question the reliability and validity of their assessments. These are common concerns with all types of assessment. With careful planning, less formal or constraining assessment programs can be developed to assure objectivity and provide accountability (Gullo, 2005).

Reliability means that an instrument, such as a checklist, can be relied on to measure a child in the same way every time it is used. The reliability of a checklist is increased if other professionals are likely to come up with the same results when they use that checklist to observe the same child.

Validity means that the checklist is measuring what it is intended to measure. Validity is affected by the quality of the checklist design, but it is also affected by the purpose for which the checklist is used. For example, assessing kindergarten-aged children with a checklist that has been developed for use with second graders would not be a valid use of that instrument. Homemade checklists usually do not have data that support the reliability of the checklist. Using only a portion of a checklist or combining parts of two or more checklists are more likely to result in a checklist that lacks validity and/or reliability.

As pointed out earlier in this book, in many of the schools from which examples were collected, there was a comprehensive, performance-based assessment system in place. Checklists were completed at regular intervals, children's work was collected in a systematic way, and there was a planned system for review of the observational data and the children's work. Documentation from projects or other learning experiences provided rich, informative work samples and observational notes that were then incorporated into those processes. Several of the teachers who shared the work of the children in this book used the Work Sampling System. This system has reliability and validity research (Meisels, Liaw, Dorfman, & Fails, 1995), which enables teachers to feel confident about the validity and reliability of the conclusions that they draw from the assessment process. A number of other developmental checklists also have data on reliability, which can be found in the manuals accompanying the checklists.

Avoiding Bias. When using informal methods of assessment, it is important to avoid bias and address the issue of equity and fairness. *Bias* is defined as "any attitude, belief, or feeling that results in, and helps to justify, unfair treatment of an individual because of his or her identity" (Derman-Sparks, 1989, p. 3). Teacher bias can result in inaccurate observations or faulty interpretations of data. According to Cohen, Stern, and Balaban (1997),

> Teachers often have feelings about children whose ethnic, racial, or cultural group differs from their own. Negative or fearful reactions to children in wheelchairs, to children who cannot see or hear, or to children with other disabilities such as those resulting from Down syndrome, cerebral palsy, autism, or spina bifida may arise in teachers. Disapproving opinions about gays and lesbians are sometimes projected on children or children's parents. Teachers may ascribe particular behaviors as acceptable for boys but unacceptable for girls. Bias is at work when a teacher describes an inquisitive boy as "bright" and an inquisitive girl as a "chatterbox." (p. 4)

Bias in assessment can have devastating consequences because it affects teacher decision making. One way teachers can be biased is through embeddedness in their own culture (Greenfield, 1997). As noted earlier, Lynch and Hanson (2004) urge that anyone working with children and families strive to develop *cross-cultural competence*, a way of thinking and behaving that enables members of one cultural, ethnic, or linguistic group to work effectively with members of another. They recommend that professionals develop competence in three ways:

1. By developing self-awareness, an understanding and appreciation of their own culture and how that culture has affected how they think and behave
2. By developing culture-specific awareness and understanding of children and families with whom they work through reading, talking with members of the cultures, and sharing daily lives
3. By learning about cross-cultural communication, the differences between cultures of both verbal and nonverbal communication

Bias can also occur when children do not have an equal opportunity to demonstrate a skill or knowledge. This inequality can come from a child's prior knowledge, cultural experiences, language proficiency, cognitive style, or interests (Lam, 1995). Bias may result when these elements do not match the norms of a classroom. In the types of documentation discussed in this book, assessment can occur in a variety of ways to meet a variety of individual needs in such a way that bias should be reduced. Children are assessed as they are engaged in active, meaningful learning that has relevance to them and their lives. It is possible, however, for teachers not to look for the variety of ways that a child might demonstrate knowledge, for example, by focusing only on one type of documentation, such as language products. In this case, the teacher will need to try other methods of documenting the child's knowledge. The teacher needs to be cautious in concluding that because she has not documented a skill for a specific child, that it is nonexistent. An undocumented skill or area of knowledge should be a warning to the teacher to try another way to document, since the chosen method may not have given the child an opportunity to reveal a skill or knowledge. The teacher also needs to guard against thinking that a child's development in one area, such as verbal fluency, means that he is equally advanced in all other areas, such as mathematics, when this may not be the case. Systematically observing and collecting children's work from each learning area or domain throughout the year can ensure that the teacher will look at the whole child and each skill area independently.

Bias can also occur if a child has not been asked or chosen to participate in a project or learning experience: Engaged problem solving cannot be observed when the child has not had an opportunity to demonstrate it. All children at the early childhood level do not need to be simultaneously involved in all projects or learning experiences in a classroom. All children, however, at some time during the year, need the opportunity to do so and to have their approach to learning thoroughly documented.

Avoiding bias in the assessment process requires teacher commitment and effort. Open collegial relationships in which teachers can reflect together on the documentation can also assist in avoiding bias. It is often easier for someone else to see how bias might have an impact on our decision making.

How Much Is Enough? Teachers often ask, "How much is enough?" when it comes to documenting young children's learning. They wonder, "How many anecdotal notes do I need? How many portfolio items do I need? How much should I write when I write a narrative report on children's learning?" There are really two answers to this: "It depends on the child" and "More is not always better."

Sometimes in their efforts to be thorough, teachers become overzealous about collecting observations and work samples. Their good intentions lead them to several problems. The first issue relates to time. The point of documentation of children's learning is to inform instruction. Excessive documentation can limit the time that teachers have to spend on planning for high-quality individual and group instruction. It's important for teachers to balance the time they spend on documentation with the potential this documentation has to inform instruction. We have known some teachers who have felt that they needed to collect a work sample for every item on the Work Sampling Checklist. It is important for teachers to be certain that they have *observed* instances of the child's performance on a particular checklist item, but there is no need to have a concrete sample for every item. However, if the teacher does not believe that a child is able to perform on a particular indicator, and he wants to share this concern with families and/or colleagues, then he may want to focus on collecting additional documentation related to that indicator. Consequently, the amount of documentation to be collected depends on the questions the teacher has about that child's development.

If a teacher has collected enough observations and samples of a child's work to represent the child's typical development, then he has enough to use in deciding what and how to teach the child and to share with parents and families. Collecting and reviewing observations with a parent, coteacher, or associate teacher can help teachers be assured that they have evaluated the child's performance accurately. After such a review, if a teacher still has questions about a child's ability in a particular area, then he may want to provide the child with additional opportunities to use that ability in a regular classroom activity.

It's better to have one really good sample that represents what the child knows and can do in a particular learning area than it is to have a large quantity of samples of a lesser quality.

Staff and Families Are Knowledgeable About Assessment

When teachers use collections of children's work to document their learning in the natural classroom environment, parents are better able to understand and communicate with the teachers about their child's progress and performance. Letter grades or standardized scores leave parents with a sense of their child's performance or progress, but they do not provide insight into how the child goes about learning, what she is starting to learn and could use help with at home, or what she is not yet ready to learn. Sharing anecdotal notes and documentation through portfolios can be especially helpful in providing this additional information.

Parents can and should be partners in documenting the learning of their children, but this cannot happen unless teachers explain the "why" and "how" of documentation to them. Many teachers meet with parents at the beginning of the year to explain how documentation is used in assessment and to invite parents to join them in creating an accurate picture of their child's learning. Parents are more likely to take an active role in the school when their involvement is focused on their child's learning (Harbin, McWilliam, & Gallagher, 2000).

PART III
How to Document

CHAPTER 12

Organization and Presentation of Documentation

If reading the preceding chapters in this book has convinced you to attempt to document the learning occurring in your own classroom, we want to advise you to approach the process as if you were learning a new skill, such as driving a car. As in learning to drive, the first attempts are slow and each step has to be carefully considered and planned. Integrating comprehensive documentation into a classroom is also a skill that takes time to learn. A driver eventually becomes so skilled and confident that she can drive without consciously thinking about most of the separate tasks, like starting the car. The teacher who works at improving documentation eventually finds that documentation is such an essential part of her teaching that it becomes automatic. This chapter and Chapter 13 provide assistance for those first steps into increased documentation. However, with experience, you will discover many more strategies, especially if you share your work with colleagues.

GETTING READY TO DOCUMENT

Gathering Materials and Equipment

A teacher can prepare for the documentation process by gathering together materials that are helpful for documenting. These include Post-it notes for writing down observations and folders for collecting children's work and anecdotal notes. Some teachers find it helpful to place pens and notepads around the classroom so notes can be jotted quickly without having to leave an area where children are working. The availability of a clipboard for every child ensures that children's thoughts and representations will be captured on field trips and during in-depth investigations of topics in the classroom.

A camera with film is very useful. Any camera with a flash that the teacher feels is easy and comfortable to use will work; however, a 35-mm camera with film speed of 200 will result in good inside and outside shots on the same roll of film. Teachers will want to try different types, speeds, and brands of film to see what works best in their classroom. A zoom feature will enable closer shots without intruding on children's work space. Be sure that batteries are fresh for taking inside shots.

Digital cameras with automatic focus and zoom features are now available with good resolution. These cameras have several advantages. They enable educators to take multiple shots in sequence without worrying about making each shot count so they can still keep their focus on supporting learning. Later the best photos can be saved and the rest deleted, or they can be viewed immediately and retaken to be sure important moments are not missed.

In addition, it is easy to crop, enlarge, and correct lighting and contrast with digital photos. They can be quickly and easily inserted into newsletters, displays, websites, and electronic presentations. Digital photos allow immediate sharing with children, parents, and media. In the long run, digital photos save money and time for schools and centers. In choosing a digital camera, it is important to select one with a high resolution and one that can be used easily.

A battery-operated tape recorder that is small and can be placed inconspicuously near children working will help capture conversations. These recorders have become more affordable and have increased in quality. Recorders with a detachable microphone enable the teacher to place the microphone in the children's work area but start and stop the recorder from a distance. If a teacher wants to record a particular child, a small wireless microphone can be attached to the child to pick up his words, although this technology may be too costly for many. It is important to try out a tape recorder to see if it can record over the high noise level in an early childhood classroom.

Using a video camera at certain times enriches documentation, especially when it is used for studying pedagogy or with professional learning communities. Many digital cameras also have video capabilities. These short clips are surprisingly good for capturing children discussing, constructing, or working. These can be inserted in electronic portfolios or shared in presentations. An added advantage of these video clips is the ease of capturing them. They require no more than the push of a button on a digital camera.

For video that will be studied for nuances of language, nonverbal communication, or children's expression, a more formal setup is usually required. The high noise level in an early childhood classroom also affects videotaping. It is helpful if the video camera has a detachable microphone or the camera purchased is especially selected for this task. The camera also needs to be easy to carry and use and to operate without extra lights in situations of low-level light.

Videotape recorders have also become more affordable and convenient. Full-size camcorders are still available and convenient, because the tapes can be slipped directly into a video cassette recorder (VCR). However, digital video disc (DVD) players are rapidly replacing VCRs, so the convenience of the VHS tapes is not as significant. Video recorders can record on digital tape, and some record on CD or DVD. Digital videotape will be more useful to a teacher who wishes to transfer the video footage into the computer for editing, and the disc will be more useful to a teacher who simply wishes to play what she has recorded directly on a DVD player without editing.

Access to a photocopy machine is so common it is often not considered as a tool for documentation; however, easy access to one enables a teacher to copy children's work that they wish to take home, reduce and enlarge samples so they can be more easily displayed, and make multiple copies of children's books or project history books for children to check out and share at home. If access requires setting aside a special time for a trip to the end of the building or to a photocopy store, teachers will be discouraged from documenting.

A computer with a simple desktop publishing program will enable the teacher to make displays and narratives that look professional. A scanner greatly simplifies the process of making books, displays, and newsletters. It enables the teacher to scan children's work directly into the computer, reduce it so that it is manageable, and share it in a variety of ways. If a multimedia computer system is available, the teacher, older children, or a parent can produce their own multimedia record of projects or other learning experiences. The importance of this material and equipment in the schools of Reggio Emilia is seen in this statement from Vea Vecchi (1998), *atelierista*, in the Diana School:

> Yet, this method takes much time and is never easy. And we know that we have much to learn. The camera, tape recorder, . . . video camera, computer and photocopying machine are instruments absolutely indispensable for recording, understanding, debating among ourselves, and finally preparing appropriate documents of our experiences. (p. 142)

There is no doubt that all of this material and equipment is helpful. They encourage documentation because they enable the teacher to be more efficient and the documentation to look more professional. However, many teachers begin documenting with just a spiral notebook, some notecards, an inexpensive camera, and an organized system for collecting children's work. Chapter 13 includes a list of recommended materials and supplies for documentation, "Getting Ready for Documentation."

Identifying Curriculum Objectives

In preparing to document, it is also important to obtain a copy of the goals and objectives and any curriculum guides. If the teacher is documenting for program evaluation or to demonstrate accountability, he will want to focus on the knowledge, skills, and dispositions that the school district or early childhood program wants children to develop. This will not only focus the documentation but also increase teaching effectiveness. If there is no required curriculum, a teacher might find such information in a purchased curriculum guide, report card, or developmental checklist. If the school uses standardized, group-administered achievement tests, it is important to be aware of the content and skill objectives on which the test is based. These can be found in the manuals for the standardized test. There may be several sources of goals, or several sets of standards. The first step in documenting might be to integrate these into one list so the teacher understands expectations for children or achievement goals (for guidance, see Seefeldt, 2005). A list of goals or standards can then be used not only for documentation but also for guiding selection of materials and learning experiences. An example of such a list is shown in Figure 12.1.

Once goals and objectives are identified, the teacher can think about what types of documentation would best provide evidence of achievement of these goals. A form, "Plan for Documenting and Sharing Students' Achievement of Curriculum Goals and Standards," is provided in Chapter 13 for analyzing standards, curriculum goals, or checklists and thinking about the most appropriate type of documentation to be used. This form can be used by a faculty or professional learning community. For example, if the objective is for children to be able to meaningfully count five objects by the time they leave a 4-year-old prekindergarten program, a teacher could then look at the web showing types of documentation (refer to

Figure 12.1. Benchmark Index, assembled from the Illinois Early Learning Project lists of standards and benchmarks (http://www.illinoisearlylearning.org/standards).

Language Arts

- Understand that pictures and symbols have meaning and that print carries a message.
- Understand that reading progresses from left to right and top to bottom.
- Identify labels/signs in the environment.
- Identify some letters, including those in own name.
- Make some letter-sound matches.
- Predict what will happen next using pictures and content for guides.
- Begin to develop phonological awareness by participating in rhyming activities.
- Recognize separable and repeating sounds in spoken language.
- Retell information from a story.
- Respond to simple questions about reading material.
- Demonstrate understanding of literal meaning of stories by making comments.
- Understand that different text forms, such as magazines, notes, lists, letters, and story-books, are used for different purposes.
- Show independent interest in reading-related activities.
- Use scribbles, approximations of letters, or known letters to represent written language.
- Dictate stories and experiences.
- Use drawing and writing skills to convey meaning and information.
- Listen with understanding and respond to directions and conversations.
- Communicate needs, ideas, and thoughts.
- Seek answers to questions through active exploration.
- Relate prior knowledge to new information.
- Communicate information with others.

Mathematics

- Use concepts that include number recognition, counting, and one-to-one correspondence.
- Count with understanding and recognize "how many" in sets of objects.
- Solve simple mathematical problems.
- Explore quantity and number.
- Connect numbers to quantities they represent using physical models and representations.
- Make comparisons of quantities.
- Demonstrate a beginning understanding of measurement using nonstandard units and measurement words.
- Construct a sense of time through participation in daily activities.
- Show understanding of and use comparative words.
- Incorporate estimating and measuring activities into play.
- Sort and classify objects by a variety of properties.
- Recognize, duplicate, and extend simple patterns, such as sequences of sounds, shapes, and colors.
- Begin to order objects in series or rows.

- Participate in situations involving addition and subtraction using manipulatives.
- Describe qualitative change, such as measuring to see who is growing taller.
- Recognize geometric shapes and structures in the environment.
- Find and name locations with simple words, such as "near."
- Represent data using concrete objects, pictures, and graphs.
- Make predictions about what will happen next.
- Gather data about themselves and their surroundings.

Science

- Use senses to explore and observe materials and natural phenomena.
- Collect, describe, and record information.
- Use scientific tools such as thermometers, balance scales, and magnifying glasses for investigation.
- Become familiar with the use of devices incorporating technology.
- Investigate and categorize living things in the environment.
- Show an awareness of changes that occur in themselves and their environment.
- Describe and compare basic needs of living things.
- Make comparisons among objects that have been observed.
- Describe the effects of forces in nature (e.g., wind, gravity, and magnetism).
- Use common weather-related vocabulary (e.g., rainy, snowy, sunny, windy).
- Participate in recycling in their environment.
- Identify basic concepts associated with night/day and seasons.
- Begin to understand basic safety practices.
- Express wonder and ask questions about their world.
- Begin to be aware of technology and how it affects their lives.

Social Science

- Recognize the reasons for rules.
- Participate in voting as a way of making choices.
- Develop an awareness of roles of leaders in their environment.
- Identify community workers and the services they provide.
- Begin to understand the use of trade to obtain goods and services.
- Recall information about the recent past.
- Locate objects and places in familiar environments.
- Express beginning geographic thinking.
- Recognize similarities and differences in people.
- Understand that each of us belongs to a family and recognize that families vary.

Physical Development and Health

- Engage in active play using gross motor skills.

- Engage in active play using fine motor skills.
- Coordinate movements to perform complex tasks.
- Follow simple safety rules while participating in activities.
- Participate in developmental activities related to physical fitness.
- Exhibit increased endurance.
- Follow rules and procedures when participating in group physical activities.
- Demonstrate ability to cooperate with others during group physical activities.
- Participate in simple practices that promote healthy living and prevent illness.
- Identify body parts and their functions.
- Act independently in caring for personal hygiene needs.
- Use appropriate communication skills when expressing needs, wants, and feelings.
- Use acceptable ways to resolve conflict.
- Participate in activities to learn to avoid dangerous situations.

Fine Arts

- Dance: Investigate the elements of dance.
- Drama: Investigate the elements of drama.
- Music: Investigate the elements of music.
- Visual Arts: Investigate the elements of visual arts.
- Describe or respond to their own creative work or the creative work of others.
- Dance: Participate in dance activities.
- Drama: Participate in drama activities.
- Music: Participate in music activities.
- Visual Arts: Participate in the visual arts.
- Use creative arts as an avenue for self-expression.

Foreign Language

- Maintain the native language for use in a variety of purposes.
- Use and maintain the native language in order to build upon and develop transferable language and literacy skills.

Social/Emotional Development

- Describe self using several basic characteristics.
- Exhibit eagerness and curiosity as a learner.
- Exhibit persistence and creativity in seeking solutions to problems.
- Show some initiative and independence in actions.
- Use appropriate communication skills when expressing needs, wants, and feelings.
- Begin to understand and follow rules.
- Manage transitions and begin to adapt to change in routines.
- Show empathy and caring for others.
- Use the classroom environment purposefully and respectfully.
- Engage in cooperative group play.
- Begin to share materials and experiences and take turns.
- Respect the rights of self and others.
- Develop relationships with children and adults.

Figure 3.1) and think of the types of documentation that could provide evidence of the ability to count to five. Possible documentation might be an anecdotal note of a child's participation in the process of counting the number of children at a table for snack or a dictated narrative about a block construction in which the child counted the blocks. Anticipating the need for documentation by making a list of knowledge or skills to be documented will make this easier. A teacher can also make signs with this information and place them in the classroom where he can see it and remind himself of what to collect.

This may be especially helpful in assuring others that the teacher will be addressing this list of goals and objectives, even though he may be teaching in a different way from his colleagues and may be involving his children in more direct, active, or interactive experiences, as described in Chapter 1.

Beginning with required standards, curriculum, or goals is also important in the selection of a portfolio system. Any portfolio system adopted must be compatible with these requirements. If there is no portfolio system, these requirements can be used to develop a portfolio collection process. In Chapter 13, there are three forms to help you in this process: "Developing a Portfolio System," which asks questions to guide decision making about portfoliios; "Individual Portfolio Items to Be Collected," which guides selection of specific learning area items; and an "Individual Portfolio Item Collection Record," which assists in tracking portfolio item collection.

Many teachers also find it helpful to make multiple copies of blank forms with a list of the names of all the children in their class. The forms can have names down one side and blank columns. When the teacher needs to observe or assess whether each child has mastered a specific skill or concept, she can write the concept in one of the columns and check it off or write a date observed in the square by the child's name. An example of this would be to have a form listing the names of the colors. These are also useful when the teacher wants to collect the same thing from each child, such as in Core Items for a portfolio (see Chapter 6). In Chapter 13, there is also a form, "Portfolio Sharing Plan," for planning how to share a portfolio with parents.

Planning for Documentation

It may be advisable for a teacher to review the web of types of documentation in Figure 3.1. This will help the teacher to keep in mind the variety of ways that she can document and then plan for collecting the documentation. In Chapter 13, there is a form, "Plan for Documenting a Learning Experience," which helps teachers think about documentation of a specific learning experience such as a project. Using the form, teachers anticipate the main events that are likely to occur, what types of documentation would be appropriate, the equipment and materials needed, who will document, and who will be responsible for the duties that the documenter normally does. For example, on a trip to a grocery store, an appropriate type of documentation might be photos of children asking questions and sketching the layout of the store. For this you will need a camera (and film if it isn't digital), batteries, clipboards, and pencils. You will also need someone who is responsible for taking the photos. If you select a teaching assistant to be in charge of taking photos and distributing and collecting clipboards, that aide is not able to keep track of the challenging child that he normally keeps focused. Someone else will need to be assigned that responsibility. If any of the items listed are not there, if the batteries are dead, or if the aide has to attend to the child, then the documentation will not get done and the opportunity to capture the learning experience will be lost.

Many teachers find it helpful to incorporate plans for documenting into their written lesson plans. Three sample lesson plans are provided in Chapter 13. One is based on a time schedule, and the other two are based on weekly planning using domains. Each includes documentation in the planning process. It is not necessary to use these planning forms. They may not fit with your program; however, we have found that lesson plans are the most frequently requested tools during documentation training, so these are shared as a help but not as a prescription.

Another consideration in planning is for the teacher to try to anticipate what she may want to do with the documentation. For example, if a teacher makes an observation that will go into a portfolio as a Core Item, it may be easiest to record that directly on a Core Item sheet instead of on a Post-it note. It is important, however, not to be too narrow during the collection process. Documentation is often used for several purposes later in a learning experience, so sometimes it is better if the documentation is saved in a format that is easily adapted to a variety of uses.

Another consideration in planning for documentation is to capture evidence of children's knowledge and skills at the beginning of an ongoing learning experience such as a project. As explained in Chapter 7, having children make a web or a list of what they know about a topic provides a written record. Some teachers plan on students adding to or altering the web as the learning experience progresses as a visual record of their learning. Recording or writing down the exact words of the children in statements and questions at the beginning and end of a learning experience also enables assessment of change in vocabulary and understanding.

Setting Reasonable Goals for Documenting

When teachers are first focusing on documentation in their classroom, they often make the mistake of thinking that everything that occurs in the classroom must be documented. It is easier if a beginning documenter focuses on one or two domains. A teacher can identify one or two things that he will collect and when he will collect them throughout the school year. Writing samples are a good place to start. Another way to narrow the focus is to set a goal of documenting one learning experience from beginning to end, such as a project or a unit.

Another fairly common mistake that is easy to correct is trying to capture all learning in photographs or to photograph activities for which other documentation has already been gathered. Again, it may be helpful for the teacher to revisit the web to see the variety of ways besides photographing that children's learning can be documented.

Other reasonable goals that a beginning documenter may choose are setting aside a certain time to observe each day, focusing observations on one child per day, or focusing observations on one child in one area daily over an extended period of time. As the teacher becomes more adept at documenting, she may set goals to increase documentation, such as increasing observations of children's learning in a particular area of the room.

Anticipating Displays

It is at this time that a teacher might also need to think about what kinds of displays will result from a learning experience or from documentation of a particular area of learning. This is a good time to revisit the windows framework in Chapter 2 and to project what audiences might be viewing the displays. The teacher can ask herself if the purpose of the display is to provide a window on a child's development or to share a learning experience such as a project. It is also helpful to think about what different points of view the audience for the display is likely to have.

PREPARING CHILDREN FOR DOCUMENTING

There are many advantages to involving children in the documentation of their own learning. In preparing for documentation, and even during documentation, the teacher should plan some time for preparing children for documentation. She can introduce and directly teach skills that children may need to document their own learning. One of these skills is using a web to record what they know and then what they have learned. Another skill is using writing to record their thoughts. Even preschoolers can help make lists of materials needed. Teachers can model questioning and hypothesizing so that children learn how to phrase questions for research. The questions and answers can then be documented. Practice in construction skills such as taping, stapling, and building things will enable children to better represent their knowledge through making products.

As in all areas of documentation in which they participate, it is important for children to have easy access both to materials and equipment for documenting and to storage places for their items. Milk crates with hanging files are popular with many teachers for portfolios because they encourage student involvement in the collection process.

It is important that children also understand that they should be encouraged to express what they are learning in many ways. In addition to webs and lists, types of documentation that they can understand and readily use are narratives such as conversations, written stories, and books; writing such as captions and signs; constructions such as block structures, play environments, dioramas, and models; and artistic expressions such as drama, drawing, painting, sculpture, musical expressions, and photography.

Children should be encouraged to do as much writing and drawing as possible about what they are observing and learning. Keeping their clipboards readily available for independent use supports their drawing and writing. As discussed earlier, the teacher can encourage children to revisit, redraw, and rewrite in order to help them solidify knowledge, become aware of their own learning, and demonstrate to others the extent of the learning occurring during a project or other experience. If first attempts (or sketches) and final copies are displayed prominently, then this documentation can be very powerful.

DOING THE DOCUMENTING

When beginning the documentation process it may, once again, be helpful to review the web in Figure 3.1 to keep the variety of ways to document in mind.

Recording and Reflecting

There are two processes that the teacher has to work into her schedule when documenting. One is time to record information and collect children's work; the other is time to reflect.

It is easy to assume that recording and collecting will happen throughout the day; however, it is important that the teacher carefully consider how this process will occur. As noted previously, placement of recording materials (notes, pencils, tape recorders) is critical because the teacher does not have time to stop and search for them in the middle of teaching. An excellent plan is for the teacher to simply record thoughts in a spiral notebook as they occur throughout the day. Other teachers use a form similar to "Documenting Individuals' Work During a Group Activity," which is provided in Chapter 13, to record notes when children are all together and they need to get much information down quickly. In Chapter 5, we provided information about the Early Childhood Standards Project, which enables teachers to utilize technology to record their observations.

It is helpful for the teacher to watch for opportunities to collect documentation of several children at one time. Recording and transcribing a conversation and making multiple copies of the conversation provide documentation of the language skills of each of the children involved in the conversation.

Many teachers take time each day to outline what was done that day. This may focus on the class, an individual child, the project, or the teacher and the teaching strategies. As pointed out in Chapter 10, time should also be set aside daily to summarize and reflect on the observation data and items collected. Documentation can guide the teacher in planning what resources to access, experts to bring in, or field experiences to be initiated. Any skills identified as needing to be taught can also be planned for other teaching times.

Photographing

Often teachers are disappointed in the quality of the photographs they take when documenting. Morgan and Thaler (1996) give some simple rules that can result in more interesting and effective photographic documentation.

In selecting the view to be photographed, it is important to see the scene as the camera sees it. People have selective vision; cameras do not. Clutter, dirty dishes, flashy bulletin boards that are not noticed in real life seem to dominate when the photograph is developed. The teacher can look at the background through the camera, then reposition himself so that the picture has fewer distractions. Or the teacher can get closer to the children or activity being photographed so that they can fill the picture and block out the background.

Photographs of large groups of children or posed photographs do not show enough detail or expression to provide evidence of learning. The focus should be on small groups, individuals, and candid shots. Also, photographing at different angles can be effective. For example, a child working on a structure might be photographed from above, showing the top of the structure, and then at the eye level of the child.

Composition can pull viewers into the story being documented by following the rule of thirds:

> Just imagine your viewfinder has two sets of parallel lines going through it; two running horizontally above and below the center and two running vertically to the right and left of center. Each pair of lines divides the frame into three equal parts, hence the name the rule of thirds. If you frame your pictures so that . . . your children are located where any two lines intersect, or along any of the lines, the picture will be more visually appealing . . . more natural and lifelike, and the photo will be more interesting if you point the lens below their heads. That way, their faces will be in the upper third of the frame. (Morgan & Thaler, 1996, p. 27)

The rest of the photo can show the child's work or project. Figure 12.2 shows the rule of thirds.

Remember also to take photographs that tell a story. It is helpful to take a series of photographs, especially when there is problem solving and building and construction going on. The series can provide an indication of the thought processes of the children and enhance everyone's understanding of what occurred. It can be very valuable to involve children in photographing their own work. More tips for taking good photos are included in Figure 12.3 (see also Helm & Helm, 2006, Chapter 9).

Figure 12.2. Rule of thirds digagram.

Be sure to take the time to examine photos soon after taking them and not wait until projects or units have been completed. Photographs provide a wealth of knowledge about what is happening in the classroom and what children are learning. This information can affect the decisions you make about the next step in the learning experience. Too often teachers later express remorse over a missed learning opportunity or the ignored yearning on a child's face to participate in a special way. A form, "Photo Analysis," is provided in Chapter 13 for use by individuals or a professional learning community to learn how to examine and talk about photographs.

Tape Recording

Tape recording, both video and audio, is helpful for documenting children's learning and for a teacher's reflection on her own teaching. Putting an audio recorder near children and letting it record is simple and can be effective. Capturing conversation accurately in a busy early childhood classroom is assisted by using equipment that allows the teacher to separate the microphone from the recording equipment. It may also be helpful to have small group or individual activities set up in an area in

Figure 12.3. Tips for taking good photos.

Hold the camera steady when taking the photograph. Press the buttons gently and slowly.

Focus on one child or a small group of children, rather than a large group shot from a distance.

Feature children's work. Arrange the photo so the work has a prominent place in the photograph.

Show children in action, creating, studying, or sharing their work with others.

Stand close enough to the subjects to capture their expressions.

Pay attention to the background so that it does not overwhelm or distract.

Take close-ups of sculptures or structures to show the details of construction. Check the camera manual to learn the closest distance at which the camera will take sharp pictures. The closest distance at which you can get a sharp picture for most point-and-shoot cameras is 4 feet from the subject.

Take photographs in a series to show the progress of constructions or development of skills.

Position the camera level with the body or head of very small children.

In outdoor shots, aim the camera away from the sun so children's faces are not in darkness.

When using flash, stay within the "flash range." This is the range of the distance that the flash will illuminate. Typical flash range is 4 to 12 feet. Check your manual.

the classroom where there is less noise or even to use a section of the hallway or a conference room. It is especially meaningful for children to tell about their work and to have their narrative taped.

Many video cameras are now small enough that a teacher can hold and operate the recorder with one hand while continuing to interact with the child or children she is taping. Tripods and other accessories are also available. The sound quality on video recorders is equal to or better than that of many tape recorders, and some teachers find that when they can both see and hear a child, they are better able to understand his words. Seeing the child in context also provides more information for the interpretation of his words. Facial expressions and body language can be taken into account, as well as actions of other children that may have influenced the child's words. Seeing the child in context also allows the teacher to consider the influence of his physical surroundings on his behavior.

Capturing Sound. All camcorders have a built-in microphone, and it is important to learn how to use it correctly. Active classrooms where children are engaged in many activities have high noise levels that make it difficult to capture conversations. To learn how well a particular built-in microphone will pick up individual conversations in a classroom, a teacher can record an adult reading to the children. She can then slowly back away from the reader and shoot video about every three or four steps. After completing the recording, the videotape can be viewed to note at what point she can no longer hear the reader well enough to distinguish the words. If a teacher wants to capture whole-group conversations or instruction, she should not videotape in her classroom any farther away than that point. If she repeats the microphone test at a time when children are engaged in a number of activities throughout the room, she will be able to note the farthest distance that she can video and still pick up the audio in this noisier situation.

Sometimes a camera's built-in microphone will require the teacher to be so close to the action that it would intrude or alter the learning experience. There are other ways to get good sound and video:

- Use a tripod and an external microphone placed near the child or group of children being taped and use the zoom feature to bring intimacy to the visual images.
- Consider investing in a cardioid or shotgun microphone and earphones for the operator if she will be doing a lot of videotaping and analysis.

- Arrange small-group or individual work in quieter, carpeted, or more secluded areas of the room. For videotaping concentrated sequences or learning experiences, consider using conference rooms or carpeted hallways.

To capture sound when videotaping outside, it will be helpful to shield the microphone from the wind by using a wall or tree. If a camcorder has an automatic level control (ALC), adjusting it for low-level sound may be of benefit. A thorough review of the manual will be valuable.

Composing Video Shots. Even though a video image is constantly changing, it is important for a teacher to think carefully about the composition of the picture, just as in still photography. This is especially important when videotaping a stationary object or children in a fixed location. It will be helpful for teachers to consider the following tips:

- Plan what to videotape before starting to tape.
- Be sure that the background behind the children isn't distracting or cluttered.
- When children are in front of a bright light, such as the sun or a window, move the camera so that the light source is to the side and not directly behind the children.
- Apply the rule of thirds to video composition as you would to still photographs.
- Before looking through the camcorder, look at the color of the background and the subject to be sure the subject stands out. If your viewfinder is black and white, it will be especially hard to judge this through the eyepiece.
- Use the remote control with the camera on a tripod when the operator needs to be in the action.
- When videotaping children who are moving or running, use a tripod and rotate the camera on the tripod to get a smooth shot.

Videotaping Projects or Other Learning Experiences. Video documentation of children engaged in meaningful work can be useful for both teacher and child reflection. Tips that will assist teachers to successfully videotape documentation of projects or other learning experiences include the following:

- When taping field trips and other group experiences to "revisit" with the video, be sure to capture the whole scene or large features such as buildings. To do this, use panning (slow horizontal movement to show a whole scene) or tilting (slow vertical movement to show a tall object). The camera should be held still for a short time at the beginning and end of a pan or tilt. Avoid rotating more than 90 degrees.
- When recording the progress of a project, have one tape for each project and use the automatic date recorder at the beginning of each day's videotaping.
- Zoom in to show details of children's work or to show faces indicating emotion or involvement with a project; don't zoom too fast or too often.
- Remember the child's point of view. Objects that appear large or frightening to children can be panned for close-up viewing on video later.
- Be alert for interesting sounds to record as well as visuals. (A video of the train station trip is more meaningful when children can revisit the sound of the train coming into the station.)

Video Capture. Advances in the development of software have made it easy for teachers with minimal technical knowledge to capture segments or "clips" from longer videotapes and save them electronically. Teachers can use these clips as a basis for discussion about individual children or group learning experiences, and they can be saved inexpensively on CD or DVD so that significant observations taken "in the action" can be shared with parents or colleagues. Children, too, love to take their own video footage, and they can select segments of footage that they would like to include. Planning their own documentation or narrative video adds another dimension to the learning experience for older children.

Webbing

Webbing can occur with the whole class, during small-group times, or with individual children. The value of the record that it provides is increased when it is revisited and revised, so it is important to provide opportunities for that to occur. One method that some teachers have found productive is to photocopy the first web and keep it; then add to the original and copy it again, and copy that one, and so on. The series of webs shows the growth of knowledge and understanding.

At the end of each project, the teacher can go back to her list of required content. After making a copy of it, she can highlight all those content objectives covered in the project work. Displaying this list prominently with other project documentation will help others viewing the documentation see the relevance of the work to the goals and objectives of the school.

Journaling

Journaling is the process of reflecting and then writing about that reflection. Although a teacher may gather notes and write narratives of what occurred, this activity will not have as great an effect on teaching as journaling will. A teacher new to documenting can begin a teacher journal by taking 5 minutes to think about something significant that happened each day and writing about its significance, how it informs the teacher's knowledge about the child, or the implications for teaching and learning. This focus of thinking could be the class, an individual child, a study such as a project, or the teacher himself and his teaching strategies.

ORGANIZING DISPLAYS OF DOCUMENTATION

When the teacher collects children's work and reflects on it, she often becomes eager to share the knowledge she has gained with others. Many teachers, however, are hesitant about displaying their work. There is much to learn from the Reggio Emilia preschools about the importance of display, as we have already noted. The displays of the projects done in those schools have traveled the world as "The Hundred Languages of Children" exhibit and have convinced many viewers of the importance of their philosophy of education. Edwards, Forman, and Gandini (1998), in their discussion of the exhibit as a form of communication, identify three key functions of documentation and display:

> [They] provide children with a concrete and visible memory of what they have said and done in order to serve as a jumping off point . . . provide educators with a tool for research and a key to continuous improvement and renewal, and provide parents and the public with detailed information about what happens in the schools as a means of eliciting their reactions and support. (p. 9)

The exhibits of the preschools of Reggio Emilia have been successful in fulfilling those functions. Another exhibit is "The Power of Documentation: Children's Learning Revealed," which was sponsored by the Chicago Metro AEYC, the McCormick Tribune Foundation, and Best Practices, Inc. The exhibit was mounted by the Chicago Children's Museum in 2003 and continues to be viewed as it travels around the country. Together, these exhibits have provided teachers with encouragement to be brave about sharing the learning that occurs in their own classrooms.

A teacher can begin displaying children's work simply by moving outside the confines of the classroom and into the hallways of the school. According to Loris Malaguzzi (1998), in the preschools of Reggio Emilia, "Throughout the school the walls are used as spaces for both temporary and permanent exhibits of what the children and teachers have created: Our walls speak and document" (p. 64).

However, displays should not be limited to the school environment. Again, the preschools of Reggio Emilia have pointed the way. Loris Malaguzzi (1998) tells about first moving displays outside the school.

> I remember that, after a few months, the need to make ourselves known became so strong that we planned a most successful activity. Once a week we would transport the school to town. Literally, we would pack ourselves, the children, and our tools into a truck and we would teach school and show exhibits in the open air, in the square, in public parks, or under the colonnade of the municipal theater. The children were happy. The people saw; they were surprised and they asked questions. (p. 52)

Teachers quickly move from collecting and reflecting to displaying. Displays are eagerly received by parents, administrators, and the community as a whole when they are placed in community locations. Such displays of documentation are much more meaningful than bulletin boards. Just putting up children's work, however, does not mean that it will be meaningful to viewers.

In Figure 12.4 is a bulletin board style of display. It uses an attention-getting teacher-made shape along with commercial bulletin board art (the apples) to show pictures of a learning experince at an apple orchard. In contrast, Figure 12.5 shows a

Figure 12.4. Bulletin board on apples.

documentation display with an emphasis on what the children learned from this expereince.

A new opportunity for display has become available through the technologies of the Internet and the World Wide Web. The University Primary School at University of Illinois has used its website (http://www.ed.uiuc.edu/ups/) to share the documentation of projects that are going on in its classrooms. Nancy Hertzog, the director, meets with the teachers and together they select documentation that Dr. Hertzog then scans onto the website. Parents, children, and other interested individuals can follow the development of projects, viewing children's products, reading project narratives and teacher journals, and seeing photos of children working. A new dimension of interactivity is added by the ability of viewers to respond to the documentation by e-mail to the class.

Matching Displays to Audiences

One of the first things to consider when a teacher is beginning to process his documentation, with the idea of displaying it, is to consider which windows in the framework he wants to open.

- Is he interested in looking closely at an individual child's development and sharing that view with others?
- Is he interested in showing the process of a particular learning experience?
- Is he interested in focusing on his knowledge and skills as a teacher?

The teacher may also want to provide a variety of windows at some time or another from the same set of documentation materials, for example, from a

particular project. In Chapter 13 the form "Opening Windows: Plan for Displaying/Presenting Documentation" can be used by a teacher to think about the main events that occurred in a learning experience, the documentation that was collected, and which windows might be opened. By examining the documentation and thinking about the windows, often the teacher will be able to identify curriculum goals or standards that can be emphasized, or a narrative theme will emerge. It is important to think of who will be looking through the window and then plan the display according to the interests of the projected audience. For some audiences, evidence of achievement of standards may be extremely important; for other audiences, this may not be important. For additional information on how to strategically plan communication, the reader is referred to *Building Support for Your School: How to Use Children's Work to Show Learning* (Helm & Helm, 2006).

It is also important for the teacher to revisit the point-of-view experience described in Chapter 3 and to remember that those viewing the display will come with a variety of perspectives. Interests, ability to understand, and motivation will vary.

Teachers will often change the location of a display. Selected items may be displayed in the room for children's use, then gravitate to a hallway or public area when the teacher wants to communicate to others what children are learning. Displays in classrooms are often working displays that are evolving and in which children are involved in documenting.

All displays benefit from written descriptions that include the significance of what is displayed, such as what the children have learned, why the item was chosen to be displayed, the process the class used, or what an individual child learned. The description can provide the viewer with an understanding of the educational value of the experiences. Adding to a display, as children's work advances and projects or learning experiences progress, increases its value and maintains the interest of observers.

Again, students will benefit from being involved in the display process. Even the youngest children can assist in making a book that tells the story of the project, which can also be used for a display. Older students can evaluate and select the best work for the display and write their own descriptions. As displays are put up or books made, teachers will find it meaningful to provide opportunities for children to reflect on their learning by viewing the displays. When children reflect on their learning experience as they review the documentation, their words can be recorded and added to the narratives accompanying the display. This documentation of the documen-

Figure 12.5. Documentation display of apples.

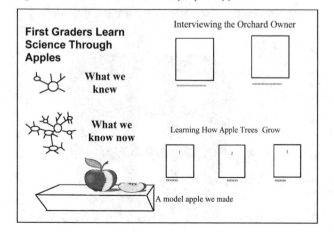

tation process can provide valuable insight for the teacher in planning additional learning experiences.

It is important for the teacher to plan when and how to share documentation with parents. Parents are significant partners in teaching. Two handouts are provided in Chapter 13 to share with parents. The first is "What Is Documentation?" This handout is a letter that can be shared with parents at the beginning of the year. It explains the concept of documentation. It also sets realistic expectations for the parents so they understand that children and their work will be spotlighted. Their child's work will not always be shown, but sometime during the year, she, too, will be in the spotlight. This has worked well in the programs that use documentation and has developed a healthy appreciation of all children's learning among parents. Another handout is "How to View a Project Display." This handout is helpful when there are many documentation displays for parents to see, such as at a project night or end-of-the-year event. This helps parents understand how to view large displays of children's work.

These events that focus on documentation can motivate parents to take time to look at children's work. Assuming that all parents will see a wall display in the normal course of the school week is probably not realistic. Calling attention to the display, having an open house to view displays, and sharing documentation at parent-teacher conferences are all ways to be sure that parents have an opportunity to experience the joy of watching their children grow and develop. Books about projects, videos, and newsletters can be sent home with children. This is especially helpful for parents who may find it difficult to visit the school.

Principles of Display

When designing a display of documentation, it is important to consider the aesthetic appeal of the exhibit. The use of the term *exhibit* is appropriate. It may be helpful for the teacher to visualize exhibiting her children's work in a museum rather than to think about displaying work on a bulletin board. A teacher may wish to visit a museum and observe the way that curators display aesthetic and historical objects. Museum displays provide a good model for teachers in how to display without having the mechanics of the display overwhelm the subject.

There are principles of display common to museums that may be helpful for teachers. Eric Douglas articulated 10 commandments for museum exhibitors, which are especially applicable to a teacher planning a display:

- Have a plan for your exhibit and make it immediately clear to the visitor.
- Remember that the human eye is lazy and usually looks only ahead and down.
- Do not allow "eye-catchers" in your exhibits or around them to distract attention from the specimens.
- Always show objects in their functional position or suggest it to some degree.
- Always keep your display equipment and mechanics as inconspicuous as possible.
- Do not arrange monotonous rows of things on shelves or crowd your cases.
- Compose your displays in three dimensions, using asymmetrical balance as much as possible.
- Avoid tacking objects flat; hang objects slightly away from the background with the aid of a block.
- Use labels which approximate the color of the background.
- Writing should be in large contemporary type and placed below eye level. (Douglas, quoted in Neal, 1976, p. 147)

Many of these recommendations are directly applicable to documentation displays. Having an overall plan for a display can enable the teacher to be sure that viewers will understand the display. A clear starting point for the display is helpful. In the display of projects at several of the schools described in this book, the project summary form (refer to Figure 4.2) was used at the beginning of each display. This form gives the viewer an overview of the project. Framing it in a black mat allows parents and other teachers who regularly view displays to identify this summary as the place to start. Another popular form was a handout entitled "How to View a Project Display," which is provided in Chapter 13.

The most effective displays are those that focus the viewer on the documentation. We feel that teacher-created or commercially created artwork, colorful borders, backgrounds, and posters waste space and time by visually distracting the viewer. Unlike posters for events or print media such as magazines, documentation displays should be designed to encourage the viewer to study the display, not glance at it.

For the same reason, the use of brightly colored or strongly patterned backgrounds is not effective. Walls or backgrounds should complement, not compete with, the work on view (Neal, 1986). It is important that the display be attractive and aesthetically appealing. Even without the commercial art, the use of many photos or monotonous rows of children's work as shown in Figure 12.6 is not very effective. Figure 12.7 shows how opening up

Figure 12.6. Diagram of bulletin board with monotonous squares.

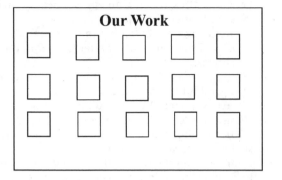

Figure 12.7. Diagram of display board with "Where do most of our birds come from?" title.

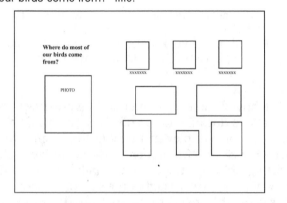

Figure 12.8. Display with two three-panel boards.

Figure 12.9. Narrative paragraphs explain the significance of what is displayed.

Figure 12.10. Three-dimensional display showing how to bring photos forward.

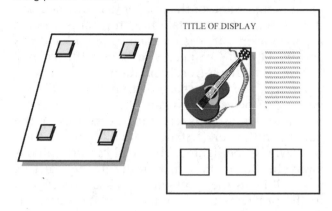

Figure 12.11. How to make a display shelf.

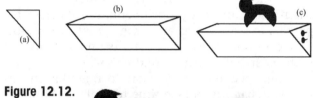

Figure 12.12. Pedestals.

Figure 12.13. Sculpture with mirrors.

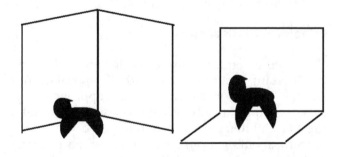

Figure 12.14. Tent card.

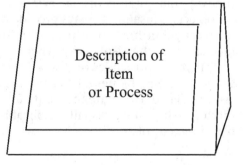

the display to provide more white space, adding a photo, and using a variety of student work increases the aesthetic appeal.

An eye-catching display can be created through the subtle use of color, texture, and/or pattern. Neal (1986) suggests using varying shades of one basic color to unify a display. Another suggestion is to match the background colors in a display or tablecloth to the content of a display. This also creates viewer interest. For example, softer nature colors complement displays that show children's study of outdoor topics. When exploring background colors, the teacher may find it helpful to examine the predominant colors in the photographs used in the documentation. For example, in the photographs of the Meadow Project, which occurred in the fall, the dominant colors were subtle greens, yellows, and browns. The teacher picked up these colors and enhanced the display by using a dry brush to stroke subtle shades of yellow-green onto the background display material. Burlap and log pieces provided a background for three-dimensional objects (see Figure 12.8). In contrast, the photographs of the Bicycle Project were mainly taken indoors and featured many pieces of metal, vinyl, and metallic colors. A good choice for the background material for the bicycle display was gray or white.

Narrative, or print, should not overwhelm the display or discourage the viewer from looking. However, a display can appear stark and clinical when it has too much white space, too little text, and a total lack of color. Print must be close to the picture or object for easy identification (see Figure 12.9).

Displays that have more than two dimensions are especially attractive (see Figure 12.10). Interest can be added by displaying children's three-dimensional products, such as sculptures or equipment created for play environments. Small shelves can be attached to displays to provide space if shelving is not available (see Figure 12.11). A spotlight can also be used to highlight an aspect of children's work and to attract attention to the display. Pedestals such as blocks of wood also increase interest in sculpture (see Figure 12.12). Matting, as long as it does not overwhelm, can enhance a drawing or painting. Transparent holders, frames, or pedestals are especially appealing and take nothing away from the children's work. Use of table mirrors for placement of objects or back mirrors enable viewers to study children's work from more than one direction (see Figure 12.13). This often reveals more of the detail that is indicative of in-depth study and new knowledge and skills. Tent cards can be used to explain the meaning of parts of displays and add a three-dimensional component to flat work placed on tables (see Figure 12.14).

Documentation displays can show the passage of time and direct the viewers' focus through the layout of the display. Figure 12.15 is a layout for a documentation panel on block play. This display presents a 3-year-old child's problem solving while building a block structure. The display was based on the teacher's sketches that were drawn as she observed the child attempting to create a house with the blocks. The sequence shows how the child selected two blocks of different sizes for the walls of the house, then discovered that the block selected for the roof of the house was slanted. The child replaced the shorter wall with a block that matched in size and was then able to put the roof on straight. The composition of this display emphasizes the passage of time. The horizontal arrangement of the narrative and the drawings of the child's block work require the viewer to look at each item individually and in sequence. The starting point for viewing the display is clearly indicated by the use of numbers. Each step of the work is explained. A photograph of the final block structure is mounted on foam-core board so it stands out from the background. It ends the display.

Sometimes displays are arranged directly on a wall area. This is especially helpful for large projects with several components. Figure 12.16 is a suggested layout for a wall display with no borders. The display still needs a starting point, indicated here by the Project Summary. Sequences and narratives are arranged in one horizontal line. Time 1, 2, and 3 sketches are grouped together with narrative. The mural in this display is irregularly shaped. Not all of the children's work must be matted or bordered.

Creative use of the photocopying machine can focus viewers on children's work. Children's work can be photocopied onto a transparency. It can then be viewed by the whole group of children, or projected onto a wall or shadow screen where children can "get into" their own documentation. The same thing can be done with slides that children or teachers have taken while documenting an experience that they shared together, such as a visit somewhere or a dance or other performance they were involved in. Photocopying can enable the teacher to have additional copies of a document that can be displayed in a variety of ways. In Figure 12.17, photographs of Kendra pretending to be a butterfly were copied. One set was cut out to display a three-dimensional sequence that enabled viewers to understand her expression of movement in a static display.

Using the computer also simplifies and enhances documentation displays. Multiple copies of documentation that apply to more than one child provide a copy for each child's portfolio. Narratives can be used to enhance wall displays, then reprocessed on a

Figure 12.15. Layout for documentation panel on block play.

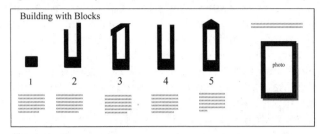

Figure 12.16. Display layout for a wall (mural or group project display).

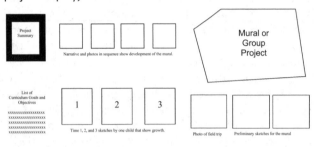

Figure 12.17. The teacher copied photographs and made a three-dimensional display to show the child's movement.

computer as a narrative for a children's book to take home. It is possible to make a book for both parents and children by changing the type fonts to differentiate the portions of the narrative intended to be read to the child and those intended to be read by the adult. Use of different fonts or different-colored print will also key viewers in to what is most relevant for their purposes when materials are used in displays.

The computer also often has the added advantage of a spell-checker and grammar-checker. To ensure credibility, proper spelling and grammar are important in narratives, captions, and signs shared with the public.

SETTING ASIDE TIME FOR REFLECTING ABOUT DOCUMENTATION

Documentation cannot inform decision making if it is not thought about, and thinking reflectively is not automatically a part of the teacher's day in many of today's schools. In some schools, thinking about what children are learning occurs only periodically when standardized group achievement tests are given or once a year when state- or district-required assessments are completed. These assessments are not immediately available to the teacher, and teachers are not accustomed to reflecting in-depth about children's learning or relating information directly to daily decision making. In addition, in many schools, documenting and reflecting on the meaning of the documentation are neither expected of teachers nor reinforced; therefore, they are not a priority in allocation of a teacher's time.

In addition to modeling high-quality documentation, the Reggio Emilia schools have also provided a model for the importance of taking time to reflect on that documentation and to engage in dialogue with colleagues about children's learning. Reflection and engagement of colleagues in discussion deepen the teacher's understanding and can have a significant impact on the growth and development of children.

As emphasized earlier, setting aside a special time for reflection and journal writing may be the best way to ensure that they are given priority. Making a habit of writing in a journal at a regular, specified time, such as the end of each day, can assure that reflection will occur. Sometimes the end of the day is not the best time because the teacher may be tired or have other pressing duties. Other times that have worked for some teachers are during the lunch hour or early the next morning. If it is difficult to set aside a block of time each day for reflection, the teacher can shorten the time by making quick notes of thoughts about the day, documentation gathered, and topics to think about at a later time. Then, once a week, the teacher can set aside a longer time period to review the short daily notes and write observations.

Sharing with colleagues is an important way to reflect. Loris Malaguzzi (1998) points out the importance of reflecting with colleagues:

> teachers must leave behind an isolated, silent mode of working that leaves no traces. Instead they must discover ways to communicate and document the children's evolving experiences in school. (p. 69)

One possibility is to work out an informal agreement with a colleague to meet and discuss reflections. If the teacher has a teacher associate or aide in the classroom, the opportunity to see experiences from two different viewpoints is very valuable. Sharing with colleagues can be on-the-fly, sharing during activities or experiences, at the end of the day, or at a designated time during the day. It is very helpful to set a policy to ask each other daily, "How did we do?" This can become very powerful if the answer is focused on children's learning that has been observed and documented instead of general global feelings of the flow of routine.

When a portion of staff meetings is designated for sharing observations and reflections or a professional learning community is formed, as described in Chapter 10, teachers are provided with an impetus to prepare by gathering together any relevant documentation and deciding on specific events or observations to share. A teacher can determine what kind of input she would like from her colleagues, for example, problem solving, advice on a different way to respond, or ideas for extending a child's experiences. This will focus the discussion and provide a meaningful experience for the teacher. However, everyone should make it a point to be open to other insights or points of view as they emerge while examining the documentation. Keeping a written record of the discussion will provide opportunities for everyone to see the similarity of experiences. Review of the discussion notes at a later time will also document the teacher's growth in dialoguing and observing.

Sometimes it is appropriate to ask a colleague to gather documentation for the teacher by observing or collecting while she is teaching or interacting with children. This can provide rare insight if the teacher tells the colleague what focus she desires. If colleagues are unavailable when an event occurs for which the teacher desires observation and reflection, audio or video recordings can enable joint observation and reflection at a later time.

It is important that reflection with or without colleagues occur on a regular basis, not just at the end of a learning experience. Organizing and reflecting on a regular basis on the photos, notes, and student products provide the basis for adjusting the learning experience, challenging children's thinking, and introducing opportunities for skill development. If reflection is delayed until after a display is assembled or a culminating event occurs, then the experience cannot be altered to achieve maximum growth and development.

Teachers with experience in documenting children's work have found that it is helpful to provide a way to make their documentation readily available for reflection. Tacking documentation on the walls of the classroom or in a staff room, even without explanations or notes, during an experience will help the teacher visualize the process and reflect. Telling others about the significance and the insight provided will elicit additional reflections. These can be used to write more formal summaries and become part of a more public display at a later time.

Another technique that teachers have found to encourage reflection is to regroup different pieces of documentation for making different types of decisions. For example, a documentation of a child learning a skill could become an individual portfolio item but could also be used to show the value of a particular learning experience. As these are used in displays or shared with others, some teachers have found it helpful to make photocopies for multiple use. As the teacher reflects on the documentation, she may color code her reflections to indicate the viewpoint or the focus of the reflection. Highlighting and adding borders are other ways to let viewers know the significance of the documentation.

Organizing and collecting documentation is a long process. It takes commitment by the teacher. If the teacher is sharing the documentation as she "lives it" with her children, she will find that she is able to understand in greater depth what is occurring in her classroom. As she gains a greater understanding, she will find that she is changing her way of making decisions.

TEACHING WITH INTEGRITY

Learning how to document children's work has been a successful and fulfilling experience for many of the teachers described in this book. Perhaps the most powerful effect of documentation is that children gain satisfaction from their own efforts and see the appreciation of those efforts by parents and other adults who are important in their lives. Teachers who document have observed that as they increased the attention given to documentation, children have become more careful about their work and more evaluative. For example, we have seen that documenting children's first, second, and even third attempts at a task such as drawing and labeling a vegetable has resulted in children's talking about the growth that has occurred. The time and effort that teachers devote to gathering information on children's work has communicated clearly to the children that what they are doing is important. Even the youngest children have come to understand the excitement that evidence of their learning can generate in their parents.

Teacher Judy Cagle documented a 4-year-old's writing about his mother's reaction to the documentation of a project on reflections that was displayed in the hallway. Perhaps copying the writing that he had seen his teacher do when making anecdotal notes, Dion wrote a series of letterlike shapes that the teacher then collected as a writing sample for documenting growth in language and literacy. Mrs. Cagle had written the following note and dictation on the sheet on which she mounted his story.

> Dion used letters and letterlike forms to write about his mother's visit to the class to see the Reflections Project. His writing says, "My mom saw reflections in the hallway. Her said, 'Wow!'"

Any careful systematic documentation requires teacher commitment and effort. Many teachers may hesitate to step in and try it. However, it is important to remember our image of the school and our view from afar and to recall the many challenges to both the school and the community surrounding it. These challenges are not likely to vanish quickly. Documentation as described in this book can help meet those challenges.

One of the ways we can help people understand the value of early childhood education and what schools do is to throw open the windows and invite people to look. We may have reached the point where, in the words of Loris Malaguzzi, "the need to make ourselves known became so strong" (Malaguzzi, 1998, p. 44) that we, like the teachers in Reggio Emilia, need to make the effort to document our children's work.

In closing this chapter, we want to quote Steven Carter's (1996) definition of *integrity*. He divides it into three parts:

1. Discerning what is right and what is wrong;
2. Acting on what you have discerned, even at personal cost; and
3. Saying openly that you are acting on your understanding of right and wrong. (p. 7)

In today's climate of accountability, how we assess children, how we make decisions about their education, and how we present early childhood education to the public have become issues of integrity, issues of what is right and wrong with significant consequences for children and families. We encourage you to think about the right thing to do when teaching and assessing children, and join the teachers whose work is described in this book in their efforts to capture the active, engaged learning occurring in their classrooms.

The success of their documentation to inform their teaching and communicate with others can be seen from the many examples in this book. It was worth the investment of time and energy. However, a side effect, not predicted but perhaps the most valuable, was the frequently reported increase in their joy in teaching and the parents' joy in their children's learning.

CHAPTER 13

Teacher Materials for Documenting Young Children's Work

This chapter is designed to help teachers begin documenting. In Chapter 2, three windows provide a framework for thinking about documentation: a window on a child's development, a window on a learning experience, and a window for teacher self-reflection. While working with teachers who are learning to document, we developed many lists, shortcuts, handouts, and forms to help the teachers implement the ideas described earlier in the book within their own classroom and school. In this chapter, we share these forms to speed the process of learning to document, to aid in planning documentation for accountability, to reduce teacher preparation time, and to enable teachers to collect and display professional documentation the very first time they incorporate the exciting process of documentation into their own classrooms and teaching. All forms may be photocopied. Most teachers will develop their own forms and layouts as they become more comfortable with documentation. Included in this chapter are resources that help teachers:

- Think about documentation (processes, procedures, and organization)
- Inform others about the value of documentation and how to view documentation
- Document children's learning
- Prepare documentation for display or presentation

These resources include four types of forms that teachers may photocopy and use: preparation forms, documenting forms, analysis forms, and presentation forms.

Preparation forms provide tools that will help teachers get ready to document, including a material and supply checklist, forms for thinking about curriculum and documentation, and forms for setting up a simplified portfolio system. These forms coordinate with Chapters 3, 6, 7, 8, 11, and 12.

Documenting forms provide resources to guide the teacher's collection process. Included are forms for planning documentation of standards/curriculum goals, weekly planning forms that include space for documentation goals, and forms for capturing documentation for all three windows. These forms coordinate with Chapters 3, 5, 6, 7, 8, 11, and 12.

Analysis forms assist teachers in focusing on and discussing documentation with colleagues. Forms included are a teacher reflection journal page, photo analysis form, and a form to aid in sharing documentation with a teacher's professional learning community. These forms coordinate with Chapter 10.

Presentation forms aid the teacher in displaying documentation in a variety of ways, including documentation display planning, window sharing forms, project/learning experience summaries, and handouts for documentation viewers. These forms coordinate with Chapters 2, 4, 8, 10, and 12.

Getting Ready for Documentation

You can become a more efficient documenter by organizing your materials, supplies, and equipment to match the types of documentation you will collect and store. Use the lists below to develop a plan for selecting and organizing materials for documentation. Keep in mind that if your organizational plan fits your own unique organizational style, you will be more likely to follow through with it. See Chapter 12 for an in-depth look at organization and presentation.

What types of portfolios will I develop? What will they keep a record of?
- ☐ Individual child
- ☐ Adult-selected work
- ☐ Areas of learning
- ☐ Group learning experiences
- ☐ Child-selected work

Recording Observations

What tools or combination of tools will I use to capture and share my observations of children? Will I be able to photocopy, photograph, or scan samples of the children's work?

- ☐ Post-it notes
- ☐ Index cards
- ☐ Self-adhesive file or address labels
- ☐ Pen on a rope
- ☐ Apron with pockets
- ☐ Clipboard

- ☐ 35-mm camera
- ☐ 35-mm film
- ☐ Digital camera
- ☐ Digital image editing program (e.g., Photoshop)
- ☐ Polaroid camera
- ☐ Polaroid film

- ☐ Video camera
- ☐ Blank videotapes or DVDs
- ☐ Cassette/digital audio recorder
- ☐ Blank cassette tapes
- ☐ Photocopy machine and paper
- ☐ Scanner
- ☐ Photoquality paper

Developing a Portfolio

Where will I keep my observations? Will I include them in the same folder with samples of the child's work?

- ☐ 8½" × 11" folders
- ☐ 8½" × 11" folders
- ☐ 8½" × 11" expandable file
- ☐ 8½" × 11" expandable file
- ☐ File crate

- ☐ File cabinet
- ☐ Hanging files
- ☐ Index card box
- ☐ Pocket chart
- ☐ Slide album

- ☐ Photo album
- ☐ Photo file box
- ☐ Video cassette storage box
- ☐ DVD/CD storage box
- ☐ Digital image organizing program

How will I store smaller samples of the child's work?

- ☐ Loose-leaf notebook
- ☐ Transparent notebook pockets

- ☐ Large expandable files
- ☐ Scan them to computer disk

- ☐ Photograph them
- ☐ Layer them in a box between sheets of tissue paper

How will I store large samples of the child's work?

- ☐ 28" × 22" folders
- ☐ Hanging storage
- ☐ Horizontal storage shelves

- ☐ Vertical storage shelves
- ☐ Photograph them

- ☐ Scan them to computer disk
- ☐ Reduce them on copier

Tips on Obtaining Inexpensive Documentation Materials and Supplies

- Place needed supplies, such as film, on official lists of supplies the children are required to bring with them at the beginning of the school year.
- Solicit businesses for donations of materials, such as notebooks, folders, and ink cartridges.

- Buy supplies in quantity and split order with colleagues.
- Ask families of children to take turns picking up and paying for photographs at the developer.

- Shop for office equipment and supplies at "going out of business" sales.
- Locate office supply stores and developers that give a discount to teachers.

Considerations in Creating a Wall, Bulletin Board, or Trifold Display

- How much space will I have to use?
- Will I need to provide a new background?
- Will I create and border my text on computer, or will I mat my handwritten or typed text?
- Will I be able to use enlarged versions of original photos?
- Will I be able to create the display in a smaller format (i.e., 8½" × 11") and have it enlarged at a copy place?

- Will I attach bulky or heavy artifacts to the display?
- How will I prevent tearing of a child's work if I move and reuse it in another location or display?
- Will I be able to display three-dimensional items on or near the wall display? How will I support them?
- Will I hang any three-dimensional constructions?
- Can I use mirrors or lighting to add interest to part of my display?

Select supplies and equipment from the following list to help you create the display you have planned. For more ideas on using materials to create displays, see Chapter 12.

- ☐ Desktop publishing software
- ☐ Color printer
- ☐ Color scanner
- ☐ Color copier
- ☐ Foam-core panels
- ☐ Foam-core trifold panels
- ☐ Poster board panels
- ☐ Ruler
- ☐ Double-stick tape
- ☐ Spray adhesive

- ☐ Dry adhesive sheets
- ☐ Glue gun
- ☐ Small clip-on lights
- ☐ Transparent plastic display stand
- ☐ Clear acrylic box frame
- ☐ Corner mirrors
- ☐ Large fabric pieces (muted tones, various textures)
- ☐ Art knife
- ☐ Self-sealing cutting mat

- ☐ Scissors
- ☐ Paper cutter
- ☐ Straight edge
- ☐ Matting in colors keyed to the background
- ☐ Yardstick
- ☐ Table
- ☐ Transparent plastic pocket-style holders for three-dimensional items

Tips for Organized Storage of Displays

- Use a box such as the kind poster board comes in to organize and store display panels.
- Use a large cardboard box to store foam-core displays. Cut the top part of the sides at a 45-degree angle to make "flipping through" the displays easier. Label each panel on the back as to project, date, and so forth.
- Use cardboard mailing tubes to store large items such as murals.
- Create displays for enlargement with computer publishing software and store on DVD/CD.

Displaying in Other Places

For many people, seeing is believing. When we display documentation of the learning that is taking place in our classrooms, we demonstrate our accountability and open the door for dialogue about best teaching practices with the people in our community. Which of the following locations could you use to share your display? What others can you think of?

Local

- ☐ Staff or professional learning community meeting
- ☐ Staff meetings at other schools or community centers
- ☐ School or community center board meetings
- ☐ Meetings of fellow early childhood educators
- ☐ School or center institute days
- ☐ Public library
- ☐ Community center
- ☐ Chamber of commerce
- ☐ High school child development department
- ☐ County home extension meetings
- ☐ Meetings of local women's or men's clubs
- ☐ Meetings of local professional clubs with related interests, such as the Arts Council or the Retired Teachers Association
- ☐ Meetings of local service organizations
- ☐ Bank lobby display areas
- ☐ Newspaper office
- ☐ Mall
- ☐ Children's bookstore

- ☐ Business related to the topic of the display (e.g., a learning experience centered on cars might be set up at a local car dealership)
- ☐ Retirement centers
- ☐ Museum

Extended

- ☐ Local college and junior college display cases
- ☐ Area education agencies
- ☐ Professional meetings at the area level
- ☐ Professional meetings at the state level
- ☐ Professional meetings at the national level
- ☐ World Wide Web
- ☐ Professional journals
- ☐ Popular magazines

Additional Sites

Developing a Portfolio System

An individual portfolio for each child is a means to organize a child's work and provide the teacher with a window on the child's development. A well-planned systematic portfolio system can be one of a teacher's most valuable tools for collecting and assessing children's individual progress. See Chapter 6 for further information on portfolios. Use this form to help you plan your own individual portfolio system. Carefully reflect on each question as you answer it and begin your planning.

The Vision of the Portfolio System

- How will I use my portfolio system? What is its purpose?

- How will I share the value of my portfolio system with others? How will it enhance my ability to fulfill the curriculum needs of my classroom?

- What areas of learning will my portfolio include?

- How will I assess a child's individual portfolio?

- Who will see a child's individual portfolio?

The Organization of the Portfolio System

- How will I organize each individual portfolio? What will I use to store an individual portfolio's contents? How will the contents be organized?

- How and when will I file individual items in a child's individual portfolio?

- How will I organize all of the portfolios? Where will they be stored? What will I store them in?

- How will I organize the portfolio so that it will be easy to share it with others? Will each individual item have a cover sheet? Will the individual portfolios have a summary sheet that can be shared with families?

- What will I do with a child's individual portfolio contents at the end of the year?

The Evaluation of the Portfolio System

- How will I evaluate the effectiveness and efficiency of my system?

- How and when will I make changes in my system? For example, will I change an individual item to be collected in midyear if I find that the specific item being collected does not reflect what I wanted to assess?

Individual Portfolio Items to Be Collected

Deciding what to include in an individual portfolio is an important step in the planning process. The items chosen to be collected will be used to assess a child's growth, strengths, and areas of need. In addition, each item will serve as a window on the learning that is occurring in your classroom. Reflect on the vision of your portfolio system and the areas of learning that you wish to study. Carefully consider your curriculum goals. Individual items in each area of learning may reflect one or more of these goals. Items may be included that reflect the uniqueness of an individual child. After considering the value of an individual item to be collected, reflect briefly on what it will take to collect that item. Remember that any individual portfolio item may be changed if it does not reflect the goals that you have set for it. Use this form to record your plan:

1. Write down the areas of development, learning, or content for which you wish to collect examples from individual children (i.e., Language, Writing, Reading, Spelling, Math Concepts, Science, Social Studies, The Arts, Physical Development, Social Development).
2. Decide how many specific portfolio items you will collect to represent each area. Write a brief description of each individual item that will be collected.

Learning Area:

Portfolio Item Description:

Learning Area:

Portfolio Item Description:

Learning Area:

Portfolio Item Description:

Learning Area:

Portfolio Item Description:

Learning Area:

Portfolio Item Description:

Learning Area:

Portfolio Item Description:

Individual Portfolio Item Collection Record

Collection Period: _____ to _____

Child's Name: _____

	Portfolio Item:	Portfolio Item:	Portfolio Item:	Portfolio Item:	Portfolio Item:	Portfolio Item:	Portfolio Item:	Portfolio Item:	Portfolio Item:	Portfolio Item:	Portfolio Item:	Portfolio Item:	Portfolio Item:

Use this form to record the individual items that you have collected for each child in your classroom.

1. Write the beginning and ending date of your collection period in the spaces provided.
2. Write a brief description of each specific portfolio item above each column.
3. Write the name of each child in your classroom in the spaces provided.
4. When you collect an individual portfolio item, write the date or place an × in the box corresponding to that child's specific portfolio item.

Portfolio Sharing Plan

Sharing a child's individual portfolio with his family gives his family the opportunity to view the child's development through a common window with the teacher. Individual portfolio items can serve as catalysts for discussions on a variety of topics, such as developmentally appropriate practices or a child's strengths. Planning for the sharing of the portfolio allows you the opportunity to make the most out of the family-teacher relationship. Use this form to help you organize what information you want to share during a conference. The form can also serve as a cover sheet for a child's individual portfolio.

Child's Name: _____

Age: _____

Collection Period: _____ to _____

Strengths of the child evidenced by the documentation in this portfolio

Areas of significant growth

Areas of concern and plan of action to meet these concerns

Child development knowledge to be shared with the family (Use one or more individual portfolio items as a means to share some knowledge of child development with the child's family.)

Plans for the future (individual developmental goals, upcoming projects, family involvement plans, etc.)

Plan for Documenting and Sharing
Students' Achievement of Curriculum Goals and Standards

Use this form to plan how required curriculum objectives can be documented and how you can show others that children are learning required knowledge, skills, and dispositions and/or meeting standards.

1. Copy one page for each learning area in your required curriculum, child developmental checklist, or standards.
2. List the concept, skill, or disposition objectives or standards to be documented for that area in column 1.
3. Review the web of the five types of documentation in Chapter 3.
4. Write specific items or strategies you can use that would most effectively document achievement or growth for each objective.

Based on:　　☐ Curriculum Goals　　☐ Standards　　☐ Child Development Checklist

Learning Area: _____

Concepts, Skills, or Dispositions to Be Documented	Portfolio Items	Narratives	Observations of Performances and Progress	Child Self-Reflections	Products (Individual or Group Work)

Plan for Documenting a Learning Experience

Use this form to help you think about how a learning experience such as a project, unit, or a learning experience of a shorter duration might develop in your classroom and how you can document its events. Thinking ahead will enable you to organize materials and equipment, and effectively use your preparation time, so opportunities for documentation are not lost. It is important to plan who will document and how duties of the documenter will be covered to maintain the classroom.

1. List the main events you anticipate in your project.
2. Review the types of documentation in Chapter 3.
3. Figure out what equipment or materials you will need.
4. Plan who will do the documenting.
5. Consider how to cover the documenter's other regular duties, if necessary.

Anticipated Main Events of the Learning Experience	Possible Types of Documentation	Equipment or Materials Needed	Assigned Documenter	Coverage of Documenter's Other Responsibilities

Lesson Planning Forms for Documenters

Many teachers have asked how to include documentation in lesson planning. The following three weekly planning forms were developed by teachers who use active, engaged, and extended learning experiences in their classrooms. You may wish to enlarge one of the planning forms on a copy machine and use it to create your own planning book, or perhaps combine ideas from each form and create your own form using computer publishing software.

The first form is from Kathy Steinheimer's preprimary classroom and is arranged for planning on a daily schedule. A large space is provided in the middle of the form for flexibility in planning. The space can be used to document teaching strategies for specific students' learning goals (target zones); planning project work, such as the Movie Theater Project in Chapter 9; planning extended work experiences, such as building a city in the block center over a period of several days; or planning for extensions of child-initiated learning experiences (emergent learning experiences). Documentation goals or jobs are recorded in the right-hand column. In addition, the planning form includes a space for recording teacher self-reflections. Standards covered by the lesson plans are documented in the Plan/Standards Check box. In this section, the teacher lists a Work Sampling Illinois Performance Indicator covered by a learning experience which is identified by a circled number, such as A1 (performance indicator), and 3 (experience number) with the 3 representing an experience's planning description labeled with the same circled number.

The second (primary planning) and third (preprimary planning) forms are for one week, but not specifically day by day, hour by hour. These planning forms enable teacher flexibility in scheduling. A typical time schedule is placed in the left-hand margin with a place for variations in daily schedule. These two forms are accompanied by an anticipatory planning web that shows how standards and documentation connect with concepts of the project or unit being studied (see *Young Investigators: The Project Approach in the Early Years* [Helm & Katz, 2001]).

Goals are placed in the second column for each learning area. One form is set up to coordinate with the Work Sampling domains, while the other coordinates with the Illinois Early Learning Standards. Although, of course, all areas are stimulated each day, these goals provide a focus for planning activities and selecting materials.

The center column evolves as the week goes by, enabling the teacher to reflect on observations and documentation from each day to plan materials and experiences to be ready for the next day.

The fourth column helps the teacher think about the environment and what is available to the children. This is where you may also include project experiences. It is helpful to think carefully through each area at least once a week, reviewing your goals. The primary form includes spaces for planning reading, writing, and math workshops. At the bottom of the preprimary environment plan is a box to check for literacy richness. When you have completed your planning, ask yourself: Is this environment literacy rich for children? Are there opportunities for purposeful and engaging use of reading and writing throughout the room? The last column is for planning for large-group times, to build community, communicate with each other, sharing, and so on.

On the bottom, there is a place to list books to read to groups of children (not necessarily the whole class). This will provide both a plan and a record. Don't forget to read books from various genres, including informational books. Both forms include a box for recording documentation goals for the week. What will you document? Do you have raw documentation that needs to be processed? What do you need to do to prepare for family/teacher conferences? The last box is completed at the end of the week as part of the evaluation of the week. "How did it go?" encourages reflection on the week: What worked? What didn't? What are the children interested in? What skills do they appear to have mastered? Who needs assistance? How is the assessment process going? In addition, the preprimary form includes a space for leftovers—goals, learning experiences, and so on—that did not get introduced or completed.

Teaching Team: Kathy Steinheimer and Carrie Noar | **Room: Yellow 2** | **Week of _____**

Time	Activity	Monday	Tuesday	Wednesday	Thursday	Friday
8:30	Welcome	Buffet breakfast; literature review, selection, and checkout; sign-in worktime . . .				**Got to Be There!** Newsletter:
9:30	Large Group					Family Contracts:
9:45	Large Motor					Documentation:
8:30 and 10:15	Worktimes 1 & 2: includes self-selected activities, teacher-directed small groups, project work, and targeted individual work with intentional strategies	Living / Block	Sensory / Discovery	Art / Performing Art	Language / Technology	Table Toys	**Reflections:**
During Large Group, Work Times, and Daily Routines	Target zones and intentional teacher strategies, project work, extended work, experiences, emergent learning experiences					**Plan/Standards Check** (List 2 corresponding indicators for each area and corresponding activity number.) Language Arts: Mathematics: Science: Social Sciences: Fine Arts: Social/Emotional Development:
12:00	Lunch	Promote and encourage a positive social environment emphasizing expressive and receptive language				
12:45	Lunch/nap transition	Lunchtime clean-up, restroom breaks, hand washing, book sharing—target individuals with limited disposition for interacting with books				
1:00	Naptime	Early risers will participate in activities including drawings, puzzles, looking at books, games, and project work				
2:30	Lights on	Wake-up call, restroom breaks, put away cots, self-selected snack, art, writing, books . . .				
Got to Be There!						

Week of: _____   Teacher: _____   Age: _____

Daily Schedule	*Completed for the Week*	*Ongoing All Week (see web)*	*For This Week*	*Daily*
Time Schedule (typical day)	**Curriculum/Assessment** Language Arts	**Plans for Learning Experiences** (Projects, Units, Investigations)	**Environment Plans** Family Living	**Meeting/Discussion Times** Monday
	Mathematics		Blocks	Tuesday
	Science		Sensory Table	Wednesday
Variations in the above schedule for this week:	Social Science		Art	Thursday
	Physical Development/ Health		Easel	Friday
Family contacts this week:	Fine Arts		Table Toys	
	Social/Emotional Development		Listening	**Documentation**
Professional development this week:			Discovery	
Planning time with colleagues this week:			Literacy Rich?	

Books (include informational)	Leftovers	How did it go?

Week of: _____ Teacher: _____ Grade: _____

Daily Schedule	Objectives for the Week	Ongoing All Week (see web)	For This Week	Daily
Time Schedule (typical day)	**Curriculum/Assessment** Personal/Social	**Plans for Learning Experiences** (Projects, Units, Investigations)	Environment	**Meeting/Discussion Times** Monday
Variations in the above schedule for this week:	Language/Literacy		Reading/Writing Workshop Focus	Tuesday
	Mathematical Thinking		Math Workshop Focus	Wednesday
Family contacts this week:	Scientific Thinking		Focus for Daily Journaling	Thursday
	Social Studies		M	Friday
Professional development this week:	The Arts		T	
			W	
Planning time with colleagues this week:	Physical Development		Th	
			F	
Books	Documentation		How did it go?	

Documenting Individuals' Work During a Group Activity

Documenting the work of individual children during group experiences can be difficult. Use this form to help you collect anecdotal information on individual children while you facilitate a group activity.

1. Make multiple copies of this form after you have listed the children in your class in the spaces provided.
2. Use this form to take notes on individual children's actions, verbal statements, ability to complete a certain task, interactions with the group, and so forth.

Description of Group Activity (optional):   **Date:**

Objective to Be Observed (optional):

Child's Name	Individual Notes

Recording Verbal Language

Transcriptions of children's verbalizations can provide an effective means of documenting knowledge, skills, dispositions, curriculum goals, and standards. Children engaged in a learning experience often talk so quickly or softly, in quick succession to one another or simultaneously, that it is difficult for the listener to understand what is being said, let alone consider its significance. A transcription allows the viewer to ponder the words of children and provides a sense of interaction patterns.

Tips for Collecting and Transcribing

- Keep your receipt until you test how well your new tape/digital recorder performs in a noisy classroom setting.
- Keep several small portable tape/digital recorders in various locations around the classroom, so that you can turn one on quickly with minimum disruption.
- Identify the best location for general recording in each area of the classroom. For example, the top of the refrigerator might be the best spot available in the housekeeping area.
- Self-adhesive file folder labels can be used to label tapes.
- Keep plenty of blank tapes and extra batteries on hand.
- Listen to recordings during long commutes to select sequences for transcribing.
- Verbal communication from videotape/DVD can also be transcribed and provide a record of the child's actions as well as words.

Sharing

- Select short sequences that document a concept, skill, disposition, or standard achieved by individual children or small groups of children.
- Describe the learning experience and the activities that led up to the verbal interchange.
- Describe the physical actions of children when possible, since it helps the reader to picture the context of the conversation.
- When sharing verbal language as part of a documentation display, use artifacts from the context of the conversation in the display.
- Include samples of the work children were engaged in while they were taped.
- Include your own reflections on the significance of the verbalizations.

Two forms for recording and thinking about conversations are shown on the following two pages. In the first form, each speaker is assigned a column. This format helps provide a visual sense of the amount of participation by each child. The teachers at Reggio Emilia used this type of format to share the language from a documentary videotape with us at a summer institute in 1996. In the second form, the language of the various speakers is recorded in the left column in order of occurrence, while the right column allows for notes on the movements and circumstances of the speakers.

Example of use of first form:

Teacher	Maria	Marissa	Emma
A big rubber band. Would you like a big rubber band? I'll go see if I can find you a big rubber band. Remember you've got some tape.			
	Maybe that will work.		
	I'm gonna cut some more big ones. Now Marissa, now Marissa, you have to use it.		
	How do we open the bottles?	OK.	
(Returning with rubber bands) Oh, you're taping it! Maybe that will work.		Oh let me please try this. There, I got it for ya.	

Example of use of second form:

Speaker	Notes
T: A big rubber band. Would you like a big rubber band? I'll go see if I can find you a big rubber band. Remember you've got some tape.	leaves room
Marla: I'm gonna cut some more big ones. Now Marissa, now Marissa, you have to use it.	sitting next to Marissa at table, cuts pieces of tape from dispenser and hands them to Marissa
Marissa: OK	
Marla: How do we open the bottles?	as if talking to herself
Marissa: Oh let me please try this. There, I got it for ya.	in a very mature tone
T: Oh, you're taping it! Maybe that will work.	returning to the table

Record of Verbal Language

Teacher: _____ **Date:** _____

Class: _____ **Context:** _____

Speaker 1 Name: Age:	*Speaker 2* Name: Age:	*Speaker 3* Name: Age:	*Speaker 4* Name: Age:

Record of Verbal Language

Teacher: _____   **Date:** _____

Class: _____   **Context:** _____

Speaker	*Notes*

Teacher Reflection Journal

Use this journal page regularly to reflect upon the growth and development of the children in your classroom and your own growth as a teacher. Developing the discipline to reflect regularly takes practice. This form can provide a framework for getting started. Later, open-ended pages or a spiral notebook may be sufficient to start your thinking. See Chapter 10 for more information on journaling.

Current Unit, Theme, or Project: _____

Today's Date: _____   **Areas for Focus of Thought:** _____

- Emerging knowledge, skills, and dispositons of the individual children in the class

- Emerging knowledge, skills, and dispositons of the group as a whole

- Strengths and weaknesses in providing experiences for individual children

- What went well? What didn't?

- Strengths and weaknesses in providing experiences for the class as a whole

- Ideas or plans that might provoke further growth

- Ideas for documenting further growth

- Thoughts and feelings about teaching

- What further knowledge or training might be helpful to me?

Photo Analysis

It is often said that a picture is worth a thousand words. One photograph taken to document an event in your classroom may have a similar worth. Carefully analyzing a single photograph may reveal information about a variety of topics, such as your teaching style, students' interactions, and classroom environment. Select a photograph to analyze closely. Be sure that the photograph selected has some accompanying written documentation about the event that you were trying to document. Use this form to help you analyze your photograph in-depth to discover more than it may initially reveal.

What knowledge or skills are being demonstrated by the main subjects of the photograph?

Do the expressions on the main subjects' faces reveal insight into the children's dispositions and/or feelings? If so, what?

Are there any children in the background of the photograph? If so, what learning is being demonstrated by their actions?

What does the photograph tell me about my classroom environment? Be sure to carefully study the background of the photograph, including items on shelves, walls, and so on.

Does this photograph reveal anything about my teaching style?

Does this photograph reveal anything about how I believe children learn?

Does this photograph document what I expected it to? Does this photograph document more than I expected it to?

Professional Learning Community Tuning Protocol

Norms for the Tuning Protocol

1. Stay within time frames. Begin on time, move quickly, and end on time.
2. Ask everyone in the meeting to talk a little. Do not let one person monopolize.
3. Protect one another's feelings. This is about ideas for the future, not about what a teacher should have done in the past.

Teacher Presenting:

Facilitator:

Time Keeper:

I. Introduction (5 minutes)

II. Teacher Presentation (10 minutes)

III. Clarifying Questions (2–3 minutes)

IV. Feedback (15 minutes maximum)

V. Reflection/Response (5 minutes)

VII. Debrief (5 minutes)

When will our professional learning community meet again?

Who will be the presenting teacher?

Documenting Student Achievement
Through Learning Experiences

Use the "Student Achievement Through Learning Experiences" form that follows to help keep track of the learning that takes place in the course of a learning experience (project, unit, theme). It can also provide powerful evidence of the effectiveness of your teaching, when included as part of your documentation display.

1. In the first column, record the experience that took place in your classroom.
2. In the second column, record the general area(s) of the curriculum covered in the experience.
3. In the third column, record specific standards/curriculum goals achieved by the children during this learning experience.
4. In the last column, note the type(s) of documentation available to support your observations.

Student Achievement Through Learning Experiences

Teacher:

Class:

Ages of Students:

Learning Experience	Area(s) of Learning Covered	Standards/Curriculum Goals Achieved	Documentations Available

Opening Windows: Plan for Displaying/Presenting Documentation

Use this form to help you plan a documentation display/presentation for a learning experience. Reflecting on collected documentation and planning for its presentation can enhance your ability to touch your audience.

1. List the main events of the learning experience that you want to bring forth.
2. Review the documentation collected during each event and list those you want to consider for displaying/presenting.
3. Write down the windows that the documentation can open and/or curriculum goals/standards that it may help bring out.
4. List possible narrative themes to be presented.
5. Consider possible audiences for the documentation and use your plan to create a display/presentation that will open windows onto your children's learning for those audiences.

Main Events of the Learning Experience	Documentation Collected That May Be Displayed/Presented	Window to Be Opened	Curriculum Goals/Standards to Be Brought Out	Narrative Themes

Windows on Learning Sharing Forms

Use the following three forms to open either a window onto a child's individual development, a learning experience, or your own teacher self-reflections. In addition, you may combine the forms in order to enhance the story you are presenting through documentation. The completed forms may be used as part of a child's individual portfolio, your documentation displays, or project history books. For examples and guidance on these three windows, see Chapter 2.

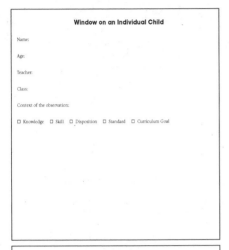

Window on an Individual Child

What insights do you have regarding a particular child's growth and development? What emerging knowledge, skills, and dispositions have you observed? Can you describe his growth in any of these three areas as a result of his involvement with a learning experience? Use the "Window on an Individual Child" form to share your thoughts on the growth of a child. Be sure to check the box that indicates whether it is growth in knowledge, skill, or disposition, or achievement of a standard and/or curriculum goal that is documented on the form.

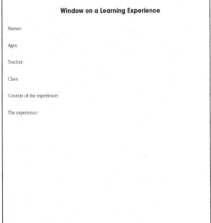

Window on a Learning Experience

What led up to the experience? Who was involved? How did the experience develop? Can you tell about the experience in story form? Use the "Window on a Learning Experience" form to share your thoughts as part of your documentation display or project history book.

Window on a Teacher's Self-Reflection

Use the "Window on a Teacher's Self-Reflection" form to share your thoughts as part of your documentation display or project history book. Use it to publicly share your reflections on children's work, or try combining it with other forms, such as the "Window on a Learning Experience" form. Frequent viewers of your documentation will quickly realize that the distinctive speech bubble shape contains teacher thoughts, and they will seek them out in an effort to get the most out of the documentation by sharing your perspective.

Window on an Individual Child

Name:

Age:

Teacher:

Class:

Context of the observation:

☐ Knowledge   ☐ Skill   ☐ Disposition   ☐ Standard   ☐ Curriculum Goal

Window on a Learning Experience

Names:

Ages:

Teacher:

Class:

Context of the experience:

The experience:

Window on a Teacher's Self-Reflection

Teacher:

Class:

Ages of Students:

Context:

Summarizing Projects and Learning Experiences

The "Project Summary" and "Learning Experience Summary" forms enable viewers of displays to get an overview of the project or extended learning experience. Use the following two forms to tell the essential story elements of the project/learning experience.

1. In the "Title and Focus of the Project" section, write a title that catches the essence of the project/learning experience and share the experience's focus in two to three sentences.
2. In the "History of the Project" section, outline the major events in the project/learning experience in the form of a condensed story. Write the history in such a way that it entices the reader to continue viewing and reading your project/learning experience's displayed documentation.
3. In the "What the Children Learned" section, connect events with concepts, skills, and dispositions gained or standards achieved by your students as a result of participating in the learning experience.
4. In the "Plans for the Future" section, share some of the next steps that you and your students may take to extend the learning experience, explore areas connected to the experience, or begin a new investigation.

Project Summary

Teacher(s):

Room:

Age Level:

Time Span:

Title and Focus of the Project:

History of the Project:

What the Children Learned:

Plans for the Future:

Learning Experience Summary

Teacher(s):

Room:

Age Level:

Time Span:

Title and Focus of the Project:

History of the Project:

What the Children Learned:

Plans for the Future:

What Is Documentation?

Dear Family:

This school year, I will be documenting your child's growth and development and the learning experiences that we have in our classroom. Documentation will enable me:
- To study individual children and follow their development/achievements
- To study the learning experiences that occur in our classroom
- To study my own teaching so that I can continuously improve

What is documentation?

Documentation has many forms: individual portfolios for collecting the work of each child, project history books that you can check out and share with your child at home, wall displays in our hallways and our classroom, collections of comments made while working and in group activities such as circle time, and the work products of the children. Products include webs (a type of diagram) that we make before and after children study a subject, play environments that they create (such as stores), block structures, drawings, paintings, stories, songs, and dances.

Will your child's learning be documented?

All children will have their work documented. We will document the work that children do together in large and small groups. Individual portfolios will hold children's individual work. In addition, individual children are sometimes the focus of in-depth study, as one in which we strive to learn more about how children learn and develop. At some time during the year, your child may also be the focus of a documentation display.

Will you see the documentation?

A major purpose of documentation is to share what is happening in the classroom. Many displays and books are made especially for families. We hope that you will come and view the displays with your child. We may ask to keep the children's work for our archives, so that we can study it again in the future. In most cases, you will be able to take the documentation home.

Can you be involved in documenting?

There are many opportunities for family members and other volunteers to help document. Family members can transcribe audiotapes into written transcripts, set up displays, make books, photograph or videotape, and take dictation from the children.

I'm looking forward to sharing our documentation with you.

How to View a Project Display

1. Read the project summary

When a project is on display, there will be a project summary near the display. It has a black border and will tell you the age of the children, the focus of the project, and what the children learned. This will provide an overview for understanding the rest of the display.

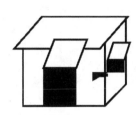

2. Find a web or list that shows children's knowledge about the topic.

A web is a diagram of children's knowledge about a topic. Webs are usually the children's thoughts and words written down by the teacher. Lines and circles indicate how children's thoughts are related. Teachers do webs when they begin to study a project to find out what children know and to plan the project. There may be several webs displayed: a beginning web, an ending web, or a planning web. Lists are sometimes substituted for webs.

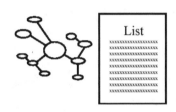

3. Look for any large structure or play environment.

Large structures and play environments are often the results of in-depth study. These are usually large items constructed by several children working together. The process of making these structures requires problem solving and working as a group and develops children's skills in building and doing research. Children plan the structure with preliminary designs and field sketches. Extensive problem solving occurs as children try to represent their ideas using the media. Problem solving is largely trial and error until the children learn to think ahead.

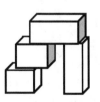

4. Look for children's representation of their learning.

Representing what they are seeing and learning about is very beneficial to children. Representations take the form of drawings, block structures, murals, sketches, songs, and children's writing. Representing helps children organize their knowledge. Children are encouraged to redraw or rewrite as their knowledge increases.

5. Look for teacher documentation of the development of knowledge, skills, dispositions, and/or standards achieved.

The development of knowledge, skills, dispositions, and achievement of standards is monitored through documentation. A developmental checklist, curriculum guide, and list of standards helps the teacher focus on the knowledge and skills that children are learning at this age level. Evidence of growth in these areas is often provided by marking on the checklist when knowledge and skills are observed and by collecting children's work into portfolios. When developmental checklists/standards lists are displayed, concepts that were observed during the progress of the project are highlighted. Samples of children's work that will eventually go into their portfolios are also often on display. These items show how children are learning required curriculum.

Reflections on Our Sharing of the Children's Work

Thank you for coming to our evening of sharing! Your interest in the children's work is greatly appreciated. In addition, I am interested in your evaluation of this evening's event. Please take a few moments to fill out this short evaluation of our time together. Your feedback will help me in planning our next event.

What did you learn new this evening?

What did you like best about this evening?

Is there anything you would like to see done differently next time? If so, what?

Is there anything that we discussed tonight that you would like to know more about?

References

Allen, D., & McDonald, J. (2003). *Tuning protocol: A process for reflection on teacher and student work.* Retrieved May 1, 2006, from http://www.essentialschools.org/cs/resources/view/ces_res/54

The American heritage dictionary (4th ed.). (2000). Boston: Houghton Mifflin.

Bagnato, S., Neisworth, J. T., & Munson, S. M. (1997). *Linking assessment and early intervention: An authentic curriculum-based approach.* Baltimore: P. H. Brookes.

Barrett, H. (1998). Strategic questions: What to consider when planning for electronic portfolios. *Learning & Leading with Technology, 26*(2), 6–13. Washington, DC: International Society for Technology in Education.

Barrett, H. (2005). Researching electronic portfolios and learner engagement. In *Information about electronic portfolio development and digital storytelling.* Retrieved May 1, 2006, from http://www.electronicportfolios.com/

Berk, L., & Winsler, A. (1995). *Scaffolding children's learning: Vygotsky and early childhood education.* Washington, DC: National Association for the Education of Young Children.

Black, P., Harrison, C., Lee, C., Marshall, B., & William, D. (2004). Working inside the black box: Assessment for learning in the classroom. *Phi Delta Kappan, 86*(1), 11–23.

Bodrova, E., & Leong, D. (1996). *Tools of the mind: The Vygotskian approach to early childhood education.* Englewood Cliffs, NJ: Prentice-Hall.

Bowers, A. (1995). *Portfolios for assessment and instruction.* Greensboro, NC: ERIC Clearinghouse on Counseling and Student Services.

Bowman, B. T., Donovan, M. S., & Burns, M. S. (Eds.). (2001). *Eager to learn: Educating our preschoolers.* Washington, DC: National Academy Press.

Bredekamp, S. (Ed.). (1987). *Developmentally appropriate practice in early childhood programs serving children from birth through age 8* (Expanded ed.). Washington, DC: National Association for the Education of Young Children.

Bredekamp, S., & Copple, C. (Eds.). (1997). *Developmentally appropriate practice in early childhood programs serving children from birth through age 8* (Rev. ed.). Washington, DC: National Association for the Education of Young Children.

Bredekamp, S., & Rosegrant, T. (Eds.). (1992). *Reaching potentials: Vol. 1. Appropriate curriculum and assessment for young children.* Washington, DC: National Association for the Education of Young Children.

Bredekamp, S., & Rosegrant, T. (Eds.). (1995). *Reaching potentials: Vol. 2. Transforming early childhood curriculum and assessment.* Washington, DC: National Association for the Education of Young Children.

Bruner, J. (1996). *The culture of education.* Cambridge, MA: Harvard University Press.

Carter, S. (1996). *Integrity.* New York: Basic Books.

Chandler, R. (1997). *Raymond Chandler speaking.* In D. Gardiner & K. S. Walker (Eds.). Berkeley: University of California Press.

Chard, S. (1994). *The project approach: A practical guide, I and II.* Edmonton: University of Alberta, Instructional Technology Center.

Chicago Metro Assciation for the Education of Young Children. (2004). *Professional Learning Communities.* Chicago: Author.

Children's Defense Fund. (2004). *The state of America's children.* Washington, DC: Author.

Clearinghouse on Early Education and Parenting (Producer). (2004). *Rearview mirror: Reflections on a preschool car project* [DVD]. (Available from the Clearinghouse on Early Education and Parenting, University of Illinois Children's Research Center, 51 Gerty Drive, Champaign, IL 61356)

Cohen, D. (1993, January 20). Assessment alternative for younger students seen honing teachers' skills, observation. *Education Week, 12*, 6–7.

Cohen, D., Stern, V., & Balaban, N. (1997). *Observing and recording the behavior of young children* (4th ed.). New York: Teachers College Press.

Derman-Sparks, L. (1989). *Anti-bias curriculum: Tools for empowering young children.* Washington, DC: National Association for the Education of Young Children.

DeVries, R., & Kohlberg, L. (1990). *Constructivist early childhood education: Overview and comparison with other programs.* Washington, DC: National Association for the Education of Young Children.

Dichtelmiller, M. L., Jablon, J. R., Dorfman, A. B., Marsden, D. B., & Meisels, S. J. (2001). *Work sampling in the classroom: A teacher's manual.* New York: Pearson.

Dichtelmiller, M. L., Jablon, J. R., Marsden, D. B., & Meisels, S. J. (2001). *Preschool through third grade: Omnibus guidelines.* Ann Arbor, MI: Rebus Planning Associates.

Dodge, D. T., Colker, L., & Heroman, C. (2002). *The creative curriculum developmental continuum for ages 3–5.* Washington, DC: Teaching Strategies.

Dyson, A. H. (1990). Symbol makers, symbol weavers: How children link play, pictures, and print. *Young Children, 45*(2), 50–57.

Edwards, C. E., Forman, G. E., & Gandini, L. (Eds.). (1998). *The hundred languages of children: The Reggio Emilia approach advanced reflections* (2nd ed.) Greenwich, CT: Ablex.

Epstein, A. S., Schweinhart, L. J., DeBruin-Parecki, A., & Robin, K. B. (2004, July). *Preschool assessment: A guide to developing a balanced approach.* (Preschool Policy Matters, Issue Brief No. 7). New Brunswick, NJ: National Institute for Early Education Research.

Fisher, D., & Frey, N. (2001). Access to the core curriculum: Critical ingredients for student success. *Remedial and Special Education, 22*(3), 148–157.

Forman, G. (1994). Different media, different languages. In L. Katz & B. Cesarone (Eds.), *Reflections on the Reggio Emilia approach* (pp. 41–53). Urbana, IL: ERIC Clearinghouse on Elementary and Early Childhood Education.

Forman, G., Lee, M., Wrisley, L., & Langley, J. (1993). The city in the snow: Applying the multisymbolic approach in Massachusetts. In C. Edwards, L. Gandini, & G. Forman (Eds.), *The hundred languages of children* (pp. 359–374). Norwood, NJ: Ablex.

Gandini, L. (1993). Fundamentals of the Reggio Emilia approach to early childhood education. *Young Children, 49*, 4–8.

Gardner, H. (1983). *Frames of the mind.* New York: Basic Books.

Gardner, H. (1991). *The unschooled mind: How children think and how schools should teach.* New York: Basic Books.

Gardner, H. (1993). *Multiple intelligences: The theory in practice.* New York: Basic Books.

Gardner, H. (1999). *The disciplined mind: What all students should understand.* New York: Simon & Schuster.

Gardner, H. (2000). *Intelligence reframed: Multiple intelligences for the 21st century.* New York: Basic Books.

Goldhaver, G., Smith, D., & Sortino, S. (1996). Observing, recording, understanding: The role of documentation in early childhood teacher education. In J. Hendricks (Ed.), *First steps toward teaching the Reggio way* (pp. 198–209). Upper Saddle River, NJ: Prentice Hall.

Golomb, C. (1988). Symbolic inventions and transformations in child art. In K. Egan & D. Nadaner (Eds.). *Imagination and education* (pp. 222–236). New York: Teachers College Press.

Grace, C. (1992). *The portfolio and its use: Developmentally appropriate assessment of young children.* (ERIC Document Reproduction Service No. No. EDO-PS-11)

Greenfield, P. M. (1997). You can't take it with you: Why ability assessments don't cross cultures. *American Psychologist, 52*(10), 1115–1124.

Gullo, D. F. (2005). *Understanding assessment and evaluation in early childhood education* (2nd ed.). New York: Teachers College Press.

Harbin, G. L., McWilliam, R. A., & Gallagher, J. J. (2000). Services for young children and their families. In S. J. P. Shonkoff & S. J. Meisels (Eds.), *Handbook of early childhood intervention* (pp. 387–415). Cambridge, UK: Cambridge University Press.

Hart, L. (1983). *Human brain and human learning.* Oak Creek, AZ: Books for Educators.

Helm, J. H., & Beneke S. (2003). *The Power of Projects: Meeting Contemporary Challenges in Early Childhood Classrooms—Strategies and Solutions.* New York: Teachers College Press.

Helm, J. H., & Helm A. (2006). *Building support for your school: How to use children's work to show learning.* New York: Teachers College Press.

Helm, J. H., & Katz, L. G. (2001). *Young investigators: The project approach in the early years.* New York: Teachers College Press.

Hendricks, J. (Ed.). (1996). *First steps toward teaching the Reggio way.* Upper Saddle River, NJ: Prentice Hall.

High/Scope Educational Research Foundation. (2003). *Preschool child observational record* (2nd ed). Ypsilanti, MI: High/Scope Press.

Hills, T. (1992). Reaching potentials through appropriate assessment. In S. Bredekamp & T. Rosegrant (Eds.), *Reaching potentials: Vol. 1. Appropriate curriculum and assessment for young children* (pp. 43–63). Washington, DC: National Association for the Education of Young Children.

Howard, P. (2006). *The owner's manual for the brain: Everyday applications from mind-brain research.* Austin, TX: Bard Press.

Illinois Resource Center. (2005). *The early childhood standards project.* Retrieved April 13, 2006, from https://www.pdaobserve.org/

Illinois State Board of Education. (2001). *Work sampling assessment, Illinois: Preschool—4 guidelines.* New York: Rebus.

Illinois State Board of Education, Division of Early Childhood Education. (2002). *Illinois early learning standards.* Springfield, IL: Author.

Jalongo, M., (1991). *The role of the teacher in the 21st century.* Bloomington, IN: National Educational Service.

Jones, E. (Ed.). (1993). *Growing teachers: Partnerships in staff development.* Washington, DC: National Association for the Education of Young Children.

Kamii, C. (1982). *Number in preschool and kindergarten: Educational implications of Piaget's theory.* Washington, DC: National Association for the Education of Young Children.

Kamii, C., & Ewing, J. K. (1996). Basing teaching on Piaget's constructivism. *Childhood Education, 72*(5), 260–264.

Katz, L. (1985). Dispositions in early childhood education. *ERIC/ECE Bulletin, 18*(2), 1–3.

Katz, L. (1987). Early education: What should young children be doing? In S. L. Kagan (Ed.), *The care and education of America's young children: Obstacles and opportunities* (90th Yearbook of the National Society for the Study of Education, Part I, pp. 50–68). Chicago: National Society for the Study of Education.

Katz, L. (1990). Impressions of Reggio Emilia preschools. *Young Children, 45*(6), 10–11.

Katz, L. (1995). *Talks with teachers of young children: A collection.* Norwood, NJ: Ablex.

Katz, L., & Chard, S. (1996). *The contribution of documentation to the quality of early childhood education.* Champaign, IL: ERIC Clearinghouse on Elementary and Early Childhood Education.

Katz, L., & Chard, S. (2000). *Engaging children's minds: The project approach* (2nd ed.). Norwood, NJ: Ablex.

Keats, E. J. (1968). *A letter to Amy.* New York: Harper & Row.

Knapp, M. (Ed.). (1995). *Teaching for meaning in high-poverty classrooms.* New York: Teachers College Press.

Kotulak, R. (1993). Unlocking the mind [Series in the Chicago Tribune].

Kotulak, R. (1996). *Inside the brain: Revolutionary discoveries of how the mind works.* Kansas City, MO: Andrews & McMeel.

Lam, T. (1995). *Fairness in performance assessment.* Greensboro, NC: ERIC Clearinghouse on Counseling and Student Services.

Losardo, A., & Notari-Syverson, A. (2001). *Alternative approaches to assessing young children.* Baltimore: P. H. Brookes.

Lowenfeld, V. (1987). *Creative and mental growth* (8th ed.). New York: Macmillan.

Lynch, E. W., & Hanson, M. J. (2004). *Developing cross-cultural competence: A guide for working with children and their families* (3rd ed.). Baltimore: P. H. Brookes.

Malaguzzi, L. (1998). History, ideas, and basic philosophy: An interview with Lella Gandini. In C. Edwards, L. Gandini, & G. Forman (Eds.), *The hundred languages of children* (pp. 49–97). Norwood, NJ: Ablex.

Mayesky, M. (1990). *Creative activities for young children.* Albany, NY: Delman.

Meisels, S. (1993). Remaking classroom assessment with the Work Sampling System. *Young Children, 48,* 34–40.

Meisels, S. (2000). On the side of the child: Personal reflections on testing, teaching and early childhood education. *Young Children, 55*(6), 16–19.

Meisels, S. J., Jablon, J. R., Marsden, D. B., Dichtelmiller, M. L., Dorfman, A. B., & Steele, D. M. (1994). *An overview: The Work Sampling System.* Ann Arbor, MI: Rebus Planning Associates.

Meisels, S., Liaw, F., Dorfman, A., & Fails, R. (1995). The Work Sampling System: Reliability and validity of a performance assessment for young children. *Early Childhood Research Quarterly, 10*(3).

Merriam-Webster dictionary (6th ed.). (2005). Springfield, MA: Merriam-Webster.

Mills, R. (1989). Portfolios capture rich array of student performance. *The School Administrator, 47*(10), 8–11.

Morgan, T., & Thaler, S. (1996). *Capturing childhood memories.* New York: Berkeley Publishing Group.

National Association for the Education of Young Children [NAEYC] & National Association of Early Childhood Specialists in State Departments of Education [NAECS/SDE]. (2003). *Early childhood curriculum, assessment, and program evaluation: Building an effective, accountable system in programs for children birth through age 8.* (A Joint Position Statement) Washington, DC: National Association for the Education of Young Children.

National Board for Professional Teaching Standards. (2001). *National Board for Professional Teaching Standards Early Childhood/Generalist Standards.* Southfield, MI: Author

National Board for Professional Teaching Standards. (2002). *National Board for Professional Teaching Standards Early Childhood/Generalist Portfolio.* Southfield, MI: Author.

Neal, A. (1976). *Exhibits for the small museum: A handbook.* Nashville, TN: American Association for State and Local History.

Neal, A. (1986). *Help for the small museum: Handbook of exhibit ideas and methods.* Boulder, CO: Pruett.

Neisworth, J. T., & Bagnato, S. J. (2005). DEC recommended practices: Assessment. In S. Sandall, M. L. Hemmeter, B. J. Smith, & M. E. McLean (Eds.), *DEC recommended practices: A comprehensive guide for practical application in early intervention/early childhood special education.* Longmont, CO: Sopris West.

New, R. (1990). Excellent early education: A city in Italy has it! *Young Children, 45*(6), 4–10.

New, R. (1991). Early childhood teacher education in Italy: Reggio Emilia's master plan for "master" teachers. *Journal of Early Childhood Teacher Education, 12*(37), 3.

Paulson, F. L., & Paulson, P. (1994). Assessing portfolios using the constructivist paradigm. In Fogarty, R. (Ed.), *Student portfolios: A collection of articles.* Palatine, IL: IRI Skylight Training & Publishing.

Pellegrino, J. W., Chudowsky, N., & Glaser, R., (Ed). (2001). *Knowing what students know: The science and design of educational assessment.* Washington, DC: National Academy Press.

Perrone, V. (1991). Association for Childhood Education International: Position paper on standardized testing. *Childhood Education, 67,* 131–142.

Project Zero, Cambridgeport School, Cambridgeport Children's Center, Ezra H. Baker School, & John Simpkins School. (2003). *Making teaching visible: Documenting individual and group learning as professional development.* Cambridge, MA: Project Zero, Harvard University Graduate School of Education.

Rankin, B. (1992). Inviting children's creativity: A story of Reggio Emilia, Italy. *Child Care Information Exchange,* No. 85, 30–35.

Roberts, S., & Pruitt, E. (2003). *Schools as professional learning communities: Collaborative activities and strategies for professional development.* Thousand Oaks, CA: Corwin Press.

Sandall, S., Hemmeter, M. L., Smith, B. J., & McLean, M. E. (Eds.). (2005). *DEC recommended practices: A comprehensive guide for practical application in early intervention/early childhood special education.* Longmont, CO: Sopris West.

Scott-Little, C., & Martella, J. (2006, March). *Early learning standards: Now that we have them, what next?* Paper presented at the National Smart Start Conference, Greensboro, NC. Powerpoint retrieved April 10, 2006, from http://www.ccsso.org/projects/SCASS/Projects/Early_Childhood_Education_Assessment_Consortium/

Seefeldt, C. (2005). *How to work with standards in the early childhood curriculum.* New York: Teachers College Press.

Smith, F. (1990). *To think.* New York: Teachers College Press.

Stiggins, K. (1994). *Performance assessment.* Greensboro, NC: ERIC Clearinghouse on Counseling and Student Services.

Sylwester, R. (1995). *A celebration of neurons: An educator's guide to the human brain.* Alexandria, VA: Association for Supervision and Curriculum Development.

Sylwester, R. (2004). *How to explain a brain: An educator's handbook of brain terms and cognitive processes.* Thousand Oaks, CA: Corwin Press.

Vecchi, V. (1998). The role of the atelierista. In C. Edwards, L. Gandini, & G. Forman (Eds.), *The hundred languages of children* (pp. 139–147). Norwood, NJ: Ablex.

Vermont Department of Education. (1988). *Working together to show results: An approach to accountability for Vermont.* Montpelier, VT: Author.

Vermont Department of Education. (1989). *Vermont writing assessment: The portfolio.* Montpelier, VT: Author.

Vygotsky, L. S. (1978). *Mind in society: The development of higher mental processes* (M. Cole, V. John-Steiner, S. Scribner, & E. Souberman, Eds. & Trans.). Cambridge, MA: Harvard University Press.

Who measures what in our neighborhood: Phase three. (2002). (University Primary School, Department of Special Education, University of Illinois at Urbana-Champaign.) Retrieved July 29, 2006, from http://www.ed.uiuc.edu/ups/curriculum2002/measure/phase3narr.shtml

Wiggins, G. (1990). *The case of authentic assessment.* Washington, DC: ERIC Clearinghouse on Tests, Measurements, and Evaluation.

Wolfe, P. (2001) *Brain matters: Translating research into classroom practice.* Alexandria, VA: Association for Supervision and Curriculum Development.

Wood, A., & Wood, B. (2001) *Alphabet adventure.* New York: Blue Sky Press.

York-Barr, J, Sommers, W. A., Ghere, G. S., & Montie, J. (Eds.). (2001). *Reflective practices to improve schools: An action guide for educators.* Thousand Oaks, CA: Corwin Press.

Zull, J. (2002). *The art of changing the brain: Enriching the practice of teaching by exploring the biology of learning.* Sterling, VA: Stylus.

Index

About the Authors

Judy Harris Helm, Ed.D. assists early childhood and elementary schools in integrating research and new methods through her consulting and training company, Best Practices, Inc. She began her career teaching first grade and then moved on to teaching 4-year-olds. She has also directed and designed early childhood programs and trained teachers at the undergraduate and graduate level. She is past president of the Illinois chapter of the National Association for the Education of Young Children. Included in the seven books she has authored are *Young Investigators: The Project Approach in the Early Years* (with Lilian Katz) and *Building Support for Your School: Using Children's Work to Show Learning* (with Amanda Helm). The Chicago Children's Museum developed an exhibit based on her work called "The Power of Documentation: Children's Learning Revealed" that is touring the country. Her work has been translated into five languages and she provides consultation and training throughout the country and internationally.

Sallee Beneke is a resource specialist for STARNET Regions I & III and a doctoral student in the Department of Special Education at the University of Illinois. Active in early childhood education for over 30 years, Ms. Beneke has been a master teacher, prekindergarten at-risk teacher, early childhood special education teacher, center director, and head teacher in several childcare centers. She was lead teacher for the Valeska Hinton Early Childhood Education Center in Peoria, Illinois, when this study began. Sallee received her Ed.M. in Curriculum and Instruction from the University of Illinois.

Kathy Steinheimer teaches 3- and 4-year olds at the Valeska Hinton Early Childhood Education Center. She is a national board–certified teacher in the area of Generalist/Early Childhood. Ms. Steinheimer has taught for 19 years and worked in a variety of settings, including private child care and hospital child care. She completed an undergraduate degree in accounting, but found that her real love was working with children. After several years in child care, she decided to continue her education, obtaining certification for elementary and early childhood education and a Master of Arts in Human Development Counseling at Bradley University. Ms. Steinheimer has been especially interested in multi-age early childhood programs, implementation of the project approach, and working with children with special needs. She enjoys sharing what she has learned with other early childhood professionals who work in school and child care settings.